THE BIG FIGHT

MY AUTOBIOGRAPHY

SUGAR RAY LEONARD

EBURY
PRESS

3 5 7 9 10 8 6 4 2

First published in 2011 by Ebury Press, an imprint of Ebury Publishing
A Random House Group company
First published in USA by The Penguin Group in 2011

The Random House Group Limited Reg. No. 954009

Addresses for companies within the Random House Group can be found at
www.randomhouse.co.uk

A CIP catalogue record for this book is available from the British Library

The Random House Group Limited supports the Forest Stewardship Council®
(FSC®), the leading international forest certification organisation. All our titles that
are printed on Greenpeace approved FSC® certified paper carry the FSC® logo. Our
paper procurement policy can be found at www.randomhouse.co.uk/environment.

MIX
Paper from
responsible sources
FSC
www.fsc.org   FSC® C016897

Printed and bound in Great Britain by Clays Ltd, St Ives PLC

ISBN 9780091946807

To buy books by your favourite authors and register for offers visit
www.randomhouse.co.uk

To Bernadette,

who taught me

the best prizes in life

are not won in the ring

CONTENTS

PREFACE

My eyes never lie.

They were open wide, staring back at me in the mirror of the dressing room at Caesars Palace in Las Vegas. Those eyes would reveal which of the two dueling personalities would enter the ring as I took on the most intimidating opponent of my career, Marvin Hagler. It was nearly seven o'clock on the night of April 6, 1987, the opening bell only about an hour away.

Would it be Sugar Ray Leonard, the star of numerous conquests in the past, an American hero since capturing the gold medal in Montreal more than a decade earlier, the anointed heir to the throne vacated by Muhammad Ali? Sugar Ray was resilient, fearless, unwilling to accept failure. The smile and innocence of a child, which made him a hit on TV, would be gone, replaced in the ring by a man filled with rage he did not understand, determined to cause great harm to another.

Or would it be Ray Leonard, the part-time boxer at the age of thirty, whose best was well behind him, his days and nights wasted on fights that never made the headlines, fights he lost over and over, to alcohol and cocaine and depression? This was a man full of fear and self-pity, blaming everyone but the person most responsible for his fate—himself.

In the room, with no one around, I kept my eyes glued on the eyes in the mirror. They were alive, probing, big, like flashlights. I looked at the muscles in my shoulders, my arms. They were cut, defined, powerful.

I began to slowly shadowbox, watching my legs, then my eyes, back to my legs, then my eyes again. *Pow! Pow! Pow! Pow!* I threw a left, a right, another left, another right. Sweat dripped down my forehead, my breathing heavier.

There was a knock at the door to let me know it was time. I didn't say a word. I took one last look at my eyes. I recognized them. They were Sugar Ray's.

I walked out. Surrounded by my trainer, Angelo Dundee, bodyguard James Anderson, brothers Roger and Kenny, and about a dozen others, I started the familiar procession down the aisle, a strange and special ritual unlike any other in sports, cheered on by the hungry masses out for blood, marching toward glory or shame or, worse, death. During the several minutes it took to reach the ropes, I remained unscathed, as did Hagler, our bodies honed from months of sparring and running to be ready for this one momentous night. Soon we would be unscathed no more, both forced to pay the dues for the brutal profession we had chosen, or, as many of us in the Sweet Science prefer to believe, had chosen us.

I proceeded as slowly as possible, savoring the feelings I had not experienced in almost three years, since I defeated Kevin Howard and retired again, this time, I assumed, for good. Howard, nowhere near the fighter I was, knocked me to the canvas in the fourth round. I got up right away, more humiliated than hurt, and summoned enough will to prevail in the ninth. But my heart was not in the fight game anymore, and if one is not committed, disaster is certain to strike. Lacking the motivation wasn't a problem against Hagler. From the moment I decided in the spring of 1986 to take him on, I was sure of one thing: I wanted to tear the man apart.

The odds were heavily against me, and why wouldn't they be? Boxing was filled with proud warriors who came out of retirement only to discover that they should have stayed away forever, their skills never the same after the long layoff, the saddest example being the legendary Joe Louis, the hero to my father and millions of African Americans, beaten eventually by a much younger Rocky Marciano in 1951. I knew I would be assuming the same risk as the others before me, and not only to my body. At stake at Caesars was something just as important—my reputation. When I first retired as a pro in 1982, I prided myself on being the rare exception in my sport, the fighter wise enough to get out before it became too late. If I was whipped by Hagler, a very real possibility—he hadn't lost in eleven years—I would join the long list of disgraced ex-champions, leaving one lasting, pathetic image for the public I worked endlessly to impress.

Over the previous five years, I spent less than twenty-seven minutes in the ring while Hagler took on eight opponents (fifty-seven rounds) during the same period. While I trained more vigorously for Hagler than for any prior opponent—I sparred for well over two hundred rounds—no amount of effort on the speed bag, the heavy bag, jumping rope, and running could compare to an actual fight against a man coming from the opposite corner whose prime objective is to inflict as much damage as is humanly possible. My sparring partners never let up. They had careers they were hoping to build.

ilton Head, South Carolina, I felt in control of
....ngs. There was a plan I stuck to every day. On
right night in Las Vegas, I felt in control again, but didn't know if the plan
would work. A fighter never knows till the bell rings.

There was also the injury to my left eye, which had led to the initial
retirement. The official diagnosis was a partially detached retina, which
could have left me, if the doctors did not operate as soon as they did,
blinded in that eye for life.

The possibility of reinjuring the eye was on my mind during the
Howard bout and in the months leading up to the encounter with Hagler.
What if I thought about the eye again, if for only an instant, during the
fight itself? Marvin Hagler was no Kevin Howard. He said if I was "fool-
ish" enough to take him on, he was "foolish enough to rip" my eye out.
He meant it.

Hagler's bravado didn't frighten me, though it did get to my family, who were already alarmed enough to begin with. They never actually came out and shared their concerns for my safety, yet I saw the
look in their eyes, just as I saw it among the members of my camp. They
were afraid I might get seriously hurt. Nobody was more ferocious during the 1980s than Hagler. In 1981, he gave Mustafa Hamsho such a
thorough pounding that he required fifty-five stitches to plug the cuts
in his skin.

Perhaps more worried than anyone were members of the Nevada State
Athletic Commission, which held jurisdiction over the bout. Not every
state gave a license to a fighter with a detached retina. If my eye suffered
permanent damage, the commissioners, picked by the governor, would
be the ones dealing with the fallout. To protect itself, the commission

asked me to take one final exam. I wasn't crazy about the burning sensation caused by the drops the doctors put in my eyes to dilate them, but I agreed. I had come too far over the past eleven months to let the opportunity slip away. I passed the exam. The fight was on.

I t was just after eight P.M. As the challenger, I was the first to climb under the ropes.

Wearing a short, Elvis-style white jacket, I received a warm reception from the fans and enjoyed every second of it. Life after boxing can be rewarding in many ways, but nothing comes close to the sound of applause, and any ex-fighter who claims he doesn't miss it is lying. Hagler was next, starting his procession down the aisle, the familiar scowl planted firmly on his face, accompanied by "War," the anti–Vietnam War anthem from the late sixties.

What was *he* thinking? Did this most macho of fighting men have any doubts of his own? Did he worry about a different Hagler showing up on this, the most important night of his career? We all attempt to hide what's most vulnerable about us. Perhaps Hagler's fierceness was related to something equally frightened within the man himself.

At first, Hagler wasn't sure about fighting me. After I went public in May 1986 with my decision to challenge him, he took several months to offer his response.

What did Hagler need to prove? He owned the middleweight belt and was recognized by the press and fans as the toughest pound-for-pound fighter on the planet. What else could he possibly gain by beating a has-been like me? On the other hand, he could lose everything and perhaps never get a chance to redeem himself. Yet what Hagler did not own was true stardom, and the only way he could attain it was to expose me, in his view, for the fraud I had always been, the slick, made-for-TV package who stole the spotlight that should have been his.

I did the commercials. I appeared on the talk shows. I made millions while Hagler, for much of his career, risked his life for thousands. These slights, as well as the promise of making at least $10 million, were why, in the summer of 1986, he accepted my challenge. He would put an end to the Sugar Ray Leonard hype machine, once and for all.

I came up with a plan as I waited for him. Since the fight was made official I had worked on messing with Hagler's psyche, and here was one more chance. I wanted to know which Hagler I would be facing, the invincible one or the insecure one. After he entered the ring and received his ovation, every bit as generous as mine, I slowly glided toward his general direction, shuffling my feet and shadowboxing. As I crept closer, I began to think like a choreographer on Broadway, carefully plotting my steps.

The two of us were soon only a few feet apart, headed for a certain collision. If Hagler backed off to avoid me, I kept thinking, I would win the fight. If we bumped into each other, I would lose. He was the champion defending his turf and I was daring to take it away. It went back to the code in the hood, where the strongest person on the streets stood his ground against any threat.

It was a matter of respect: Did Marvin Hagler respect me or not? It then dawned on me: He was not going to move. I screwed up and I was going to pay the price.

Please fuckin' turn, I thought. *Now!*

At the last possible second, he did, darting to the side to avoid contact while I did not budge one inch. I was relieved. Hagler was mine.

We met in the center of the ring for referee Richard Steele's instructions. I looked down at the canvas, not at Hagler. I was in my zone and did not want to be disturbed.

We retreated to our respective corners, soaking up the final words of wisdom from the boxing lifers who had done everything they could to prepare us for the moment, which was only seconds away. It was now up to the two of us, half-naked and half-scared, ready to kill or be killed.

The bell rang.

1

Palmer Park

My eyes didn't lie when I was a kid, either, and what they revealed to me in the mirror when I got home on that unforgettable day was no major surprise. I was hurting. I was hurting bad. To make things worse, I needed to clean up the marks on my face before my dad, Cicero Leonard, would notice. He was a fighter in his day, and he wouldn't think too highly of a son of his who got beat up pretty good the first time he stepped into a ring. Gaining his respect meant everything to me and it was never easy.

I was seven or eight years old. I don't recall exactly what inspired me to take on the skinny kid at the No. 2 Boys Club in D.C., several blocks from our small apartment on 210 L Street. Proving something to my dad, and myself, was probably the reason. Daddy didn't talk much, but when he did, he loved to reminisce about his favorite fighter of all time, "the Brown Bomber," Joe Louis. He talked about growing up in the town of Mullins, South Carolina, when he used to sit by the living room radio in other people's homes—his family was too poor to purchase one—listening as Louis put away his latest victim. Louis, the undisputed world heavyweight champion from 1937 to 1949, offered black people hope that a brighter future was coming, that they wouldn't be condemned to second-class status behind the white man forever. As the radio announcer described the action, my dad mimicked the champ's every move, dreaming of his own glory in the ring. He loved to fight from the day he could walk.

Besides Joe Louis, my dad's other inspiration growing up was his father, Grandpa Bilge. How many of the stories about Grandpa are true and how many are myth I suppose I will never know, such as the time he knocked down Belle, his prized mule, with a single belt. If this really did happen, then Bilge, six feet three and 240 pounds of pure muscle, not the grandson he never met, was the best puncher in the Leonard family. After a long week of work, Bilge spent Saturday nights with his buddies, drinking home-brewed corn liquor and bragging about his strength.

My dad, like many black kids in the Deep South, never made it out of elementary school in the early thirties. Bilge, needing every healthy hand, put him to work plowing the fields of a large farm owned by another man. My grandparents were sharecroppers, which meant they grew crops on rented land for a percentage of the farm's production. The owner supplied the equipment and mules, and cash or credit for them to live on until the crop could be harvested. For ten hours a day, six days a week, Daddy hauled tobacco and cotton and sweet potatoes, Grandpa Bilge keeping very close watch. If he did not do what he was told, he got a good whuppin'. Bilge would wait until Daddy was in bed, and beat him with a switch, the branch of a tree. My grandma Sally, as much as it pained her, did not object. She knew her place.

Everybody did their share on the farm, including Grandma, all four feet two inches of her. The story goes that on the very next day after giving birth to one of her fourteen children, Sally was back in the fields.

As exhausted as my dad was, on Sundays, his one day off, he took on any kid from the county who was courageous enough to fight him in a ring he built by himself in his front yard using plow line ropes, an oak tree, and wood-cut staves, narrow strips of wood forming the sides. He sometimes fought as many as three or four fights, with few interruptions. After he put away the competition, which he did without much difficulty, he was cleaned up by Grandma and ready for another Sunday ritual, church.

I absorbed one blow after another that afternoon at the No. 2 Boys Club. I didn't quit, just as my dad wouldn't, searching for any openings to make the skinny kid feel the same pain I did. It didn't happen. I didn't land a single hard blow, while he kept connecting with lefts and rights I never saw. My head was pounding. My legs were burning. Blood was pouring from my nose. Mercifully, the slaughter ended. I was no son of Cicero Leonard. Fortunately, Daddy didn't notice the damage on my face, nor did any of my five siblings, and after healing from the wounds, I returned to the much safer world of comic books, in which the good guys prevailed over the forces of evil.

In 1941, war came and Daddy spent three and a half years in the navy, working as a cook. He expected to be sent overseas. He never was, stationed instead in Maryland and Florida. Being in the service was still a jarring experience for someone who had never slept a night away from home. Once he adjusted, he kept up with his favorite pastime, fighting.

He lost only once in forty-seven bouts, to a fellow named Little Red from Philadelphia. Little Red didn't carry much of a punch but he was fast with his hands and feet. Daddy, who fought at five feet nine and about 160 pounds, was no Joe Louis, and this was as good a time as any to find out.

Daddy battled for everything he wanted in life, including his beloved Getha, and didn't care who might be in his way.

He met Getha in 1948 in the town of Gapway, South Carolina, about two hours from Columbia, when he went to pick up his cousin Robert, who had just gone on his first date with the young beauty. On the way home, Robert couldn't stop raving about Getha and how he planned to marry her one day. Pops, also now smitten, envisioned a different future and figured he might as well stake his own claim right away.

"I'm going to take that girl from you," he told Robert.

"No, you ain't," Robert said.

They proceeded to do what any two mature young men would if they couldn't settle an argument. They fought. Without providing a blow-by-blow account, let's just say Robert never dated Getha again. Which didn't mean Daddy was going to win her over without another fight, and this one would be much tougher.

According to the rules established by Getha's mother, Nettie Elliott, boys were permitted to pay a visit only on Wednesday and Sunday nights from six to nine. At nine P.M. sharp, your ass was out the door, one way or the other. When Cicero asked Getha if he could stop by one Sunday evening, she approached her mom for permission.

"I reckon so," Nettie said.

When it came to Grandma Nettie and her daughter's love life, that was about as much enthusiasm as she could muster, and with good reason. Getha had given birth to a son, Roy, about a year before with a man who was no longer around. Nettie and her husband took on the responsibility of raising Roy until years later, when he came up north to live with us in D.C.

For about a month, Cicero and Getha saw each other—only on Wednesdays and Sundays, of course—and held hands, her parents in another room. Soon they announced they wanted to get married.

"Do you know what you're doing?" Grandma asked Momma. Momma said she did.

Yet my grandfather, in vetting a possible marriage, wanted to make sure Cicero would be a strong provider for his only daughter. He went around in his road cart to the farms in the county, asking if this Cicero Leonard was a good worker. Satisfied by the responses he received, he allowed the wedding.

For the first couple of years together, my parents stayed in South Carolina, before settling in Wilmington, North Carolina, where my dad found work on the Coca-Cola assembly line, putting bottles in crates. The move came at the perfect time. The jobs available for blacks in South Carolina in those days were mostly in farming, and Daddy figured he had spent enough time hauling tobacco. Besides, Momma was never a farm girl. The sun made her sick. Soon, the kids started to come, one after another, me being the third youngest of six, arriving on May 17, 1956. I was named after my momma's hero, the great Ray Charles, whose hit song "I Got a Woman" reached the top of *Billboard*'s R&B singles charts in 1955. A member of the church choir, she was hoping for another singer in the family.

In 1960, packing everyone in a car borrowed from my daddy's brother, Norwood, we moved again, to Washington, D.C. We lived with him until we found an apartment only a short distance from the Capitol. Uncle Norwood said there was a lot of work in town, and he was right, as Daddy landed a job at a wholesale grocery store, filling up the outdoor stands with fruit and potatoes. After a few years, we left the District to rent a house in nearby Seat Pleasant, Maryland. In the late sixties, we moved to Palmer Park, a racially mixed lower-class area about twenty minutes from D.C. We rented first before buying a place of our own, on Barlowe Road, for eighteen thousand dollars. Given the modest dwellings we had lived in, the house felt as spacious as the Hearst Castle, and I didn't mind that the rooms were cramped or that I shared a bedroom with my two older brothers. Daddy worked as the night manager of S&R, a twenty-four-hour supermarket, for about one hundred dollars a week, twice what he earned at the other store. It would be the last real job he ever held.

He worked long hours, from midnight until almost noon, and then, whatever the weather, walked the whole five miles home. Every so often, he asked for a lift, but folks always said they were headed in a different direction. I can't imagine the humiliation he must have felt when he watched the same people drive right past him. It took years before he saved enough money to buy a car. Sundays were our favorite time, Daddy taking the family for a picnic of barbecued fried chicken and watermelon or to the beach. While we played in the water, he slept on the grass, the heavy toll of the week catching up to him.

My mom didn't have it any easier, working as a nurse's assistant at Holy Cross Hospital in Silver Spring from eleven P.M. until seven A.M. After making dinner, she caught a bus to downtown D.C., where she transferred to another bus. For seventy-five cents, which was no small change, she then took a cab from the bus station to the hospital, and another back to the station on her way home. The trip took her two hours each way.

Daddy did everything in the store that no one else wanted to do, which included driving a large trash truck to the suburbs twice a week. On evenings when the truck was parked in front of our house, my brothers got so embarrassed they couldn't wait for him to drive it out of sight the following morning. Every winter, he put up the Christmas lights at the home of one of S&R's two owners, or "boss men," as they were known, who lived an hour away in northern Virginia.

Pops didn't have a choice. Good jobs for black men were not in abundance. He and Momma were struggling to feed six children and couldn't afford to alienate anybody. The boss men weren't cruel to my dad, although they didn't hesitate to put him in his place.

"Your son is too small," they said years later, after I began to attain a little success as an amateur boxer in the Washington region. "He will never be anything."

"He will," insisted Pops. "He will. You just wait."

They laughed.

When I became rich and famous, they stopped laughing.

"Do you think your son might want to buy the store?" one of the owners asked.

"No," Daddy said. "Not a chance."

He told me one of the most satisfying moments he ever experienced was when he walked into S&R for the first time as a customer instead of as an employee after I made it possible for him to retire. He was as proud as a father could be.

The feeling was mutual, even if I was slow to come around. I will never forget the day I saw Momma holding Daddy's unsteady hand, showing him how to write his name, one letter at a time. My father, my hero, could not write his own name. Eventually, though, I grew to have a deep appreciation for the sacrifices he made and how tough it must have been to survive in the world without a decent education. Yet he never felt pity for himself or allowed anyone to feel pity for him.

Palmer Park, a community of similiar one-story structures, was not the most dangerous place, although we did have our share of drug dealers and troublemakers, many of whom hung out at the Landover Mall, a couple of miles from my house. My friends and I tried to keep our distance from them but didn't always succeed. One afternoon, several of us were hanging out near the front entrance to the Palmer Park Recreation Center when we stumbled upon an argument between a thug in the neighborhood and a fat, mentally challenged kid. The guy suddenly took a wrench and pounded the kid's head over and over. The blood gushed out the way you see it in the movies. He didn't care that we were watching. He knew we weren't going to call the cops or help the kid, or we'd have the rest of his friends coming after us.

Violence was nothing new to me. I saw it in my home as well, whenever my dad taught my brothers a lesson for acting up, which was quite often, though it didn't keep them in line for very long. His methods of discipline included an extension cord and making us bend down and put our heads between his legs while he hit us with his belt. As a shy kid who mostly stayed out of trouble, I wasn't punished nearly as frequently as my brothers. Yet as much as I detested the violence, I was drawn to it. I admired the power and control held by those who resorted to it.

Worse than the cord or the belt was the stare Daddy gave us whenever we let him down.

The time I remember too well was when he bought some battery-operated race cars for me as a special present. I pestered him every day for weeks, not giving any consideration to how much they might cost for a family squeezing by from paycheck to paycheck. Sick of my nagging, he went to a jar and poured out a large pile of silver dollars. He was as excited to buy the cars as I was to play with them. The fascination didn't last, however, because by the end of the next day, after breaking the tracks, I left the cars scattered throughout the living room as I went to play outside. Daddy did not say a word. He gave me that familiar stare and walked off. I can still see the disappointment on his face and it makes me feel horrible all over again.

Money worries were a constant throughout my childhood. I wore my brothers' hand-me-down clothes and stayed home from school when my class went on field trips to the famous landmarks in D.C. The lack of any savings also prevented me from becoming a member of the local Boy Scout troop. But I wasn't to be denied. I went to the Goodwill shop and purchased an official uniform for fifty cents, a rather significant amount for a kid my age. For weeks, I wore the uniform everywhere, beaming with pride. Pretending was better than nothing. We felt the impact of our situation most acutely during the holidays with the absence of any expensive gifts under the tree.

On one particularly grim Christmas, we received only the apples and oranges Daddy managed to pry away from the S&R stockroom. We didn't complain. We were grateful for anything, understanding that, as African Americans in a white-dominated culture, we were different.

It was not until one hot summer afternoon, when I was eight or nine years old, that I realized *how* different.

I was walking with several friends to the Washington Monument a few miles away when we pulled up to a bar on the city's predominantly white northwest side. The others stayed outside in the shade while I went in to ask for a glass of water.

"Get the fuck out of here, *nigger*," the bartender said.

I wasn't naïve. I knew what the *N* word meant, but it had come up only in casual conversation with other kids in the hood when we chatted about how the "honkies" took advantage of black folks. Now, for the first time, I heard the word from the lips of a white man.

For some reason, I didn't tell my friends, but when I got home that night I could not wait to share the experience with my parents. They would surely sit me down and explain the long, painful history of racial prejudice in the United States, and how I should cope with similar insults in the future. No explanation, though, came then or ever. Momma shrugged the incident off. She and Daddy believed, as many blacks did who grew up back then, that "if you're white you're right, if you're black step back."

In her defense, I am certain she was merely trying to protect me from the suffering her generation endured. Still, I've always wished she and my father could have spoken about their anguish. We were living in the America of the mid-1960s and, despite the inspiring words from Dr. King and the courage of the marchers, black and white, who placed their lives on the line in the Deep South, our less-than-perfect country was not going to be less divisive anytime soon.

* * *

My parents, however, had no trouble confronting each other.

Week after week, they fought, and it normally started after one, or both, had been drinking, and often quite heavily. Nothing was as terrifying as the transformation Momma went through after she had a few drinks. She never drank in front of the children. Instead, she would disappear into her bedroom as the strong leader we depended on and come out an hour or two later angry with the whole world. There was no telling what Momma might say or do, and who might get hurt.

For years, I told myself lies, that my parents fought about money, the root of the conflict between many marriages, black and white. Only in recent years, freed from my own indulgences in alcohol and drugs, and owning up, at last, to the pain I caused my wife and two children from my first marriage, have I been able to examine the full, ugly truth: The fights between my mom and dad were about other women. My dad couldn't get enough of them.

I began to remember scenes from my childhood that I had long buried, of catching him in town with a woman I did not recognize. And I was not the only witness; Daddy did not try to keep these affairs a secret. It was almost as if he wanted Momma to find out or didn't care. The worst part, and I know I will seem racist, was that some of the women he fooled around with were white. Adultery is adultery: What difference should it make what color they were? Plenty, I felt at the time. By dating white women, he was not only hurting Momma and the family; he was altering my whole perception of race relations. I had grown up believing black men dated only black women and now I didn't know what to think.

The pushing and shoving between my parents was intense, with Momma the more aggressive one, tossing pots and pans. For a God-fearing, devout member of the church choir, Getha Leonard was one tough lady. People assume that I inherited my fighting spirit from my dad. It actually came from her. I have never met anyone with more determination, and that includes Roberto Duran, Tommy Hearns, and Marvin Hagler.

As a kid, I felt that it was my responsibility to keep my parents from killing each other. I often threw my scrawny little body between them, as a ref does, to break them up. Daddy at least knew enough to never hit Momma back.

In calmer moments, he showed her how to use a switchblade. The lessons did not go to waste. When Momma was eight months pregnant with me, according to my brother Kenny, she was walking up the steps in front of our apartment in Wilmington when a woman from the same building, for some unknown reason, started to slap her around.

"As long as I live, I will get you," Momma supposedly said.

It took only a few months. Momma saw the woman about to enter the complex one day, got her knife and went after her. The woman fell down and screamed, but survived. Momma, I was told, went back upstairs as if nothing happened. On a different occasion, she attacked another woman who kept demanding the money she owed her.

Then there was the time she used the knife on Daddy.

I was six or seven, and we were still living in D.C. The noise coming from the kitchen was louder than usual, but when I made it to the living room, he was already on his way out the door. With a knife in his back.

I followed him outside as he slowly climbed the stairs to a neighbor's apartment on the third floor.

"Can you pull this out?" he asked. The neighbor did.

The wounds were not severe enough for him to seek medical attention. Knowing my dad, he would have had to be on his deathbed to go to the hospital.

He never lost control, except when he thought someone was trying to steal his wife. One day, a stranger followed Momma home from the store. She was an extremely attractive woman, with jet-black hair down to her shoulders. The man was downstairs in front of our apartment complex. Daddy grabbed the man and threw him out into the street. When he tried to hide under a car, Daddy kicked him and pulled him out. The man started running, Daddy chasing him.

"Don't kill him," people shouted.

The man was lucky Daddy listened. I saw the entire beating and came away proud of my father. I must have told the story to everyone in school the next day.

Through the years, the two of them managed to remain together, although fresh new disputes would occasionally tear us all apart.

The most memorable one occurred one night in the early seventies, when Momma hurriedly packed our Ford LTD around midnight to take me, my sisters Sharon and Sandy, and my two-year-old niece, Ting, to my grandmother Nettie's home in South Carolina, while my other siblings stayed behind in Maryland with Daddy. Momma was exhausted, but determined, as only she could be, to get out of town. It wasn't long before everyone fell asleep, including her. At around two A.M., sitting in the front seat, I was woken up by the sound of the car careening off the road, rocking back and forth, its lights flashing on one object after another, all of us screaming. Then came the crash. I don't know if I was ever unconscious. The next thing I recall was seeing blood on the windshield, the steering wheel bent, and the jack from the trunk cutting right through the backseat. It was a miracle the jack didn't stab my sisters or my niece and that we suffered only minor injuries.

Momma, her whole lip split and looking as if it were about to peel off, took over, ordering everyone out of the car, now tipped in a ditch. She grabbed my sisters and Ting and we started walking in the dark down a dirt road, knocking on doors, scared to death. No one was home at the first place we stopped, or they didn't bother to answer. At the next place, a nice couple let us in and an ambulance arrived to take everyone to the hospital. From there, we called Kenny, who drove Roger, my sister Bunny, and my dad in his Volkswagen to take us home. How nine of us squeezed into Kenny's bug remains a mystery.

The car accident, along with the fights between my parents, gave me nightmares for decades. Forty years later, I still can't cope with any yelling and screaming, though I was unable to avoid it during my own doomed marriage. My ex-wife, Juanita, and I were no different from my mother and father.

I hadn't reached puberty and yet felt like I had seen enough violence to last a lifetime, from the fighting in the hood to the fighting at home. Nowhere did I feel completely safe, knowing the next sign of danger could arise anytime. The only escape was the fictional world I read about in comic books or invented in my head.

One spring afternoon, my survival was more at stake than ever, and it was my own fault. I went for a walk with a few friends along the creek near our house in Seat Pleasant when I slipped on the rocks and fell into the freezing water, which was at a higher level than normal after a week of heavy storms.

Unable to swim, and in a state of panic, I grabbed on to whatever objects I could—branches, logs, anything. It did no good. The current was too powerful, dragging me downstream with alarming speed toward a hole about fifty yards away where I might have easily drowned. Somehow, I clawed my way to the edge, walked through the woods, and was soon carried off by a friend's older brother to safety, to the relief of family members who had gathered in a nearby field after word spread through the neighborhood. I was brought home, where my mother put cold towels on my head. My lungs filled with water, I threw up for the rest of the day. We didn't go to the hospital because we couldn't afford to. Looking back, the experience taught me I could overcome any challenge, which was to prove vital in the years ahead.

It was six or seven years after the beating I took at the No. 2 Boys Club in D.C. when Roger convinced me to give boxing another try.

At first, I didn't see the point of beating up another human being, and I could not imagine I'd be any good at it. But Roger, three years older, did not stop nagging me, and besides, I was sick of him being the bully in our family. He used to hit me whenever I wasn't prepared for it, not terribly hard, but hard enough to make me cry. Learning how to fight, I figured, might be the way to stop him. I was also encouraged by my best friend, Derrik Holmes, who took up the sport a few months earlier.

Derrik was the coolest kid I knew in school, a tremendous athlete, and a stud with the girls. If Derrik thought boxing was a worthwhile pursuit, there must be something to it. I joined the new program at the rec center a few blocks from our house.

The program was not exactly state-of-the-art. There was no actual ring and there would not be one until 1976. Our practices were held on four mats spread out on a hard wooden floor, which made maintaining a proper balance important, and they were cut short to make room for basketball. We used only one speed bag, two heavy bags, and a cracked dresser mirror for shadowboxing. The next Joe Louis wasn't coming out of this dive. Of course, the way I appeared on that first day, it would not have made a difference if I showed up at the famous Stillman's Gym in New York. I held my hands close together in front of my face in the familiar fighting pose of John L. Sullivan, the heavyweight champion from the late 1800s. I looked ridiculous.

No matter. There would be plenty of time to pick up the sport's rich nuances. What did matter was that from that day forward, I was hooked. The appeal did not result from any desire to pound my opponent into submission. In my family, I was the one least likely to fall in love with fighting. I wasn't like Roger, who could not make it through lunch without starting a fight, or the occasionally combative Kenny. I was the reserved Leonard. I preferred to read about heroes instead of trying to be one.

What was it, then? What made me return to the rec center day after day for years? What inspired me to wake up at five each morning to run five miles in the snow with icicles hanging from my lips?

For one thing, I knew I was finally good at something, unlike my unsuccessful attempts to excel in basketball, track, and wrestling. In basketball, I was too small, and I didn't have a good enough jump shot to make up for it. In track, I seemed to pull a muscle every other day. I took up wrestling for several months but tore a ligament in my shoulder and did not wrestle again. With every sport, I was just behind my peers. Yet within a few months of boxing, I knew how to throw a jab and avoid a left hook. But picking up new skills wasn't what drove me the most. What drove me was the power it instilled, the sense that I was in control instead of being a victim. In the ring, for the first time in my life, I felt I could conquer any force. Strange, isn't it? The ring is where men try to do great harm to one another, and where I felt the safest.

Due to the tireless efforts of Dave Jacobs, Pepe Correa, and Janks Morton, the boxing program, despite its less than ideal working conditions, slowly turned boys into fighting men.

Each was indispensable in his own unique way. Jacobs, or Jake, as he was called, made us believe that we could accomplish anything, in or out of the ring, though I was a bit uncomfortable with how fervently he preached the Gospel. "Give him the victory that his heart desires, Jesus, that his heart so deserves," he would ask the Lord before sending his troops into battle. I always felt, with all the problems in the world, there was something wrong with asking God for help in a silly boxing match. When I prayed before a fight, I prayed for my safety and the safety of my opponent. I never asked for a victory.

A talented boxer, Jake won the city's AAU (Amateur Athletic Union) featherweight title in 1949 and turned pro a year later. But after winning eight of his first ten bouts, he figured boxing would never be lucrative enough to pay the bills, so he quit and landed a job at a pharmaceutical company. In 1970, he began volunteering at the rec center. He was our coach and resident cheerleader. A group of us used to go to his house almost every day to see films of the all-time greats, such as Willie Pep and Jersey Joe Walcott and Sugar Ray Robinson on his projector, Jake showing us how to execute the right cross and the left hook.

If Jake was the model of discipline, Pepe was the opposite. He spent much of his youth running from one city to the next, always just a step ahead of the law. Pepe possessed a spirit and energy that were contagious, and no one seemed more proud of his black heritage. I constantly marveled at his ability to recite verbatim Dr. King's "I Have a Dream" speech with remarkable passion in each syllable. It was as if he had been standing on the steps of the Lincoln Memorial on that historic day in August 1963, gazing at the mass of people in the National Mall, hopeful, at last, about a more tolerant America.

At six feet one and 230 pounds, Janks Morton dreamed of a career in the NFL, but started an insurance agency in the Washington area when he, too, found out the money in pro sports wasn't enough to make a decent living. The gospel for Janks, who volunteered four days a week, was honest, old-fashioned hard work. No amount of push-ups or sit-ups or jumping rope or hitting the speed bags satisfied him. The only way to be among the best, in his view, was to show more desire than your opponent. Years later, when I needed money and advice after the Olympics, it was Janks who came through.

During the first year, many kids dropped out, the demands too much, narrowing the group in the program from about forty to a rough dozen, everybody anxious to see how they might stack up against one another in the ring.

I relished every aspect of the process, from the five-mile runs in the dark and cold to the jabs I threw from one end of the court to the other to the consistent pounding of the speed and heavy bags. After school, I couldn't wait to get to the gym to see if I was any sharper with my punches or quicker with my footwork. I also developed my own special workout routine in which I sometimes ran to school instead of taking the bus. The other kids assumed I was crazy—and maybe I was—but I needed to believe the extra effort would pay off someday. I came home from the rec center on numerous occasions with a black eye or a busted lip, much to the dismay of my mother, but I always went back the next day for more. During those first sweet and painful months, I knew, somehow, that something was already changing in me—in my body as well as my head. I became dedicated to the point that many years when I needed to lose weight, I sat in the car for hours during hot summer afternoons, the windows closed, wearing a sweatshirt covered by a sheet of plastic.

Like my dad in his yard in South Carolina, I took on anyone, including kids several years older and as much as fifty pounds heavier. It didn't matter. All I cared about was improving every time I put on the gloves. I weighed only about 120 pounds, but pretended I was the heavyweight champion of the world, Smokin' Joe Frazier, getting down into his familiar crouch to bob and weave, anxious to knock people out with the left hook. But when I realized the advantages of fighting in a more upright style, the way Ali boxed, I started to score more effectively with my jab and absorb less punishment from taller fighters.

I was also drawn to Ali's magnetism, in and out of the ring. After I switched my allegiance, I never switched again. I became almost obsessed, as Ali was, with keeping my face pretty, unmarked. When I got acne, as every teenager did, I put on makeup to cover the zits.

The boxing program saved lives—it was as simple as that. By spending time under adult supervision, our group avoided a more dangerous form of violence, in which the weapons of choice were guns, not fists. Our parents knew where we were and that we would make it home safely, even if it wasn't until one or two in the morning. For many kids our age in Palmer Park, that was no guarantee.

We became brothers, although any brotherly love was put aside during the actual matches. *No friends in the ring,* we told ourselves. A healthy dose of adolescent ego also came into play. There were two ways of getting your name in the newspaper if you were a black teen in D.C.— the bad way or the good way. The bad way was through the police blotter. The good way was through boxing, the winner's picture appearing in the *Washington Post.*

Knowing how to box wasn't enough. I needed to learn how to communicate, and that's where Roland Kenner came in.

Roland ran Dave's Supper Club in Glenarden, where I made a couple of bucks helping out a few days a week. He told me and Derrik Holmes that since only the heavyweights made any serious money as pros, we had to set ourselves apart from others in our weight class, and the surest way to accomplish that was to be smart and articulate, dispelling the image in white America of the black prizefighter who could do nothing else in life. Roland conducted mock interviews with us on old reel-to-reel tapes, demonstrating how to look into a camera and answer questions:

Mr. Leonard, what will you do after you retire from the sport?

How will you change your strategy in the ring if your first plan of attack doesn't work?

What got you interested in fighting as a kid?

We also learned to dodge any questions to which we did not know the answers. I became an expert at that technique.

I didn't see the point to these sessions at first, because the white, educated world was not one I ever expected to inhabit, and neither did Derrik. What possible difference would it make how two poor black kids from Palmer Park looked into a TV camera? So what if I spoke too fast for people to understand me?

Over time, I saw the wisdom of what Roland preached and worked on my responses every night before I went to sleep. My delivery grew slower. My answers made sense. I never stopped working on this area of self-improvement just as I never stopped practicing my left jab and right uppercut. Years later, after turning pro, I spent a few minutes almost every day with a dictionary, picking up as many new words as I could.

Derrik, on the other hand, did not display the same dedication. He went pro in 1978 and did quite well for several years, piling up fourteen victories and a draw in his first fifteen bouts, including ten knockouts. With his smooth style, he was known as "Holmes, Sweet Holmes." There were no limits to what he could accomplish.

As the years passed, though, Derrik began to realize he would not be as successful as he hoped, and I believe that haunted him. He was much better than me in the beginning, but once I eclipsed him, he never caught up. After the WBC champion Wilfredo Gomez put him away in the fifth round of their super bantamweight title fight at Caesars in 1980, Derrik stepped into the ring only five more times. One of those was on my undercard in Reno in February 1982, when he fell to an unknown by the name of Franco Torregoza. Derrik came into my dressing room as I was going through my last-minute preparations to take on Bruce Finch.

"What the fuck happened out there, man?" I asked him.

"He took my heart away from me, Ray," he said. "He took my heart."

"Even if it's true, Derrik, you don't ever fuckin' tell somebody that," I said.

I was angry. I respected Derrik, but he didn't respect himself. He turned to drugs. He reached a point where he had to make a choice: Give up drugs or give up boxing. He made the wrong choice, and it cost him his freedom.

Derrik, to be fair, was no different from countless other blacks who have taken up the sport since the days of Jack Johnson and Joe Louis but have been unable to make enough money to set themselves up for the rest of their lives. There was never a Plan B for Derrik Holmes, just as there isn't one for the overwhelming majority of black boxers. He could not rely on a formal education or family connections to help him find a place in the world. Think about it: How many ever went to college? How many grew up in Beverly Hills? Boxing is a poor man's profession. It always has been and always will be. The drugs were not accessible in the gym, but on the streets, Derrik could obtain any controlled substance he desired.

The drugs didn't get rid of the anger inside him, which came to a head on a December day in 1983 when he ran into his mother, who was taking his four-year-old daughter shopping because he didn't have the money. He resolved to get some any way he could. He robbed the owner of a Christmas tree business where he had worked a week earlier, shooting the man with one thought in mind—that he needed money for the daughter he loved. Fortunately, the man survived, or Derrik would have been convicted of murder instead of attempted murder, along with armed robbery. He did twenty-three years, not getting out of prison until January 2008.

In the summer of 1986, only a few years into his incarceration, I visited Derrik at the Maryland Correctional Training Center in Hagerstown. I was scared, but not of the inmates. I was scared of my emotions. I was not sure I'd be able to contain them. When we were top amateurs, we trained with prisoners at a facility in Virginia. Being in excellent shape and very strong, they gave us quite a workout. Now, more than a decade later, Derrik and I would be together again in a similar environment. Except only one of us would walk out.

Derrik, head of the prison's boxing program, found a few middle-weights to spar with me. I took on about three or four fighters, but what I'll always remember is the smile on Derrik's face. For one day, at least, he was among his friends again. What also stands out is the compassion he showed to his fellow inmates, particularly one fighter who I nailed with a hard right. Derrik was worried that if I knocked the guy out, he would be humiliated in front of his peers and reminded about it wherever he went.

"Don't worry," I whispered to Derrik. "I won't take him out."

The session was soon over and it was time to leave. Derrik was given permission to escort me and a few others to the gate. I gave him a hug and didn't look back. The next thing I heard was the sound of the doors closing behind me. I started to cry. I didn't see Derrik again for more than twenty years.

During his first two years in the joint, Derrik felt sorry for himself, drinking a pint of liquor every chance he got, earning a new nickname, "Hennessy Holmes." He was put in lockup seven times, and was well on his way to racking up enough extra time to make sure he never got out.

It was a good thing he found the Lord. It turned his life around. He became an aide in the prison library and didn't touch another drop of alcohol. These days, he's in charge of a boxing and fitness gym in Capitol Heights, Maryland, teaching others not to follow his example. He is married to a lovely woman, Regina, and they have an amazing story. They were married before, in the mid-1990s, but the physical separation was too great for them and they got divorced. Derrik never stopped thinking about her. Three weeks after he was released, he called Regina and they got together. Soon they were back at the altar. If that isn't true love, I don't know what is.

The sport turned me into a different person, afraid of no one. One day, a bully, probably about six feet two, threw me against a locker at Parkdale High. I was almost knocked out cold.

The old me would have searched for any peaceful way to end the mismatch. The new me fired off a succession of left hooks, missing wildly. The bully began to laugh. Yet each hook kept coming closer and closer, until one put his butt on the ground. The guys who had surrounded us, expecting to see me get whipped, were speechless. For the rest of the afternoon, I walked around school as "the man," everyone spreading the word: "Did you hear what Ray did?" I looked down at my fists, seeing them in a whole different light. I realized they could operate outside the ring as well as they did inside. As for the bully, he never bothered me again.

The same went for Roger, who found out the hard way that I was not the same little brother he used to push around. The day I beat Roger up for the first time was a turning point in my life and we both knew it. He began to take such a routine whipping from me, he told Dave Jacobs that our mother did not want her sons to fight each other any longer. She never said that.

Once he couldn't beat me up, Roger realized he might as well take advantage of my new skills. With gloves hanging over his shoulder, he took me to visit others in the neighborhood. "My little brother will kick your ass," he said. I suppose you might say Roger was my first matchmaker.

This being the early seventies, when television and film still provided a lot of strong male role models, it was no surprise that I found one for myself: the martial arts star Bruce Lee. I was blown away by how much speed and power he could generate for such a small man, and how pretty he looked in the process. Lee was unbelievably intense, possessing a will to overcome any obstacle. After seeing one of his films, I went home and tried to copy his technique by driving my right fist as hard as I could into the ground in our front yard. Needless to say, I never tried *that* again. Lee inspired me for years, long after I turned pro. When I threw punches at my sparring partners, I made the same noises he did during his fierce exchanges. I wish I could have met him. He died under mysterious circumstances in 1973 at the age of thirty-two.

My love affair with boxing came as a surprise to my parents, who saw me as a sheltered child seeking to avoid confrontation at any cost.

I'll never forget the puzzled look on my dad's face when I asked him to attend my first amateur bout. Fighting was fine for Roger and Kenny, but not for his youngest boy.

"You can't fight," he said.

"Just come and watch me, Daddy," I said.

Well, after seeing me prevail handily, he never had trouble picturing me as a fighter again. I made him quite proud, though there was, of course, another boxer who received his highest praise.

"Nobody today would beat Joe Louis," he often said. My brothers and I shook our heads in disbelief but we didn't try to change his mind. There was no point. Besides, talking about his beloved childhood hero made him feel young again.

Within months, I started to bulk up. Speed provided a valuable advantage, but if I ever hoped to outduel the premier sluggers, I could not simply run around the ring for the whole time. As Joe Louis said about his rival Billy Conn: "He can run but he cannot hide." Sooner or later I would have to stand toe-to-toe, giving them everything they could handle and absorbing their best in return. Only then could I be considered a real fighter.

Bobby Magruder was one, the toughest in the D.C. region, and in the spring of '71, after his scheduled opponent dropped out a day or two before their fight, I was picked to take his place.

Bobby, a white guy of Irish and Scottish descent, was a featherweight with the power of a middleweight. Even his name was intimidating—*Bobby Magrrrrrruuuder*—and considering what he went through, no wonder he was fearless.

His father deserted him and his mom when he was only ten years old. By the time he was eleven or twelve, he was fighting once a month in illegal bouts in a strip club called The Cave in Waldorf, Maryland. As Bobby duked it out against the sons of farmers and truck drivers from outside the state, girls wearing only bikinis performed on swings overhead, serving up their own form of entertainment. Bobby earned fifty cents for every victory, along with any nickels and dimes tossed on the floor by the satisfied customers. Each cent went a long way, as Bobby's financial situation made the Leonards seem like the Rockefellers. To buy a ten-cent can of soup, he rounded up five Coke bottles a day, collecting two cents per deposit.

Bobby did not fight just in the bars. He fought in the streets, and in 1966, at the age of fifteen, he was preparing for another one of those battles when he nearly lost everything. A car belonging to a member of the gang he and his buddies were about to rumble with purposely ran into him, pinning Bobby against another vehicle. Both legs were crushed, the left leg so badly that doctors were planning to amputate—until they met a Magruder who made Bobby seem meek in comparison.

"You're not taking my son's leg," his mother insisted. "I want a specialist."

Bobby spent more than three months in the hospital, and the leg was saved.

His recovery was only beginning. For about a year, because his family did not own a car, he walked the entire six miles back and forth every day to receive physical therapy. The walk did him enormous good, building up the strength in his body. When he felt powerful enough, he went back to the sport he loved, helping to start the Hillcrest Heights Boys Club boxing team. During those bleak moments in the hospital, he made a deal with the Lord: *Let me walk again and I will stay out of trouble.*

During the late 1960s, Bobby fought in sanctioned AAU matches, knocking out everyone he faced, and made it to the 1968 Olympic Trials. It was quite a comeback.

Now it was my turn to see the legend up close. Was I concerned? You bet I was, especially after finding out that Dave Jacobs would not be in my corner because his wife was ill, leaving me in the hands of Janks Morton. I felt abandoned. Jake was my primary trainer, and nothing against Janks, but this was not the time to make such a significant change. A boxer's connection with his trainer is almost too complicated and intense for words.

Bobby was the defending Golden Gloves champion, and if that were not challenging enough, the fight was to be staged on his turf. Hillcrest Heights, or Little Italy, as it was known, was affluent, safe, and primarily white. While I do not recall any specific racist slurs, let's just say I was not greeted with the warmest reception in the world. The place was jammed, roughly 500 people squeezing into a gym fit for maybe 250, many sitting on top of one another on the windowsills, fire codes broken everywhere.

I was wrong to worry about Janks. He made me believe in myself that night as no one ever did. "We're going to do it," he said over and over.

Janks encouraged me to box, box, box, and . . . box. One glance at the confusion on Bobby Magruder's face and I could tell he never saw anyone that fast in the ring. I danced in circles, pausing for a moment to fire a jab and then darting away from his right hand. I stayed in the middle of the ring. When he got me into the corner, I spun out of his reach.

He connected with several decent shots, but I was never close to being knocked down. After I was awarded a split decision, the fans could not believe it. Their hero was not invincible, losing to, of all people, a black kid from Palmer Park!

In later years, there would be famous tussles against such legends as Duran and Hearns and Hagler, with much larger stakes, but no fight ever meant more to me than the triumph over Bobby Magruder. By defeating the man in D.C., I became the man, and if I could beat Bobby, I could beat anybody. We fought twice more, for the Golden Gloves title, and in the finals of the AAU tournament. I won both times, but it was our first duel that propelled me to the next level.

Week after week, the fights came, as did the victims, in D.C. and around the country. Some were harder than others.

One of the most memorable was an encounter with Larry Hinnant, a black fighter who was also from the D.C. region. I didn't prepare too thoroughly, as I had knocked him out before and assumed I'd have no trouble again. I soon learned never to assume *anything* in the ring. In the second round, Hinnant landed a shot out of nowhere, which almost put me on the canvas. I woke up in time to capture the decision, yet while I won over the judges, I didn't win over the spectators, who booed the verdict. I couldn't blame them. Hinnant, the underdog, fought with courage. I didn't. I was fortunate that my superior talents bailed me out.

Shortly after Hinnant came Dale Staley. Staley resembled the late actor/teen idol James Dean. Every strand of his hair was in place. When the bell rang, however, Staley turned into a savage and he made no apologies. Rules? Dale Staley did not believe in rules. He believed in using his head, elbow, knee, or any other body part to hit his opponent, and most of the time he got away with it. The fight was held at Prince George's Community College, and the gym was packed. It was like facing Bobby Magruder all over again. After my subpar showing against Hinnant, some folks figured there was a chance Staley would take me down. There was no possibility in my mind of that happening and I wasted no time proving it. I gave him a crash course in Boxing 101, connecting with one jab after another to his increasingly puffy jaw. He stayed aggressive, anxious to employ every trick he knew, but I never allowed him to get too close. The fans cheered the decision. I showed courage this time.

In 1972, as a lightweight, I made it to the quarterfinals of the National AAU Tournament. Traveling became quite an adventure, although I must admit I was very naïve back then. During my first trip on a plane, which was bound for Las Vegas, Janks Morton joked that the bottom of the aircraft was beginning to come apart. Derrik and I believed him and were scared to death. Good thing Janks didn't keep the gag going for much longer or we might have looked for the nearest parachute.

Vegas was frightening, especially at night with the lights flashing, though it didn't stop us from ignoring our curfew and walking the streets on the Strip, drinking sodas, spellbound by the strange universe we'd entered. I lost to a guy named Jerome Artis, who was superfast and talked a lot of trash, and it was, in fact, my first setback as an amateur. I wasn't too devastated. I knew I'd have to lose sometime.

The wins kept coming, along with the rewards. Despite being only sixteen, a year under the minimum age requirement, I was picked to be on the national team to oppose boxers from other countries. I lied to the people in charge, and they knew I was lying but did not care because they wanted to lead a U.S. revival in international boxing events. In Vegas, I was doing fairly well against Russia's Valery Lov, until he landed a hard right I never saw. I found myself in a place that wasn't familiar: the canvas. While I was lying there, I saw Joe Louis and the comedian Redd Foxx laughing. The Russian didn't stand a chance. Nobody laughed at me. I got up and won the fight.

Soon came the toughest test to date, the 1972 U.S. Olympic Trials in Cincinnati. At this point, capturing the gold medal was not the all-consuming goal it would become, though I was extremely disappointed when I lost a decision in the semifinals to a local kid, Greg Whaley, whom I clearly whipped. As it turned out, Whaley was hurt too severely to fight in the finals and never fought again. Did I feel sympathy for him? Not really. Everyone who signs up for this cruel sport is aware of the risks each time we climb underneath the ropes. Greg Whaley was no exception.

After the fight, Tom "Sarge" Johnson, one of the Olympic coaches, approached me in the dressing room.

"Don't worry, Sugar Man," he said, "I'm sure you'll make the team in '76. You'll be more experienced. The lessons you take home from here will make you a much better fighter."

Sarge had been telling people around me that I was "sweeter than sugar." For decades, as a result of his comment, Sarge has received credit for my nickname, and I have never bothered to correct this version. I even spread it myself. It made for good copy, as they like to say.

There's just one problem. Sarge Johnson did not come up with the nickname "Sugar Ray." I did.

I did it out of respect for the incomparable Sugar Ray Robinson, whose fights I knew almost punch by punch. Robinson, the welterweight and middleweight champion in the forties and fifties, was the most complete prizefighter in history. He could attack. He could counter. He could dance. He could do everything. Some boxing writers later took me to task, arguing that there can be only one Sugar Ray. But Robinson, in his fifties, told me he considered it an honor that I adopted his nickname, and his opinion was the one that counted.

My chance to make the 1972 Olympic team was not over just yet. It was arranged for me to join the squad representing the U.S. Army in a qualifying event in Texas, though whatever possible connection I might have had with the brave men and women who put themselves in harm's way is beyond me. My father served his country, not me.

I trained hard in Texas, too hard. I practically starved myself. For three days, I didn't consume anything but water and the juice I squeezed out of lemons. It obviously wasn't the smartest thing to do in one-hundred-degree heat. Despite my last-minute efforts, it dawned on me that, at roughly 135 pounds, I wasn't going to make weight (125 pounds) in time for my qualifying bout. Instead, I made a scene. I have never admitted this, but I faked a blackout, and, frankly, it ranks as one of my best performances—and lowest moments. I fooled everyone, including Dave Jacobs, the other coaches, and my mother, who did what I knew she'd do, pleading with the staff not to let "[her] baby fight." I was thus spared the embarrassment of not making weight. Looking back, I wish I had been honest about the weight problem from the outset. At sixteen, there was much to learn.

Especially when it came to the opposite sex.

The person I was around girls was entirely different from who I was in the ring. In the ring, I identified with the comic book heroes I read about. My favorite was Superman, who was speedier and more powerful than any force, except kryptonite. Everyone knew my name, and that I was headed to bigger things. With girls, I could not put together a coherent sentence, let alone ask them out for a date. They knew about my boxing exploits, but that didn't impress them. Winning a bunch of amateur fights was not the same as being the star quarterback on the football team or the highest scorer on the basketball team. I wondered if there would ever be a girl for me.

Then she came into my life. Her name was Juanita Wilkinson, and, like my father when he met his future bride in South Carolina, I knew right away that she was the one.

However, unlike the more assertive Cicero Leonard, I waited and waited and . . . waited. Day after day passed as I stared at Juanita from around the corner while she boarded the bus for school. Whenever I got anywhere near her, I began to shiver. Her face was that of an angel, and she sported a cute, curly Afro, and there was no way to diminish another part of her appeal, the size of her breasts. They were enormous, beautiful. I got the break I needed when her girlfriend Bobbi Massey gave me her picture and number. Of course, I waited several more weeks to get up the nerve. What could this goddess possibly see in me? She could have had any guy in school. Finally, one afternoon, I made the call. I was more apprehensive than I'd been before any fight. I was relieved when one of her sisters said Juanita wasn't home.

A few hours later, she called back. I must have become more comfortable than I realized because after I asked her if she had a boyfriend and she said she'd had a few, I told her: "You met your match this time." I called back later that evening, and we were on the phone for ten straight hours, except for short bathroom or food breaks, till about six in the morning, often whispering to make sure our parents didn't catch on. Juanita fell asleep at one point and started snoring softly, yet I stayed on the line until her father came on and hung up the phone. With the light of dawn peeking through the window, I lay awake, still not quite believing that I'd talked to the girl I'd admired from afar for months. We'd brought up every subject two teenagers could possibly think of—music, school, friends, parents. The next night, exhausted, we did it again, starting a romance over the phone. Toward the end of one of those early calls, I boldly asked Juanita if the long chats meant we were officially boyfriend and girlfriend. She paused. I wished I hadn't asked.

"I suppose we are," Juanita said.

"Okay, then, you're my girlfriend," I said. I was in heaven.

Three days later, we met in person. It happened by accident the first time as I ran into her on the street when she was hanging out with a niece and cousin. I asked if I could walk her home and she said yes. I was anxious again, to say the least. What if I wasn't as smooth as I was on the phone? The chemistry between a girl and a boy can't be faked. If I screwed this up, I would never get to first base with her, and it might go down as the shortest love affair in the history of Palmer Park.

There was nothing to be anxious about. Juanita and I walked down the street hand in hand. For the record, I did make it to first base that night, and it was fantastic. From then on, we saw each other almost every day. I would arrive around eleven thirty at night to greet her in the street when she returned from working at the gas station her father and cousins owned. After hours of pumping gas and changing oil and tires, Juanita's face was smudged with black smut and she smelled like grease. I didn't care. All I saw was the girl I loved and I could not wait to hold her in my arms. I often stayed until the sun came up. We kissed and talked and kissed some more.

One night in late August, it happened.

With my house to ourselves, she stopped by to hang out. We were sitting on the couch watching TV when, with her typical bluntness, she blurted out: "You know, I did not come over here to sit!"

It took me a few seconds to understand what she was hinting at, but once I did, I was terrified. I don't recall exactly what I said. I am certain it was something stupid. I thought I was going to hyperventilate.

I was no virgin, mind you, having done the deed sometime earlier at the local drive-in on the dusty backseat of Coach Pepe's station wagon with a girl whose name I've never been able to remember. It didn't matter. As far as real sex was concerned, I was very inexperienced.

A birds-and-the-bees talk from Cicero and Getha Leonard? You've got to be kidding. The only advice on the matter came from my brother Kenny, and, believe me, he was no Dr. Ruth. He made one point, and one point only: "Ray, whatever else you do, make sure you get out quickly," and then he cracked up. Well, when the time for me to perform arrived that evening, my whole body shrunk. *Everything* shrunk, if you know what I mean. The important thing was that I did my manly duty, although I ignored my brother's advice and the subject of protection was never discussed.

In no time, Juanita and I were having sex on a regular basis, and we never used a rubber or any other method of birth control. We did it everywhere. In the car. In my house. In the woods lying down on my jacket. Everywhere.

The inevitable came next: Juanita was pregnant. When she told me the news, one might assume that my first reaction had something to do with her physical well-being or what decisions we needed to make, as a couple, about our new, important responsibility.

Not me, not the selfish, insensitive Ray Leonard. My juvenile mind raced to *my* accomplishment, the pride *I* felt: *Damn, I'm a fucking man!* I thought.

It was not until my ego was sufficiently massaged that I focused on *our* next move. Because Juanita didn't show for four of five months, we kept her pregnancy a secret from everyone, including our parents. I was no Rhodes Scholar, but I knew Cicero and Getha Leonard would not exactly be thrilled with the idea of a surprise grandchild. At no point did Juanita and I seriously contemplate getting married, as that would have derailed my path to the 1976 Olympics. Nor did we investigate how much it would cost for Juanita to have an abortion. In any event, it soon became too late for that option, and, as I suspected, my mom and dad weren't pleased to hear the news. Incensed was more like it. They should have blamed me, but they didn't. They blamed Juanita.

The most painful example of their disapproval came on the day of November 22, 1973, when my son, Ray Jr., entered the world. After driving around eighty miles per hour to the hospital, I hung out in the waiting room with the other nervous fathers-to-be. While they smoked cigarettes, I chewed gum, a baby myself at seventeen. For several hours I watched as one new dad after another received the official word and rushed to the phone to call his loved ones. They were all crying and screaming. I never saw grown men act like that before. I would probably do the same, it occurred to me, when my turn came. It soon did, and once the nurse told me that both mother and baby were doing fine, I phoned my parents. Regardless of their initial reactions to Juanita's pregnancy, I assumed they would be excited to hear from me.

"Momma, we just had a baby boy!" I shouted into the receiver. "A boy!"

I was wrong. There was no excitement at the other end. She muttered a cold reply and promptly hung up. I couldn't believe it. My happiness turned immediately into anger.

To this day, when I reflect back on that conversation, I become hurt and confused. I don't understand why she couldn't have shown the slightest joy on such a glorious occasion for Juanita and me, the birth of our first child. She couldn't accept Juanita, and she wasn't the only one in the family who was mean to her. So was Roger. If he was on the porch when she came over to the house, he would call her a bitch or a moth- erfucker, and warn her to never show her face there again. Saddest of all was my own unforgivable role. When Juanita told me what Roger said to her, I never asked him to stop. I avoided confrontations. That's who I was. Juanita went out of her way to break down the barrier between her and Momma, but when Getha Leonard made up her mind, there wasn't a thing anybody could do.

I'd like to say I was a model father, paying regular visits to be there for Juanita and Ray Jr. in every way, but that was not the case, then or ever. Even during Juanita's pregnancy I was absent, sometimes for weeks.

Perhaps the responsibility was too great. Or perhaps I resented the possibility of anyone holding me back from my quest to win the gold. Whatever my reasoning, I was gone, physically and mentally, too busy in the gym and in the sack. I fooled around quite a bit, including with Dave Jacobs's two teenage daughters. My father went berserk when he found out about this particular fling, dragging me out of the Jacobs daughters' place one morning at five o'clock and forcing me to run fifteen laps across the street from our house. I couldn't be sure whether Pops was more upset that I was cheating on Juanita or that I wasn't training hard enough for my upcoming duel with Dale Staley. In any case, I got back to work, and after I beat Staley, I resumed my affair with the Jacobs sisters and the other women in my life.

To cheat on my girl, the mother of our child, who dropped out of high school to care for Ray Jr. and, for two years, gave me half of the forty dollars a week she earned at the gas station while I trained for the Olympics, was shameless beyond belief. At the time, I didn't confess a thing to Juanita, but she knew. She always knew. After every extended absence, I would come back to see our son and renew our romance. That she knew as well. I wish I could admit that I harbored deep regrets about my conduct, but that, too, wouldn't be the truth. I felt I was entitled to do anything I pleased in those days, from destroying other men to bedding other women, and nobody would dare try to stop me.

Yet during these times of great promise, I was also feeling great pain, and it's difficult to know where to begin. I will simply tell two stories, both similar, both equally disturbing, then and forever.

The first has to do with a prominent Olympic boxing coach. I got to know the man, who was in his late forties, when he accompanied me and another fighter to an amateur boxing event in Utica, New York, in 1971. One night, he had the two of us take a bath in a tub of hot water and Epsom salts while he sat on the other side of the bathroom. We sensed that there was something a bit inappropriate about a grown man watching two teenagers in a tub, but because he was a male authority figure, we did not question him and eventually forgot about it.

A few years later, I was sitting in the man's car one night in the deserted parking lot across the street from the rec center when he started to tell me how important the Olympics could be to my future and how I stood an excellent chance of winning. To hear a major force in amateur boxing offer such high praise was a huge ego boost, which was maybe why it took me forever to see the real reason he had me in his car. Before I knew it, he had unzipped my pants and put his hand, then mouth, on an area that has haunted me for life. I didn't scream. I didn't look at him. I just opened the door and ran. I ran as fast as I could. He was lucky I didn't have a gun or a knife because I would have killed the man and simply accepted the consequences. By the time I got to my house, which was only a few minutes away, I was drenched in sweat. I hurried to my room and stayed there for the rest of the evening. I did not want anyone to see my tears.

When I first decided to share that incident in these pages, I didn't tell the entire story. I couldn't. It was too painful. Instead, I told a version in which the abuser stopped just as he reached my crotch. That was painful enough. But last year, after watching the actor Todd Bridges bare his soul on Oprah's show about how he was sexually abused as a kid, I realized I would never be free unless I revealed the whole truth, no matter how much it hurt.

In the years following the incident, whenever I saw the man around the neighborhood, I didn't say a thing and neither did he. I looked at him and he looked at me. We both knew.

Not long afterward, maybe five or six months later, it happened again, and again with someone I trusted.

He was a short, bald elderly white gentleman with huge lips whom I became friendly with in Hillcrest. A respectable member of the community, he always wore a tie and sport coat. On about a dozen occasions, he handed me a wad of cash. The total was probably close to five hundred dollars, which was a lot of money in the early 1970s.

I didn't ask why. I didn't care why. I didn't wonder for a second if he was setting me up. All I knew was that the cash he gave me was, besides the twenty dollars a week I received from Juanita, the only spare change I would have, with every other penny going toward my boxing expenses. It took money to go to the amateur tournaments around the country, tons of it, and the only reason I went was due to the extra funds raised through bake sales and donations from folks in Palmer Park. I was grateful to him, and didn't tell a soul.

Every visit was during the day, when others weren't far away. Then, for the first time, I went to see him after dark. In his upstairs office, between puffs of a cigarette, he gave me a pep talk about my boxing prospects.

"It's going to be okay, son," he said. "Your credentials are going to be off the charts. You are going to be one of the greatest fighters of all time."

I loved to hear the praise. It was one thing to hear it from my parents, and quite another from a white man. I was also excited, as I knew more cash would shortly be in my possession. Except the man had something else in mind. He touched me on the shoulder, then moved toward my crotch.

The nightmare was back.

I wanted to scream, but didn't. I wanted to kick his ass, but didn't. Fortunately, my body grew so tense that he stopped in time, but barely. I ran out of his office. Once I was safely in my car, I started to shake uncontrollably. I don't know how I made it home without getting in an accident.

I never confronted the man, just as I had never confronted the first abuser, both of whom passed away decades ago. What would have been the point? The damage was done. As life went on inside and outside the ropes, I buried these memories as deeply as I could, as if nothing ever happened. There were too many good ones to put in their place.

Except something did happen, something horrible, something words can never describe. For years, flashbacks to these two attacks disturbed me greatly, especially when I had too much to drink, which was quite often. The defenses I worked hard to construct would come crashing down, and I would not be able to stop the tears. I'd ask myself what every victim of abuse does: Did I do anything wrong to cause these men to take advantage of me? Each time I arrived at the same conclusion: absolutely not. If I experienced any guilt at all, it was that I didn't destroy them right then and there.

I began to wonder whether the fury I sometimes displayed in the ring, which was most uncharacteristic of my true nature, might be traced to these incidents as much as the fighting between my parents.

I do not know. I am not a psychologist.

I do know that I was in a lot of pain as I chased my dream of winning the gold.

Yet chase it I did.

2

"My Journey Has Ended"

Beating Bobby Magruder and the other top fighters in the hotly competitive D.C. region was not easy. Beating the Russians and the Poles and the Cubans would be even tougher.

I would first have to deal with the throbbing pain in my hands, which started around 1973 and became worse as the months dragged on. Every time I fought, especially the long, rigorous sparring sessions, the pain, caused by calcium deposits around my knuckles, was awful, and it sometimes took me hours to fall asleep. I felt as if someone had shot me with a jolt of electricity. My trainers and I tried every possible remedy, from rubbing alcohol to Epsom salts to Ben-Gay. Nothing solved the problem. I realized the pain would be a regular companion throughout my quest for the gold, and if I wasn't prepared to accept this reality, I might as well give up before wasting more time and money. While that thought did occur to me, as it does to every boxer, I never came close to quitting. It is remarkable what one is willing to tolerate if the goal means that much.

The one remedy that did have a positive effect was winning. My hands did not seem to hurt quite as badly after I knocked someone out or earned a decision. Even when I did lose, my confidence continued to soar. Such as the time I took on Anatoli Kamnev, a talented Russian fighter, in Moscow. Not surprisingly, just as in Cincinnati, I was robbed by the judges, who awarded the decision to one of their own. To his credit, Kamnev promptly walked across the ring and handed me the trophy. In another unforgettable fight, I sent Poland's Kazimier Szczerba to the canvas three times during the final round, the last one a certain knockout. But the referee decided the punch came after the bell, which it didn't, and awarded the victory to Szczerba. I don't think he enjoyed it too much, however, as he needed to be propped up to take part in the postfight ceremony. And I thought figure skating was rigged.

Going abroad to take on fighters from other countries was the ideal preparation for the Olympics, and for my personal development. I knew very little about the world outside Palmer Park, Maryland, and without boxing, I probably would have remained sheltered forever. One day, walking by myself in Rome, I came upon a girl no older than eight or nine who stared at me for the longest time. She took off, but then returned with a handful of other kids, each with the same puzzled expression. What was wrong with me? I wondered. Had they never seen a black person before? As a matter of fact, I believe they had not, and soon there were a few dozen gathered in a circle around me. I felt like I was on exhibit at the zoo. They weren't bashful, either, touching my hair and my skin. It occurred to them that while I was different, I was a human being just like them. No one spoke to me, but I felt their love.

Going abroad was not always an enjoyable experience. In Moscow, the food was terrible. I wouldn't eat much of anything but ice cream. It became obvious that the Russians were also staring because I was black. Only, I did not feel their love. Being away from home for several weeks, the longest stretch of my life, the loneliness got to me like never before. I became depressed, asking my roommate to kneel down and pray with me on the floor by my bed, and I was not the religious type. About a year later, when I was out of town preparing for the 1975 Pan American Games in Mexico City, I called Dave Jacobs to tell him I could no longer take the isolation and wanted to come home. He talked me out of it. He said I'd come too far and was too close to winning the gold in Mexico. He was right. The victory at the Pan Am Games gave me a profound boost of confidence heading into 1976, and it wouldn't have happened without Jake's persistence. I got through a lot of lonely nights with the love letters I received from Juanita. I wrote her whenever I left the United States for a long period, and could not wait to hear back.

It was around this time when a new member joined my team—well, not officially, as his checks were signed by ABC Sports, but it sure felt as if Howard Cosell were on my side.

With Muhammad Ali approaching the end of his brilliant career, Howard was searching for his next sidekick. In me, he saw someone who could not only win his fights but also appeal to the nonboxing fans, which meant good ratings and advertising dollars for ABC. Howard covered a few of my amateur fights, setting the stage for the Games in Montreal. He and I never established the magical rapport he enjoyed with Ali, but I can't imagine how my career would have progressed without him, and where I would be today. With Howard as the announcer, ABC carried each of my fights in the Olympics, and perhaps more significant were the interviews, bringing out the best of my personality to fans all over America. I was careful, however, not to let the inevitable comparisons to Ali get to my head. The attention would vanish as fast as it emerged if I didn't perform where it mattered most, between the ropes.

I could never be Ali outside the ropes. Nobody could. As unpredictable as he was in public, that was nothing compared to the Ali I observed in private. I got to see that side of him during our first meeting in early 1976, when I was invited by the Touchdown Club in D.C. to present him with an award. I was never as self-conscious of my poor upbringing. When I pulled up in a little blue Chevy Nova and saw a parking lot filled with one limousine after another, I made a U-turn and parked on the street a few blocks away.

At the dinner table, Ali sat on my left. Leave it to him to ease any tension.

"How long do you stop having pussy before a fight?" he said, with the same delivery as if he were asking me to pass the mashed potatoes.

I almost choked on my food.

"About two days," I answered, once I composed myself.

"Two days?" he said without looking up. "You a baaaaad nigger."

In the late spring of '76, I went back to Cincinnati for the Olympic Trials. As Sarge Johnson had predicted, the lessons I learned four years earlier made me a much better fighter. In my first qualifying match, I won a decision vs. Ronnie Shields. Next up was Sam Bonds, a tall, skinny southpaw. It did not take me long to figure him out. I hit him with a jab to the body, another jab, and a right. It was over in forty-two seconds.

In the final, I squared off against Bruce Curry, the Golden Gloves state champion from Texas.

Getting by Curry was far from automatic. He was an outstanding boxer, a future junior welterweight champ, but that wasn't my major problem. It was my right hand, which hurt terribly, forcing me to throw one left after another, and he knew it. He became more aggressive in round two. Unless I showed Curry a different look, he might take control of the fight. I couldn't let that happen. Late in the second, I landed a combination. The pain was intense but I had no choice. In the third, I scored repeatedly with my left, again sparing the right as much as possible. The decision was mine.

Shortly afterward, Curry and I met again at the team's training camp in Vermont for what was known as a *box off*. If he were to prevail, we'd face each other in a third, and final, match with an Olympic berth in the light welterweight division on the line. Fortunately, it didn't come to that, as I beat Curry once more. I was going to Montreal. I owed an extraordinary amount to Dave Jacobs, Pepe Correa, and Janks Morton for getting me this far. They never stopped believing in me, and their faith was paying off. Now it would be up to U.S. Olympic boxing coaches Pat Nappi and Sarge Johnson to help me win the gold.

As the Games approached, the pressure was intense, and not just on me. In 1972, only one American boxer, light welterweight Sugar Ray Seales, captured the gold medal in Munich. We could live with the fact that other countries poured millions into their amateur programs, but we were the United States of America, producing such outstanding Olympic champions as Muhammad Ali, Joe Frazier, and George Foreman, in 1960, 1964, and 1968, respectively. Winning only one gold was something we could not live with.

There were plenty of reasons to believe we wouldn't suffer a similar fate in Montreal. In addition to me, the squad included the two Spinks brothers, Michael (middleweight) and Leon (light heavyweight), Howard Davis (lightweight), and Leo Randolph (flyweight). Another positive was the experience we had gained in taking on the best boxers from other nations, often on unfriendly soil. We were familiar with their styles and strengths, primarily the Europeans. Nonetheless, the experts didn't expect us to dominate. There were too many other good fighters.

In Vermont, we learned how to be a team, not a collection of gifted individuals out for their own glory. As usual, I was shy in any group setting, although the earlier overseas trips, as well as the Cosell interviews, loosened me up to the point that I was selected as captain.

Of course, being young and immature, our egos collided. Howard Davis and I were sparring innocently when, as a CBS TV crew filmed us, he went after me hard, giving me a black eye. I didn't retaliate at the time, but that night I complained to teammate Louis Curtis. My pride was definitely on the line.

"He's trying to overshadow me," I told Louis.

"Just show him, Ray," he said.

I did just that. In our next sparring session a few days later in Montreal, after he threw a lazy jab, I dropped him with a right hand. My pride was just fine.

In general, everyone got along superbly. We laughed together—the tap dancing by Chuck Walker, the lone white boxer, was a source of constant amusement—and we cried together, rallying around Howard after his mother died suddenly of a heart attack. He thought about giving up his bid but we assured him that she would want her son to bring home the gold. Everyone shared the same goal of turning pro after the Games, earning as much money as possible before our bodies gave out. Everyone except me. I didn't waver for a minute: My dream would end in Montreal. That was the promise I made to my mother, Juanita, and myself.

Boxing was a path to the future. Boxing was not *the* future.

* * *

On July 17, 1976, along with more than six thousand athletes from ninety-two countries, I walked into a scene unlike any other I've ever witnessed—the opening ceremony of what was known officially as the Games of the XXI Olympiad. Starting with Greece, the delegations from each nation paraded into Olympic Stadium, their flags raised, their hopes even higher. Queen Elizabeth II, in respect to the people of Quebec, gave the welcoming address in French. Moments later, thousands of pigeons were released to signify the opening of the Games. It's too bad that I remember very little. My mind was busy on the task ahead. With the endorsements I was likely to receive if I was successful, I'd be set financially, and free to pursue my next goal of being the first in my family to earn a college degree. The classroom would be no easier than the ring.

Each night, as I stayed in the Olympic Village, protected by hundreds of armed security guards and numerous iron gates—it was only four years since the devastating attack on the Israeli athletes in Munich—I went to sleep thinking about my next fight, and about Juanita. She didn't go to Canada with me. Girlfriends weren't allowed in the Village, and besides, she and I were in one of our frequent cooling-off periods, dating back a few months. I can't recall what broke us up on that occasion, but it's safe to assume I was to blame, another episode of womanizing the likely cause. Yet while I kept messing around, first with a girl in Vermont and then one in Montreal, Juanita was the only one I truly loved. I wrote poems to her every week and taped her picture on my sock for the whole world to see. Not for one moment did I imagine she and I were done for good, so deep were my feelings for her, even if I had a strange way of expressing them. It was clear to everybody around me that I needed her there for moral support.

Dave Jacobs seized the initiative, persuading a reluctant Juanita, who left behind little Ray and an offer to become the assistant manager at a clothing store to join about a dozen others in a borrowed camper to make the all-night trek from Palmer Park. The trip turned out to be about a hundred miles longer than necessary after they took a wrong turn and were headed toward Toronto before realizing their error. Daddy was perhaps the most excited of everyone, going on the long journey despite the fact that his boss men warned him that he would lose his job if he went. He didn't care. Nothing was going to prevent this navy vet from watching a son of his represent his beloved country. After they arrived in Montreal midway through the competition, the camper parked only about four blocks from the Village, I went to visit them every chance I got. One thing you could safely say about the Leonards: They weren't very interested in keeping a low profile. Pictures of me were plastered on the windows, signs proclaiming: RAY LEONARD FAN CLUB, PALMER PARK, MD. I was a bit embarrassed, but loved it. Having them around after being on my own for two months was a source of great comfort. The men slept in the camper while the women shared a room in a motel.

In my opening bout, I faced Sweden's Ulf Carlsson. I knew very little about him except that he was a typical European fighter, always coming forward, displaying almost no lateral movement. I was patient, scoring repeatedly with the left jab. In round two, I landed a series of combinations and thought the Swede might go down, but he hung on. The decision was never in doubt. Next came southpaw Valery Limasov from the

Soviet Union, quicker than Carlsson and one of the favorites for the gold. Early on, he gave me trouble with an effective right lead, and I couldn't get inside. I finally did in the second, connecting with hard rights and lefts, and rallied late in the third to advance. I then defeated England's Clinton McKenzie, finishing strong again, causing a standing eight-count with about forty seconds left in the third round.

In the quarterfinals against East Germany's Ulrich Beyer, I was aggressive from the start and controlled the opening round, though I didn't land any real heavy blows. In the second, Beyer held his own, but I connected late in the round with a powerful right uppercut that pushed his head back. I then kept up the pressure in the third and coasted to victory. In the semis, I faced Kazimier Szczerba, the fighter from Poland whom I lost to when the referee ruled that my knockout punch came after the bell. I was intent on leaving no room for human error in our rematch, and I couldn't waste any time. That was perhaps the most critical difference between the amateurs and the pros. With only three rounds to make an impression, every second counted.

With about a minute left in the first round, after carefully measuring him, I started to get through his defenses on a consistent basis. In the second, I scored with my left over and over. Szczerba didn't come close to going down, but I dictated the tempo and secured the decision. There was nothing the judges could do this time.

Finally, the day arrived, Saturday, July 31. After 149 fights, which included 144 victories, there was only one left and it would be the most important of all.

I didn't get much sleep the night before and was up early, around seven o'clock, three or four hours before the weigh-in. After I made weight, I spent the early afternoon walking around the grounds with my family.

Around three or four o'clock, someone suggested I go back to my room and get a little rest. It wasn't that simple. For four years, I had dreamed of this moment and sacrificed everything. Now it was almost here.

There were still two major obstacles standing in my path.

One was the condition of my hands, which hurt more than ever, the result of five fights in twelve days. The pain was so bad in my right hand that I could barely make a fist. The other was Andres Aldama, the fierce Cuban fighter I would face in the final.

There was little I could do about my hands. I soaked them in ice for hours to bring down the swelling, but knew the first punch I threw would bring the pain right back.

Aldama was another matter. He was so dominant in the semis against the Bulgarian Vladimir Kolev—the poor guy was taken out of the ring on a stretcher after he was knocked unconscious—that as I watched a tape of the fight in a screening room at the Village, I overheard another athlete say, "Oh, shit, *this* is the guy fighting Sugar Ray next? He is going to destroy him." I snuck out the back of the room.

I could understand the sentiment. Yet I was not deterred. I was never deterred. Not in the ring.

The strategy against Aldama was to take advantage of my superior lateral movement and hand speed. If I failed to maintain a safe distance, Aldama would discover his range, deliver his shots, and I might be the one leaving on a stretcher.

My mind wandered a lot during those final hours as I lay on my bed. I dozed off, eventually.

* * *

It was time to leave for the arena. The team boarded the bus for the short trip. I didn't say a word. I don't think anybody did. What was there to say? We knew what we had to do.

In the locker room, Sarge Johnson, speaking in his familiar deep voice, led us in prayer.

Our dreams began to come true. Leo Randolph took home the gold and Howard Davis did the same. His mom would have been proud. Now it was my turn to keep the streak going. Four years of hard work were about to come down to nine minutes. It almost seemed unfair.

I bowed to the fans in each corner of the stadium, which I did before every fight.

The bell rang.

In the first round, my plan worked beautifully, as Aldama, referred to as "the Cuban" by Cosell and analyst George Foreman, did not come close to inflicting any serious damage, while I scored with a few solid left hooks. Still, I didn't do anything foolish, as I found out real fast how hard Aldama could hit. Nobody had ever hit me that hard. I also figured that Aldama would tire himself out, which was exactly what happened. I closed strong with a series of stinging combinations, giving him something to think about during the one-minute break between rounds. He wasn't sending me away on a stretcher.

In round two, I showed more movement, darting to Aldama's right to avoid his left. Then it happened, a sudden left landing right where I was aiming—Aldama's head—catching him, Cosell, and the crowd in Montreal by surprise. Aldama stood for a split second, then went down on one knee. He was not badly hurt, but that wasn't the point. The point was that I seized a sizable lead and needed only to stay on my feet in the final round to win the fight—and the gold. This was no time for heroics.

Requiring a knockout to win, Aldama came after me more aggressively, but his desperate attack made him more vulnerable. So much for being conservative. I landed five straight punches, which eliminated any possibility of a last-ditch comeback.

The seconds couldn't go by fast enough. Finally, the bell rang, and there was no need to wait for the official verdict (5–0). The stadium went crazy. My supporters went crazy. I went crazy. The gold medal was mine, one of five the U.S. boxing team won in Montreal, only one less than the entire track squad, along with a silver and a bronze. Howard Davis was chosen as the Games' most outstanding fighter. I didn't care. The shame of 1972 was avenged at last. No boxing team to represent America in the Olympics has surpassed our success, and that includes the 1952 group that featured future world heavyweight champion Floyd Patterson.

Nonetheless, I made it clear again that I was done with boxing. The exact words were: "My journey has ended. My dream is fulfilled." And I meant it.

During the ceremony when they played the national anthems for the three medal winners, one might assume I was euphoric, able to let go of the emotions bottled up for years. That's not what happened. No doubt I was filled with great satisfaction, the kind that can come only after investing every ounce of one's being in a difficult mission. I was proud, as well, for those who believed in me—my coaches, friends, family, and fans. It was their triumph as much as mine.

Yet I felt as empty as I'd ever felt. It dawned on me that my career in boxing, which had changed me forever, was over. So focused was I during the last days in Montreal, I didn't stop for a second to absorb it all, and it was probably a good thing, as I needed to put my energy completely toward beating my opponents. Any mental lapse might have been disastrous.

Now reality was sinking in and I wasn't ready for it, the end of a life that gave me more than I could ever imagine, more than a medal and fame. Boxing was an escape from the places I dared not enter. How would I find peace now?

As I surveyed the fans, decked in red, white, and blue, waving American flags, I decided I would cry to show them how much capturing the gold meant to me. Strange, isn't it, that I felt the need to *create* a reaction instead of being comfortable with the one that came to me naturally? It said a lot, I believe, about who I really was behind the mask of smiles and sweetness. I was sad and lonely, always searching for approval and a way to protect myself. If I assumed command of my emotions, no one could hurt me. If I let myself be vulnerable, the pain would be unbearable.

After the ceremony wrapped up, I headed for the exit. Now that I owned the gold, there was little to do except go back to Palmer Park. Still wearing my trunks and sweat suit, the medal hanging from my neck, I waited in the camper by myself while my parents and friends searched everywhere, until Jake figured out where I was. It felt like hours, but it probably was no longer than thirty minutes. I must have downed five sodas. I kept touching the medal to see if it was real.

"Let's leave now," I said after everyone climbed excitedly on board. "I'm ready to go home."

"Ray, what are you talking about?" they said, referring to the possessions I left behind in my room, which included trunks, shoes, and T-shirts.

I didn't care. After two months on the road, I couldn't wait to be back in my own bed, and although I owned a plane ticket for the next day, and might have arrived home before the camper—it was a fourteen-hour drive to Palmer Park—I needed, for my own peace of mind, to leave Montreal right away. We were soon on the highway, my head cradled in Juanita's loving arms. It wasn't very long before I received the first indication of my new celebrity status. At the border crossing between the United States and Canada, one of the guards, noticing the SUGAR RAY signs on the windows, asked to see the medal, kissed it, and then let us proceed. The hours went by in a hurry, everybody talking about the fight with the Cuban, and the fights before. The only downer during the ride was the condition of my hands. They hurt so badly that we went to a hospital about an hour from Palmer Park to have them X-rayed. We then stopped at a gas station a few miles from home. I combed my hair and was ready for my close-up.

When the camper arrived in Landover, we were given a police escort for the final stretch. I could not believe it. Police escorts were for presidents not fighters. In no time, we were at the shopping mall, where a welcoming ceremony had been planned. I saw the proud faces of the men and women who had given their time and energy to make my dream possible.

Over the next few days, I received mail from fans throughout the world, and our phone rang off the hook, many callers claiming to be "friends" when the truth was that I barely knew them. Strangers rode by the house hoping to get a peek at the local boy who had been on TV. Chalk it up as my first lesson in the Price of Fame 101.

Some lessons were harder to learn than others, such as the one that began with an article in the *Washington Star* a few days after we returned from Canada.

The headline said it all: COUNTY STUNS SUGAR RAY WITH A SURPRISE BLOW.

It was a surprise blow, all right, the sobering news that the Prince George's State's Attorney's Office had filed a paternity suit against me in court as part of a general crackdown against welfare cheaters all over the country. I was informed that the filing was standard procedure because Juanita had applied for public assistance, requiring authorities to verify the identity of the father and determine if he could provide financial support. Without the suit, a woman would not be eligible to receive the help she needed for herself and her child.

The assurance meant nothing. People would still believe I was no better than other members of the supposedly lazy black race, eager to shirk my responsibility at any cost. I found the timing of the story— a low-level county bureaucrat must have leaked the suit to the press— bizarre, to say the least, and then it made perfect sense: a deliberate reminder from the ruling white class that, gold medal or not, I still was, and always would be, a nigger. To be treated with such disrespect after helping U.S. boxing recapture the prestige it lost in the 1972 Olympics was inexcusable. Plus, I never tried to hide the fact that I was the father of a two-year-old boy. I was proud of Ray Jr., and everyone knew it.

As usual, I kept these feelings of betrayal to myself. I was not an Ali or a Jesse Jackson, who confronted racism whenever they saw it. Just because, thanks to Pepe, I knew many of the words of Dr. King's "I Have a Dream" speech, didn't mean they resonated deeply in my soul. I may have been articulate, but I was still wary of confrontation. The feelings did not go away. They helped me understand the barriers I would need to overcome in whatever career path I chose.

Other reminders of my place in the world followed in the weeks ahead, especially in the singular issue that has long epitomized the wide gap between the two races, the almighty dollar.

Thanks to Janks Morton, a meeting was arranged with the two of us and Mike Trainer, an attorney who worked out of a small second-story office in the D.C. suburb of Silver Spring. Janks knew Mike from playing on the same recreational softball team. He asked him to help me explore options for how to earn money after Montreal. Mike, who ran a general practice, wasted little time. He was extremely serious, which automatically made me uncomfortable. It took me years to realize this was how business was conducted. I hardly spoke during the entire meeting.

Mike gave Janks a bewildered look, as if asking, *What the heck is wrong with this guy? Does he know how to talk?*

"Don't worry," Janks said. "I'll call you later."

Thanks to Mike, who knew somebody high up at the school, I was awarded a nonathletic scholarship to the University of Maryland, where I planned to pursue a degree in business administration. I also wanted to help kids just as I was helped.

The first day of classes was weeks away. In the meantime, I'd cash in on my new fame just as swimmer Mark Spitz did in 1972, perhaps appearing on the front of the Wheaties box. To help me sift through the offers, we contacted public relations specialist Charlie Brotman. Charlie knew everyone in town, working wonders with the Washington Whips, the soccer franchise, and the Tapers, the professional basketball squad. If Charlie could generate awareness for these rather obscure outfits, he would make a fortune for an Olympic gold medalist and TV star.

I waited for a letter in the mail or a knock at the front door from somebody offering me $1 million, and it couldn't happen fast enough. I thought back to the night early in my courtship with Juanita when I asked her to the movies. I went to Kenny and my mother to borrow a car. They turned me down. With nobody else to approach, I had to tell Juanita we couldn't go. I was ashamed and determined.

"Juanita," I said, "one day, I promise you, I'll have enough money that I won't have to ask anybody for anything. They're going to have to come to *us* for money."

In the aftermath of Montreal, that day had arrived.

Or so I assumed. As the summer wore on, the glow from the gold fading by the hour, it became evident that Madison Avenue did not picture me as the right person to promote its products to Middle America.

"We loved watching Ray in the Olympics," was the standard response, according to Charlie, "and we know he has a great future ahead of him, but . . ." The "but" had to do with the paternity suit. As I feared, they didn't bother to check the facts.

In their view, there was no room in a family company for a black spokesman—a difficult sell to begin with—who had a child out of wedlock and didn't fulfill his obligations as a father. It didn't help that fighters had never been seen as ideal role models. Poor, uneducated, inarticulate, they would not appeal to average, hardworking Americans. Instead, the only offers I got were for appearances at local businesses, with the payoff very little—a few hundred dollars, tops—or, at times, none at all. I went anyway. I accepted every free dinner I could. That's what growing up the way I did will do to you.

I was, to put it mildly, not organized. I reached into my pockets once and handed Charlie dozens of phone numbers and appointments hurriedly scribbled on torn napkins and matchbook covers. I had no clue as to what I agreed to, with whom, and when, often committing myself to be in two places at one time.

Charlie never stopped working the phones. One deal he arranged took the two of us to Hollywood, where I signed pictures at an automobile show, "The World of Wheels." For every autograph, I was paid a buck or two, Charlie stuffing the bills into his pockets and socks. When we got to our hotel room, he dumped the entire pile on the bed. I started to count. "We're rich," I told Charlie, the total several hundred dollars, at least. I jumped up and down and tossed the cash in the air. As thrilled as I was, Bruce Jenner, the decathlon winner from the Montreal Games, was raking in the real dough, pitching every product on the planet. I had no problem with Bruce doing so well. He earned it. But there was no doubt in my mind that if I were white, I would have done a lot better, paternity suit or no paternity suit.

Once again, I kept my opinions to myself. Bringing up my race was never going to do me much good. If anything, it might make my situation worse. I was not as reserved, though, when it came to the matter of how my family responded to the suit. They found someone to blame instead of the county. Juanita, of course. She was perceived as a gold digger before there was any gold to go around. Never mind that I was the one who got her pregnant and didn't have the money to support our child.

I should have stood up for her and explained why the county filed the suit, but the other Leonards, as thickheaded as ever, wouldn't have backed down anyway. I was fighting a losing battle, and it didn't matter that my mom actually accompanied Juanita the first time she applied for welfare. The atmosphere grew so tense she stopped coming by the house. I couldn't blame her.

That was not the worst of it. The worst were the incredibly harsh comments the girls Juanita knew from high school made to her face, such as: "You tried to trap him with a baby, but it's never going to work," or, "I want him, you little shit, and I am going to fight you for him." She'd be walking down the street and someone would point her out: "There goes the bitch that did it to Ray." When a few girls threatened to beat her up, I was concerned for her safety. Yet, in her own feisty manner, Juanita was as tough as I was, never abandoning her faith in the bond we maintained with each other. She could withstand any insults as long as she believed we'd be together.

The controversy also kept Juanita from going with me and my family to visit President Gerald Ford in the White House. I saw no need to put her in the spotlight. But I was glad I went. The pride my parents showed was something I'll always cherish. Growing up in the Deep South, they never imagined they would one day be having a conversation with the president of the United States.

Howard Cosell was there, too, and was most gracious.

"Don't worry about it, Ray," Howard said, referring to the paternity suit. "It will blow over." Howard was a true friend.

As the days wore on, the story did not blow over. Nor did the emptiness in my soul since returning from Montreal. I wanted to believe that the void was directly related to the suit, and the negative reaction it generated among the fans of mine who felt betrayed.

I knew better. The truth was that, without chasing the gold medal as a distraction, I was lost.

I didn't realize how lost until the night I almost made the worst mistake of my life. I get chills when I think about it.

The first thing I did wrong was to call up a friend from D.C. who hung around with a much different crowd—the crowd I spent my high school years doing all I could to avoid. I knew they committed crimes. I just didn't know which ones. I didn't *want* to know.

I could have called a lot of friends to be with, but for once I didn't gave a damn about doing the right thing. I had done the right thing in representing my country, in bringing home the gold, and what good had it gotten me? I wasn't a hero. I was a nigger. And if I was a nigger, I might as well hang out with the other niggers.

I drove to an apartment in the northeast part of town where a friend of his lived. About ten people were already there listening to music and smoking weed. I knew a few of them.

"What's up, Sugar?" they said when I arrived. I could tell they were a little surprised to see me.

After exchanging small talk for about a half hour, I noticed several guys heading toward the bathroom. They were gone for a while before I began to investigate.

The door was closed. I knocked.

"It's me, man," I said. "Let me in."

When the door opened, I saw them brushing against one another, handing a long needle down the line, from one to the next.

They were doing heroin. I was naïve about drugs but I wasn't *that* naïve.

"Do me, man," I pleaded. "Do me!"

Almost immediately, one of the guys prepared to tie a piece of rope around my arm. The needle was slowly headed my way.

Just then, my friend realized what was happening.

"Ray, I am not going to let you fuck up your life," he said. "It is too late for us. Our lives are already fucked up. You *are* somebody. You're an Olympic champion."

Those words hung awkwardly in the crowded bathroom, but they were exactly the words I needed to hear. No, I was not going to fuck up my life. I took off as fast as I could, my arms spared the needle marks that would have done more damage than I could ever contemplate.

As the weeks went by, however, and I was still not offered any exciting money-making opportunities, I started to believe that maybe I wasn't somebody after all. Janks Morton warned me I'd feel this way. He spent a lot of time around former NFL players, seeing how their sense of worth crumbled after they could no longer make a tackle or catch a pass.

"Ray, you need to take advantage of your name because you are hot right now," Janks pointed out. "It won't be this way forever. If you don't do something about it soon, it will be too late."

I did not agree. People would come around eventually. After all, I had brought the gold to Palmer Park. I was chosen by the famous Howard Cosell as the successor to Muhammad Ali. I was . . . Sugar Ray Leonard!

In early September, Janks, frustrated with my inability to grasp reality, asked me to accompany him to a busy D.C. intersection at lunch hour.

"I bet you could stand here for hours and few people will recognize you," Janks said.

"That's insane," I shot back. "People will stop to ask for my autograph. I was on television!"

I stood there forever, the minutes turning into hours, hundreds of people passing by as if I were invisible. In total, less than a dozen mentioned they had seen me on TV or congratulated me for capturing the gold. I kept changing where I stood to give them a better angle, almost blocking their path. It made no difference. I became more and more discouraged. I wasn't as popular as I thought. I was Ray, not Sugar Ray, Leonard. Once I conceded the point, Janks and I headed back to Palmer Park.

It was not the decline in my popularity, however, that made me begin to reconsider my future. It was the decline in the health of my parents. Both became ill around the same time and didn't have the money to pay the medical bills that piled up every day. My father was already feeling bad in Montreal but didn't say a word. That was how he was brought up, and he figured I had enough to worry about. When we returned to Maryland, he felt worse. It got to the point where he couldn't digest any food or urinate, and was slurring his words. Pops insisted that it was just a cold. Yeah, some cold. He slipped into a coma and was rushed to the hospital. He suffered from spinal meningitis and tuberculosis, and lost forty pounds. There was talk that he might not make it.

As usual, I buried my emotions. Until the day I couldn't.

The doctor was speaking to my father while he played with a dollar bill, as if he were a little boy. He was having another of his hallucinations.

I looked into his eyes and thought, here was my rock, the strongest man I had ever known, and he was totally out of it. I cried, and seeing the pain in my mom's face only made me cry harder. Yes, they fought like hell. Yes, they almost broke up over and over again. But Cicero and Getha Leonard loved each other. They loved each other from the time they got past my grandparents' rules and started dating in South Carolina, and now their future as a couple was in serious jeopardy. As for Momma, a short time before the Olympics, she had been briefly hospitalized for a heart ailment, forcing her to miss work.

After every visit to the hospital, the same idea kept racing through my mind: Perhaps I should turn pro. Only in boxing could I earn the money to help pay my parents' medical expenses. As a boy, I took it upon myself to put my skinny body between them when they fought while my older brothers and sisters did nothing. I believed it was a matter of life and death. As a man, I felt the stakes were the same.

Was it a difficult decision? Absolutely. Instead of becoming the first in our family to earn a college degree, I'd be embarking on a vastly different sort of education, learning how to beat other people's brains in.

It was one thing to be an amateur fighter with the noble goal of representing your country in the Olympics. It would be quite another to harm other human beings, and risk ending their lives, for money.

Before making a final decision, I was invited, along with the other gold medalists, by the well-known boxing promoter Don King, to Yankee Stadium to attend the heavyweight title fight in late September between my hero, Ali, and one of his rivals, Ken Norton.

I couldn't accept quickly enough. Not only would I see Ali fight in person for the first time, I would be introduced to the crowd as the

Olympic light welterweight champion. After being ignored at the D.C. intersection a few weeks earlier, my ego could use the boost. I went with Charlie Brotman, who saw an excellent opportunity to get my name out again in the public eye, whether I turned pro or not.

Ali was not the Ali from his early years as a pro, who dazzled opponents with his speed. He now relied on his will, typified by his struggle with Joe Frazier in the "Thrilla in Manila" in 1975. He lost to Norton back in 1973, when his jaw was broken, before narrowly beating him in their rematch six months later. The fight at Yankee Stadium was sure to be another one that could go either way.

In the end, Ali was very fortunate to exit the ring with his belt, and his faculties, still intact.

But that's not what I remember most about the evening. It's what took place before the bell rang.

Charlie and I were at ringside when Cosell motioned from a special box seat for us to come say hello. I was always honored to visit with Howard.

After we hung out for a while, we got off on the wrong floor on the way back to our seats and wound up in the stadium's basement. The door opened and a massive security guard gazed at us rather menacingly. For a second or two, I thought we might not see the fight after all. Thank goodness, the guard realized who I was, smiled, and politely asked if I might want to see "Muhammad." Was he kidding? Of course I did, though I wondered: Why would Ali spend a second with me this close to the start of a championship fight? Didn't he need to focus every ounce of attention on the task at hand?

Apparently not. A few minutes later, Charlie and I were hanging with the champ in his locker room. It had been only eight months since Ali asked me at the Touchdown Club the question about having pussy in the days before a fight. It's a good thing I didn't remind him. It wasn't the right time.

"Are you turning pro?" Ali said.

"I'm thinking about it. I haven't made a final decision," I said.

Ali stared at me, his quiet eyes like giant black saucers.

"Well, if you do turn pro," he said, "just make sure that you don't do what I did. Don't let anyone own you. Remember, you are the one in the ring, and most of the money you earn should belong to you."

He added that if I did go pro, I should hire his trainer, Angelo Dundee.

"He has the right complexion and the right connections," Ali said.

Ali's handlers were getting a little anxious.

"Hurry up, champ," one said. "It's time to go."

Nobody rushed Muhammad Ali.

"I'll be there in a few minutes," he said. "I'm talking to my friends."

"My friends?" Muhammad Ali was referring to me as one of his friends!

I still was not ready to make a decision. Yet sitting in Yankee Stadium that night, I found myself mesmerized by the whole spectacle—the pressure, the applause, the electricity, all of it. I pictured myself in the ring, performing, winning—the welterweight version of Ali. Bailing out my parents was the initial motivation to turn pro, but I'd be lying if I said it was the only one.

In New York, I went to meet Don King, who gave me a tour of his properties, including his luxurious penthouse apartment. Coming from Palmer Park, I felt like I was entering a new world I didn't know existed.

It didn't take long for Don to make his pitch. Patience was never his forte.

"Ray, I can make you a fortune," he said, "and you'll be the world champion."

Don rambled on as only he can. He offered me a deal that would, as he promised, make me wealthy. The numbers, and I don't recall exactly what they were, would have set me up for a long time.

There was only one problem. I kept hearing a voice in my head:

"Don't let anyone own you."

Which is precisely what would have happened if I had signed with Don. He would have had the right, for example, to renew the contract if at any point during its last year I was ranked in the top ten of my division. I rejected the offer, and that was the end of our "negotiations." Over the years, I ran into Don on fight nights and we got along fairly well.

In one typical rant, he said: "Ray, you are very rich but you are still a nigger and you always will be a nigger. The white man is gonna take everything from you." I usually laughed during his tirades. Not this time.

"Shut the fuck up," I said. "You have more white attorneys working for you than anybody in this business."

King was speechless for the only time I can remember.

Another millionaire to approach us was Abe Pollin, the owner of the Washington Bullets and Washington Capitals. The Pollin group offered a $25,000 loan at first and later increased it to a $250,000 signing bonus. However, Pollin would have eventually owned half of my future earnings. No deal.

Meanwhile, as my parents' medical bills continued to rise, it was no longer a matter of *if* I was going to turn professional. It became a matter of *when* and *how.* More specifically: How would I afford it?

Maintaining distance from the boxing establishment meant that there was no capital to subsidize such an unpredictable venture. Winning the gold was no guarantee that I would succeed at the next level. The history of the sport is littered with promising amateur talents who never made it in the big leagues.

I could think of only one person to manage my new life and career, one person who had any sense of how the world really worked. That was Mike Trainer.

I didn't know Mike too well at the time, but what I did know impressed me to no end. There was not a trace of BS in anything he said. If he could get something done, he'd tell me. If not, he'd tell me that, too. Maybe it had to do with the fact that he was similar to me in one fundamental respect. He worked his way through law school, bagging groceries and delivering mail. He attended the University of Maryland, not Yale or Harvard. He earned his breaks, every one of them.

Mike put together a shrewd business plan, which he referred to as "a community-oriented investment organization." He installed me as the lone stockholder of a new corporation, Sugar Ray Leonard, Inc., asking twenty-three friends, who were businessmen in the Washington area, to lend the company a total of about $20,000. Mike also put in $1,000 of his own money. I was the president, chairman of the board, and chief executive officer. Our meetings did not last long.

The loans would be repaid in four years at 8 percent interest, and here was the part that made the arrangement most appealing: None of the investors would own a piece of me. They would not tell me whom to fight or when or for how much. When one potential investor inquired whether, in return, I might go with him on his sales route, he was immediately shot down by the others. The enterprise was designed to give me the best opportunity to make it as a professional boxer, not as a professional pitchman. These men weren't going to get rich off me, and that was fine with them. They might not even get their money back. What if I could not compete at the highest level? What if I couldn't sell tickets? We would find out soon enough.

On October 12, 1976, I made it official. Boxing was my future after all.

"I'm doing it for my parents," I told the press. "They're kind of down now and I'm capable of lifting them back up. I want to put them in a good financial position."

One last piece of the puzzle remained and it was a vital one: We needed someone with legitimate credentials in the fight game to navigate past the numerous pitfalls bound to emerge. Nobody on our team—Jake, Janks, Mike, Charlie, or I—understood how the industry, corrupt since the dawn of time, operated, and we couldn't afford to learn on the job. One major slip-up, in or out of the ring, and we might never recover.

After doing his research, Charlie narrowed the field of potential candidates to be my manager and trainer to three strong finalists: Eddie Futch, who guided Joe Frazier after the passing of Yank Durham; Gil Clancy, who oversaw the development of former welterweight and middleweight champ Emile Griffith and others; and Dundee, the indispensable presence in Ali's corner since his second fight in 1960. Futch and Clancy would have been good choices, but Angelo could not be topped. As Ali said, he had the right complexion and the right connections. He knew the judges and the reporters, and there was no telling when those connections might make a huge difference.

"Ray, you got to give time to the press," Angelo used to tell me. "Even if I'm really tired, I talk to them. They'll have the last say."

Angelo also knew, perhaps better than any trainer in history, the adjustments to make in the corner on fight night during the crucial moments when the wrong decision can cost your man the belt. Such as the night in 1963 when he secured for Ali extra time in his tough battle with England's Henry Cooper by enlarging a split that had already opened up in his fighter's gloves. A loss to Cooper would've certainly put a halt to Ali's bid for the crown. One year later, during his first championship fight against Sonny Liston, when a solution presumed to have been applied to the champion's face somehow got into Ali's eyes during the fourth round and blurred his vision, Dundee refused his demand to cut off the gloves and end the fight. He pushed Ali toward the center of the ring and told him to hang on until his sight was back to normal. Before round seven, when Liston didn't get off his stool, Muhammad Ali was crowned as the new heavyweight champion of the world.

Angelo Dundee comprised the final member of a team I was convinced would someday make me a world champion as well.

So much had transpired in the short three months since Montreal.

So much was yet to come.

3

From Vega to Vegas

ngelo Dundee came aboard in November, agreeing to a deal for 15 percent of my earnings. A few weeks later, I left D.C. to train at his base, the historic 5th Street Gym in Miami Beach. I was in awe. I could not believe I would be working out in the same ring where Ali hung out all those years. I had heard of the place for so long I almost expected gold locker rooms and new, shiny equipment. Instead, the gym was the same as any other, except for one difference. I could smell its greatness.

Angelo observed as I went through a standard workout, hitting the bags, jumping rope, and doing a little sparring. He offered a few pointers afterward but was generally pleased with my technique.

"We're not going to change nothing in his style," Angelo had told the reporters in D.C. "We're just going to add a few touches. The Sugar Ray Leonard who was good enough for the Olympics is good enough for the pros."

Angelo estimated it would take about three years before I'd earn a shot at the title. With each of his fighters, he selected opponents to challenge them, but not too severely or too quickly. If that meant a delay in vying for the crown, so be it. Ali didn't take on Liston until his twentieth fight, more than three years after he turned pro. A loss to any combatant at an early stage in his career could derail a young promising boxer for years to come, and perhaps cause irrevocable damage to his fragile psyche.

The man chosen for my pro debut was Luis "the Bull" Vega from Ponce, Puerto Rico. At five feet seven and 141 pounds, Vega, to be blunt, appeared to be no bull. A loser in eleven of his prior twenty-five matches, he would not pose a serious threat, which was just what we aimed for on opening night. The scheduled six-round duel was slated for February 5, 1977, at the Baltimore Civic Center, which put together a more attractive offer than Abe Pollin and the Capital Centre group.

I was thrilled to launch my new life in Baltimore. Roughly forty miles from Palmer Park, Baltimore was close enough for my fans and family to attend, including Pops, who, sitting in a wheelchair near ringside, was given a one-day pass from Leland Memorial Hospital in Riverdale. He was so excited he almost passed out.

At first, the doctors told him he was too sick to travel. Being Cicero Leonard, he did not back down. His long-term prognosis was excellent, thank God, and due to the money I would be making, he and Momma would not have to worry any longer about their bills. On the subject of money, the credit went to Mike Trainer. It was obvious from my first fight that the risk I assumed by hooking up with someone outside the close-knit boxing fraternity would pay large dividends. I stood to earn, depending on the size of the gate, as much as forty thousand dollars, an unprecedented sum for a pro debut. And I thought I was rich when I signed the autographs at the car show in Los Angeles.

Vega, on the other hand, was guaranteed only $650, becoming the first of many fighters in my career to earn a lot less than I did but as would be the case with nearly everyone I faced, he did not come close to matching me as a box office draw. My fights attracted national television coverage and fans who didn't normally follow boxing. For the first time in decades, since perhaps the original Sugar Ray, nonheavyweights made headlines. And journeymen professionals such as Luis Vega were granted a once-in-a-lifetime opportunity to pull off the upset and become famous, and perhaps rich in their own right. With Ali nearing the end of his magnificent run, someone needed to seize the throne.

The fight, to be carried by CBS, generated a terrific amount of hype, the marquee at the Civic Center reading: PRO DEBUT, SUGAR RAY LEONARD, SATURDAY FEB. 5, 4 P.M. Billboards and banners were plastered on practically every block downtown. Taking a page from the Ali playbook, I predicted a knockout in the fourth round, and figured Vega might go sooner. If that wasn't arrogant enough, I sent a letter to President Jimmy Carter inviting him to the event. Surprisingly, Carter, in office for only two weeks, found a better way to spend his Saturday afternoon.

On the day before the fight, I took Juanita and my son to see *Rocky*. The film was inspirational and instructive: I must not take Luis Vega, or anyone, for granted, I told myself.

Fight night finally arrived. Before stepping into the ring, however, I took a shot I didn't see coming. From Janks Morton, of all people.

Janks approached me in the dressing room. I expected words of encouragement, perhaps a last-minute suggestion on how I should approach this memorable night. Instead, there was only one person he was thinking about, and that was Janks Morton.

"Ray," Janks said, "make sure that Mike gives me my percentage."

His percentage? I was livid. Janks may very well have had a legitimate gripe, but this was hardly the time or the place to bring up any financial concerns.

The matter was dealt with eventually, but that wasn't the point. The point was that for the first time, I realized how money could affect those closest to me, and it would not be the last time. I loved Janks Morton, and I'll always be grateful for his generosity during those uncertain weeks after the Olympics. He handed me cash, almost every day, it seemed, that he could have easily used for his family. But that didn't excuse his self-ishness. I saw a side of him I never saw before, and it would change our relationship forever.

After kissing my father, I climbed between the ropes to a warm ova-tion and the theme song from the Olympics. I took off my purple robe with stars on the sleeves—this was showbiz, after all—and said a brief prayer.

One journey was over. Another was about to begin.

Vega was not a strong puncher, but he was fearless, withstanding the barrage of roundhouse lefts and rights I fired round after round. Despite his woeful record, he had never been knocked down. I could see why. He did deserve to be called the Bull.

His face growing red and puffy, a cut opening under his left eye, Vega kept moving forward. So this was what it was like in the pros? With their livelihoods on the line, not just their reputations, other fighters would come after me with everything they had. I danced and did the Ali shuffle to entertain the fans, cruising to the decision by winning every round on each of the three judges' cards. Yet it was not nearly as routine as it might have seemed. It rarely was.

More than ten thousand spectators showed up at the Civic Center, guaranteeing that I would make the forty thousand dollars, enough to soon pay back the investors. Mike Trainer had thought that I might have to secure a part-time job to fulfill my obligations to them, and that it could take years. It took months. We did not spend any of the money and no one ever had to lend me another dime.

I was a free man, and, after years of servitude, so was Cicero Leonard. Shortly after the Vega fight, I went to see my parents to tell them the news.

"Daddy, you will never have to work again," I said.

They were speechless.

I said I was going to buy a new home for them in the suburbs. Months later, when they moved into a four-bedroom home in Landover, Daddy and Momma could not stop saying, "God."

With my first fight in the books, Mike Trainer set out to finalize a longer deal with one of the networks. Prior to the Vega contest, he went back and forth from one section of the Holiday Inn restaurant in Baltimore to the other, meeting with CBS and ABC representatives. In the end, we signed a six-fight package with ABC for about $400,000 in rights fees. Once Mike learned the fight game, and it didn't take him long, he never wavered in his belief in my earning potential. He made deals directly with auditorium owners, increasing our share of the profits. Needless to say, the boxing insiders were not thrilled with Mike Trainer.

While Mike lined up the money, Angelo lined up the next opponent—Willie "Fireball" Rodriguez—for another six-rounder, to be held again at the Civic Center.

Willie was no Vega, winning ten of his eleven bouts, the lone setback coming against Rufus Miller, whom he defeated in the rematch. Willie possessed a solid left jab, a long reach, swift hands, and good footwork. In other words, he presented what Angelo was looking for, a test. Little did I know how much of a test.

In the fourth round, Willie landed a few solid blows, chipping one of my teeth. If the battle with Vega was a lesson in resiliency, the battle with Willie showed me the difference in punching power between the amateurs and the pros. Nobody, not even the Cuban, Andres Aldama, nailed me as hard as Willie did. What had I gotten myself into? I wondered. I had a gold medal in my possession, Angelo Dundee in my corner, and more cash than I could possibly spend, but I was a long way from taking on the premier fighters in my division. As it turned out, it was a blessing that Willie hurt me. I got mad, and when I got mad, I fought with a sense of urgency I didn't always exhibit. I held Willie at bay, registering a unanimous decision, and nearly knocked him down during the last two rounds. The fight was a turning point. At 141 pounds, I came in too light. For my next bout, I weighed 142 and was up to 145 within six months.

The hard work was only beginning. Over the next twelve months I fought nine times and starting with my fourth fight, against Frank Santore in the fall of 1977, they went from a scheduled six rounds to eight, and in the spring of 1978, to ten.

To build the extra stamina I would require if the fights went the distance, I sparred for longer periods, and more frequently. With every match I felt more confident, my delivery crisper, my defenses more alert, my footwork more elusive. I didn't punch from my toes, as I did against Vega and Rodriguez. I learned how to plant my feet properly to maximize the impact of every blow. Most fighters look directly at the target when they throw a punch. I never looked at the other man's face or his midsection. I began to see his entire body in a single frame. My fists knew where to go. I spent hours watching film of the top fighters from the past, taking mental notes of their tendencies, filing away strategies for use at a later date.

Still, the critics—and every fighter has had them—found fault with the lack of quality in my competition and the lack of power in my repertoire, and posed the question all boxers must eventually address: Could I take a punch?

The critics were dead wrong. I was doing what young fighters had done in every weight class, gradually moving up in the level of difficulty. I was knocking my opponents out, four falling in the first three rounds. What more did they want me from me? As for taking a punch, not once did I come close to hitting the deck. The real problem was that a significant segment of the written press resented the fact that I'd been discovered and promoted by television instead of in their daily columns. The balance of power in sports journalism was shifting, and they were slow to adapt.

I didn't let the criticism get to me. I saved my energy for training and disposing of whatever challenges Angelo put in front of me. I never questioned the matches he made. If he knew how to guide Ali on a steady course toward a title shot against Liston, he surely had a plan for me. I fought once a month, which was plenty. After each fight, I would take about a week off before training for the next.

That does not mean Angelo and I didn't have our moments. The one I recall most vividly took place during my thirteenth pro fight, against Dick Eklund at Hynes Auditorium in Boston. Eklund was a white guy from the city of Lowell, about an hour away. The fans were unruly for most of the night, a number of them shouting, "Nigger, nigger, nigger." I should have known the abuse was coming. Several days earlier, when I arrived at the Boston airport, I was greeted by a priest who said, "How are you, boy?" "Boy"! From a servant of God!

I tried to block the insults from my mind, but the anger kept simmering inside me to the point of affecting my performance. I could not put my normal flurries together. When I sat on the stool during one break, Angelo let me have it.

"What the hell are you doing?" he barked. "That's no way to fight. What have I taught you the whole time we've been together?"

I didn't have a problem with most of what Angelo said. He was right. I had a problem with the *way* he said it. He yelled at me, and yelling always made me angry, no doubt from the times I heard my parents raise their voices and the panic it caused. Some fighters need their trainers to berate them on occasion. I wasn't one of them. Angelo treated me as an infant, not a contender for the welterweight title.

I didn't respond. Nor did I speak to Angelo for the duration of the bout, which I won by decision. If I could have found a way, I wouldn't have gone back to the corner at all. After the verdict was announced, I bolted from the ring. I did not linger with my seconds to celebrate the victory. I didn't give a damn about the fight itself. I tracked down Mike Trainer in the dressing room.

"Angelo screamed at me," I said. "I won't accept that kind of attitude ever again. Only my father can talk to me like that."

Mike told Angelo how I felt. Mike always looked out for my feelings, as well as my finances, and, as usual, the issue was resolved. Angelo and I never spoke about it, and for the rest of our years together he never talked down to me again. If anything, we grew closer as the stakes grew higher. We would be forever linked, the white Italian from Philadelphia and the black kid from Palmer Park.

Yet there were misconceptions about the role Angelo played in my development as a fighter that I must clear up.

Angelo was my official trainer, but he didn't train me the way people thought. I'd been trained already by Pepe Correa, Dave Jacobs, and Janks Morton. I used to laugh at the stories in the paper that gave the credit to Angelo for swooping in a week or two before every fight with the magical formula to get me ready. I mean no disrespect to him, but if I did not have a strategy by that point, I wasn't going to find one in a few days. His true value was in the corner during the battle, and as a matchmaker. In those roles, there was no one else who could have served me any better.

Never was Angelo's skill as a matchmaker more critical than during the summer of 1978. After the Eklund fight, there was the possibility that I would next go against a promising young fighter from Emanuel Steward's Kronk Gym in Detroit, where I had occasionally trained as an amateur. His name was Tommy Hearns. The money would be hard to resist, around $100,000. I didn't know Tommy very well, though the two of us sparred for a few days before my sixth fight, in December 1977 against Hector Diaz in D.C., and got along just fine. I looked forward to the challenge.

Everything was moving forward—until Dan Doyle, a promoter we worked with in New England, got a call around midnight from an anxious Angelo Dundee. Angelo had just returned, according to Dan, from a fishing trip in the Florida Keys.

"We can't fight Hearns," Angelo told Doyle. "We're not ready for him."

Tommy was not a star yet—through that July, he had fought only ten times and just once outside the state of Michigan—but Angelo recognized his talent and feared the possibility of an upset. He also envisioned the day, perhaps a year or two away, when I would fight Tommy for a lot more than $100,000. In October, when Hearns demolished Pedro Rojas in the first round, Angelo appeared wiser than ever.

What would have happened if Tommy and I had fought in 1978 instead of our duel for the ages three years later? I can't be certain, though regardless of the outcome, the fight would have altered the rest of my career, and probably not for the better. A loss might have postponed my first title shot for a year, if not longer. A win might have kept Tommy from developing into the force he became, thus depriving me of my most glorious triumph.

In the opinion of Mike Trainer, however, Angelo Dundee was not doing his job, and it irritated him to no end.

After I turned pro, Mike assumed that with Angelo on board as my manager, he would return to his law practice in Silver Spring. It wasn't until much later, long after it became clear that Angelo had no intention of taking on the traditional duties of a boxer's manager, such as scheduling and contracting bouts, that Mike began to bill me at an hourly rate. Mike wrote a series of strongly worded letters urging Angelo to abide by his responsibilities but got nowhere. I would have done the same thing if I were in Mike's position, dealing with someone who expected everyone else to do the tasks he was assigned.

Most disturbing to Mike was the brief time Angelo put in at the gym. He believed Angelo needed to accept a bigger role or a smaller cut. He could not have it both ways.

Angelo wouldn't give in. My career, meanwhile, couldn't be put on hold while there was friction between the two most influential members of my team. Any delay in my progress toward a title shot could prove costly. Mike kept me posted, although to preserve my neutrality in the dispute, and my friendship with Angelo, I stayed out of the firing line. They would settle their differences later. Or so I assumed.

In September 1978, I squared off against Floyd Mayweather Sr., the father of the current welterweight star, in Providence, Rhode Island.

Providence was similar to many of the cities where I fought during the first two years of my career, and it was no coincidence. In each area where a fight was held, the national telecast was blacked out, which would have deprived us of too much revenue if it had been staged in a larger market. Another benefit was that if I could draw well in these venues, which I did regularly, in places such as Dayton, Ohio; Springfield, Massachusetts; and Portland, Maine, the networks would take extra notice of how popular a commodity I was becoming. It was no different than starting in New Haven in hopes of landing a role on Broadway.

Mayweather, ranked ninth by *The Ring* magazine, the sport's unofficial bible, presented a serious test, if not as dangerous as Hearns. The timing was perfect. It was not as if I were taking on only tomato cans, as we called the less accomplished fighters, but nor were any of them the reincarnation of Jake LaMotta. After nearly two years as a professional, I needed to find out what I knew and, more important, what I did not know. Mayweather was a slick boxer and very fast, with fifteen victories and only one defeat.

He scored well in the opening round but I was not too worried. I wanted to see what he had, and, thankfully, it was something I could handle. From then on, I owned Mayweather, pummeling him with overhand rights to the head and attacks to the midsection. That was the difference between me and Mayweather, as well as the other welterweight contenders from my era. I could dance *and* punch, despite what some members of the press believed. I knocked him down twice in the eighth, and the fight was halted, mercifully, in the final minute of the tenth, and last, round. A month later, I avenged my loss to Randy Shields, who beat me as an amateur, with a unanimous decision. I was fifteen for fifteen.

In January 1979, I took on Johnny Gant. Johnny does not rank up there with Hagler, Hearns, or Duran. Yet, like Bobby Magruder, Johnny was a star in D.C. and Maryland. Although his record was far from perfect (44–11–3), he knew how to pick his spots. Johnny was as mentally tough as they come, and given his background, it made sense. He grew up in the projects of Lincoln Heights and was sent to a youth correctional facility in Virginia when he was sixteen for driving the getaway car during an armed robbery. He served nineteeen months.

Johnny was tutored by a pretty decent trainer: Angelo Dundee. Angelo, forced to decide between Johnny and me, chose to be in my corner for the fight. He was no idiot. Johnny was thirty, an old man in a young man's profession, any realistic chance for a life-changing payday long behind him. I was only twenty-two, with many paydays on the horizon.

For some reason, I wasn't too fired up during the sparring sessions, to the point where Roger whipped me on a consistent basis. Roger had not whipped me since I was fifteen. My other sparring partners pummeled me with jabs and right hands. My efforts became so sluggish that Dave Jacobs couldn't take it any longer.

"Get out of the gym," Jake ordered. "Your mind isn't here. If you fight this way, you are going to lose."

Unlike the scene with Angelo during the Eklund fight, I did not get angry. Jake had been with me from the start. He had every right to go off.

One would assume facing Johnny Gant before a large crowd at the Capital Centre would have been enough to motivate me. The only explanation is that I was suffering from the classic burnout only other boxers can relate to: too many hours in the gym, too many miles on the road, too many aches and pains in parts of my body I did not know existed. For almost a full decade, except for maybe two months after the Olympics when my future was in limbo, I drove myself with no limitations and no excuses. After going pro, I fought seventeen times in less than two years. Everything was moving fast. Too fast.

Getting out of the gym wasn't the solution. I needed to get out of the state. If I stuck around Palmer Park, I wouldn't be able to stop myself from sparring, and given the mood I was in, that was the last thing I should do.

I flew to Vermont, where I had spent the final month of training for the Olympics. In Vermont, there was little to do but rest and hang out with friends I met in 1976. While I was not the type to bond with nature, the slow, tranquil environment, a far cry from the intensity of the gym, gave me the space to think. I asked myself: How badly did I want to be a world champion? Was I willing to do whatever was necessary? The same effort that had propelled me to win the gold would be required to win the crown. After about a week of R&R, I knew the answer. I couldn't wait to get home and back to the gym. In Palmer Park, I was a new man, whipping Roger and the other sparring partners with ease. I was ready for Johnny Gant.

On fight night, the atmosphere in the building, filled with nearly twenty thousand people, some paying as much as thirty dollars per ticket, was unlike that of any of my prior engagements. The two of us were fighting for a lot more than Washington bragging rights. I was fighting to strengthen my case for a title shot. Johnny was fighting to strengthen his case for more matches against top contenders. His window was rapidly closing. The veterans placed their bets on Johnny; the younger guys, on me.

The fight began. At the outset, Johnny called me "boy." Knowing he was out of his league, he was obviously trying to get me riled up. He did just that, but that was not a good idea—for Johnny. I respected him, but nobody called me "boy." I'd make him pay.

I battered him with an early combination and didn't let up for the rest of the evening. He landed a few strong rights to my head during the fifth round—he wouldn't be Johnny Gant if he didn't put up a fight—but I fended them off without any trouble. In the eighth, I connected with a left, a right, and an uppercut. Before long, Johnny was on the canvas.

He got up and took the mandatory eight-count, but he was in a daze. I went right at him again. I was not one to hold back when my opponent was in trouble, no matter what chance there was of inflicting permanent damage. Fights can turn in a matter of seconds, and the next thing you know you're the one who is getting beaten up, and believe me, the guy doing it will not show *you* any mercy. After a few more lefts and rights, the referee stopped the fight, and it was lucky for Johnny, who would have been seriously hurt, a fate I wished on none of my foes. Almost none. Duran will come later.

After the Gant fight, in which I made about $200,000, I knocked out Fernand Marcotte and Daniel Gonzalez, and recorded a unanimous decision over Adolfo Viruet. In May 1979 came the battle in Baton Rouge, Louisiana, against Mexico's Marcos Geraldo—and another round in the battle between Mike Trainer and Angelo Dundee. I made sure again to stay out of it. There was enough for me to deal with *inside* the ropes.

Mike was upset that Angelo had thrown me in there against Geraldo, a middleweight. I knew I was in for a rough night when I saw him at the weigh-in. All he had on was his underwear and yet he made me look like Luis Vega. He had me by nearly ten pounds.

The first punch Geraldo landed did not make me any more secure.

His power wasn't real, I told myself, each punch capable of knocking my head off. One stinging right I'll never forget shook me up so much that I started to see three Geraldos in front of me and I didn't know which one to hit. I began to dance, which was usually how I cleared my head. Not this time. I still saw three men. Fortunately, I aimed for the right one, the one in the middle, and landed enough solid blows to capture the decision. The victory came with a cost. While I have no proof, I believe the problems with my detached retina, diagnosed three years later, originated with the damage from Geraldo. My left eye was horribly swollen, and it was the first time I experienced double vision. Thank goodness I was in superb shape or I might have lost to Geraldo, and there's no telling how that would have impacted the rest of my career.

At the same time, I learned a lot about myself that night. I learned how to summon, from somewhere deep within, the extra will I didn't know I possessed. Knowing it was there, and could be tapped again, gave me the boost of confidence I would rely on for years to come. Most boxers don't go that deep, and it's not because the will can't be summoned. It can. The hesitation comes from the pain one must tolerate to do it. You become exhausted and convinced you've given your last possible breath. As Ali memorably put it, in referring to the latter rounds of the "Thrilla in Manila," you feel you're on the verge of death. That, however, is precisely *when* you must give more of yourself, no matter how much it hurts. That is what separates the good fighters from those who make history.

On the other hand, some suggest it is also when a fighter may give too much, his desire to prevail greater than his instinct to survive, and thus open himself up to the most severe consequences, his reflexes too weak to match his resilience. Yet, while a wounded fighter may be the worst judge of his faculties, he should never surrender. That's why there are three men in the ring instead of two. Allow the experienced referee to stop the proceedings if he senses one combatant is threatening to cause irreparable harm to the other. A fighter can never possess too much heart.

I went to my room, praying for the pain to go away. I lay down for a few minutes, but it did no good, so I proceeded to the hotel bar to get my mind off the fight.

When I got there, I heard the voices of Mike, Janks, and Angelo at a nearby booth. The conversation was anything but friendly.

Mike could not accept anyone, even Angelo Dundee, not bringing his A game, as I'd be the one to pay the price. The price on this night was a face filled with welts and bruises.

"How dare you not do your due diligence," Mike said. "This guy was a total monster."

"People told me that he couldn't take a punch," said Angelo, who had never seen Geraldo fight in person. "Look at all the times he's been knocked out. He's got a glass chin."

"It is *your* responsibility to check everyone out," Mike countered, "not take the word of other people."

The problems between Mike Trainer and Angelo Dundee, however, were not about to be resolved at a hotel bar in Baton Rouge, Louisiana. They were never to be resolved. Each went back to his neutral corner and that's how it remained until Angelo finally left the team in the late eighties.

With my consent, Mike rewrote Angelo's contract to pay him 15 percent of each purse, with a cap of $75,000 for a nontitle fight and $150,000 if a crown was at stake. The days of seven-figure paydays were coming soon and the last thing he wanted to see was Angelo make a fortune when he did not, in Mike's opinion, fulfill his duties. The new arrangement would wind up costing Angelo millions. In the Hearns fight, for instance, he would have received $1.8 million of my $12 million take instead of $150,000. On the day before the bout, Angelo refused to leave his hotel room after it had been reported on television that Hearns's trainer and manager, Emanuel Steward, was taking home a much larger percentage of his fighter's earnings.

Angelo complained in his book several years ago he wished I had stood up for him in the contract dispute with Mike. With all due respect, he is totally off base. I stood up for him plenty, which made Mike tread much more carefully, as he knew I admired Angelo and would never accept his dismissal. Working for me from my debut in 1977 through the Hagler fight ten years later afforded Angelo the chance to stay in the spotlight long after his first meal ticket, Ali, retired, and make a ton of money. The truth is he has no one to blame but himself. He failed to do what he was hired to do. In this corrupt business, I had to pick one person to trust, and that was Mike Trainer. He never let me down.

In the spring of 1979, before I made easy work of Tony Chiaverini and Pete Ranzany—neither fighter made it into the fifth round—Mike and Angelo moved ahead with the plans for my long-awaited title shot.

The man standing in the way of me and the belt was WBC welterweight champion Wilfred Benitez. After the two sides reached an agreement on the most delicate part of the negotiations—the money, naturally—a deal was inked for the fight to take place on November 30. What a deal it was: a whopping $1.2 million for Benitez and $1 million for yours truly, both record paydays for nonheavyweights.

The Benitez camp argued that, as the champion, he deserved more money than I did, though Mike rightly pointed out that neither of us would be anywhere near the seven-figure territory if it weren't for my ability to attract nonboxing fans, and interest from the networks. We gave in, but the contest, at least, was slated for Caesars Palace, where I loved to fight.

Before Benitez, there would be one last tune-up, against Andy "The Hawk" Price in late September, also slated for Caesars.

Price's record (28–5–3) wasn't especially noteworthy, but two of those victories came in nontitle bouts, against the highly regarded Carlos Palomino and future World Boxing Association welterweight champion Pipino Cuevas. A strong case could've been made that I was assuming an unnecessary risk by fighting a top-notch opponent on the eve of my first giant payday. What if Price, ranked eighth by *The Ring*, landed a lucky punch and pulled off an upset? Stranger things had happened. Gone would be the date with Benitez and the $1 million, and there'd be no guarantee I would receive a payday like that again. I didn't see it that way, which meant I was either naïve or arrogant, probably both. I was also greedy. I'd earn $300,000, not too shabby for an evening's work.

In preparing for Price, I studied films of his fights, depending on the strategist I trusted more than anyone: myself. That takes nothing away from the outstanding suggestions made over the years by Angelo, Jake, Janks, and Pepe. Yet it was only when I saw the grainy black-and-white footage on the screen that I could begin to anticipate how a fight might play out, round by round. I was trying to solve a riddle. If I figured it out, the other man was in trouble. If I didn't, I was. When I reflect on what I miss most about my boxing career, it isn't the noise in the arena or the articles in the papers or the camaraderie in camp. I miss the hours and hours of searching for the ways to exploit my opponent's weaknesses.

Aside from his tendencies in the ring, I knew little about Andy Price. Until Diana Ross clued me in.

I went to see Diana in concert several nights before the fight. We had been introduced a few years earlier by a mutual friend.

"Sugar, how ya doing?" Diana asked when I visited her backstage after the show. "What are you doing here?"

"I have a fight in a couple of nights," I said.

"That is so funny," she said. "Marvin Gaye told me he's managing some fighter here. I think his name is Andy Price."

"Diana," I said, "that's the guy I'm fighting!"

We both cracked up.

"Good luck, sweetheart," she said.

Price was the one who needed the luck and he didn't get it. I caught him with a vicious uppercut to the jaw in the opening round and his hands dropped to his sides. A fighter's hands usually come down in the later rounds when fatigue sets in. For his hands to fall in the first minute or two was not a positive sign for any Price fans.

I followed with a barrage of punches. Soon Price was on the deck. He tried to get up at the count of seven, but couldn't make it, and required assistance to reach his corner.

In the three years since I turned pro, twenty-five men had taken me on and twenty-five men had gone down to defeat.

One more and I would be the new welterweight champion of the world.

4

All the Marbles

In the same three years, I was neither a boyfriend to Juanita nor a father to Ray Jr. I made what I would describe as cameo appearances, showing up in their lives for brief stretches before disappearing again for days or weeks at a time. Either I hung out in the gym in pursuit of my next victory or I hung out with friends, my "boys," as I called them, in pursuit of my next piece of ass. No matter what financial responsibilities I assumed for Juanita and little Ray, I saw myself as a free man in every sense of the word and was bound to prove it . . . over and over and over. After the three of us started to live together in the summer of 1977, I rented a separate apartment that I kept secret from Juanita. Although she had heard rumors, she didn't know for sure until she tricked a friend of mine into coming clean, and I still tried to deny it. Even after I told her the truth, I didn't stop using the apartment.

The story was the same on the road, my boys taking care of the arrangements. In Baton Rouge, for example, while I trained for Marcos Geraldo, they kept a sharp lookout for any pretty women who came to the sparring sessions, or to the fight itself, jotting down their numbers and addresses. Weeks later, about ten of us, including my brothers, flew back into town to divvy up the pool of talent, and, believe me, there was plenty to go around after I got first dibs.

Looking back, I can offer no defense for my conduct. I was wrong and I have to live with these sins, and the ones to follow, every single day. They eventually cost me my first marriage and deeply harmed the relationships with my two older sons. At the same time, I wasn't the first, and I wouldn't be the last, celebrity to surrender to the irresistible temptations fame provides. Until one has experienced the full range of pleasures that most people are denied their whole lives, and that includes sex with breathtakingly beautiful women, one has no concept of how alluring they can be. If I had not been rich and famous, these women would not have given me the time of day.

The boys, now old men, tell me they miss the glory days. At the age of fifty-four, blessed with a second chance at marriage and fatherhood I didn't deserve, I do not. Still, I understand how they feel. We thought we owned the world. No possession was beyond our grasp, and there was no reason to wait for it. If I went to a car dealership and spotted a Maserati that I desired, the car would belong to me within minutes. I wouldn't sit in an office for an hour to work out the financing. "Call Mike Trainer," I'd tell the lot owner, "and make the deal." He'd hand over the tags and I'd drive away with my new toy. Cars, women, they were all toys.

Why did Juanita stick around? Why not leave me and find a man who would treat her with the proper respect? In her early twenties, she was more beautiful than ever and, just as in high school, could have attracted anyone she wished for.

Maybe it was because of our son or because she'd invested so much time in us already. Whatever her reasoning, it was a miracle that she didn't blow my brains out. If it had been the other way around, I would not have been as forgiving. When we were teenagers, I routinely beat up guys if they even looked at her the wrong way. I sent one kid under a jukebox, another almost through a windshield. In the mid-1970s, during a period when we weren't seeing each other, I went crazy when I heard she was dating somebody else. I stopped by her house at about three in the morning, practically pushed her into the car, and after driving about three or four miles, told her to get out and walk home by herself. Within a minute or two, I regained my senses and turned around to pick her up. It wasn't until the late 1980s that she stopped trying to save our marriage. I could not blame her. She gave me more chances than I deserved.

Meanwhile, with every fight—every hike in prize money—came the growing realization that to my family and friends I was no longer Ray the son, Ray the brother, or Ray the buddy. I was Ray the bank.

I was the one with riches they never dreamed of, and believed they were entitled to as well. One day, somebody might need three hundred dollars. Another day, five hundred dollars. Rare was the day that a member of my family or a friend did not seek some type of bailout, promising to pay me back, although we both knew he or she never would. We both knew they never *could*. It reached the point where I told them not to pay me back. Did I resent being my own private welfare state in Palmer Park, Maryland? You bet I did. I might have felt differently if they had made a genuine effort to earn the money themselves, however degrading the work might have seemed. They didn't. They weren't proud, like my dad, who busted his butt at a job with no chance to ever move up.

Of course, why would they be like Pops? Why would they look for honest work when they knew I'd come to their rescue every time?

"What's a little money to you, anyway?" they said. "You're going to make another fortune in six months."

All they needed was to see the signs of my success—the Mercedes Benz, the six-bedroom home in the suburbs, the television in almost every room—to know I could afford to give them whatever they wanted. They were never going to break Ray the bank.

They didn't seem to recognize when it had been only a week or so since their most recent withdrawal. If they did, they didn't care. All they cared about was squeezing another dime out of me. They went through the cash almost faster than I could give it to them, and they weren't savvy enough to use it as an opportunity to improve their lives over the long haul. Money was, like a lot of things, something they couldn't handle. Fortunately, they are better off today than they were thirty years ago because they had the good sense to marry spouses who taught them how to be responsible in middle age.

My friends and family members told the bleakest stories. Too bad Oprah wasn't around in those days.

"Ray, you know, my car is broken down," one friend said, "and there's no way for me to get to work without it. It's too far to walk."

"Ray, I'm way behind on the rent," another said, "and the landlord is threatening to kick me out if I don't pay right away."

Rent was a regular hook, not food or clothes or other basic necessities.

On and on it went, forever, it seemed. One friend had the nerve to suggest I pay him the exact sum he owed Uncle Sam. He was not kidding.

They didn't come right out and ask for money. That would be too bold. Yet the subtext of the "conversation" was obvious from the second they walked through the door.

Roger was assertive enough to ask, though not for cash. He asked for *chickens*—each chicken the equivalent of one hundred dollars.

"Ray, can you spare me a couple of chickens?" he'd say.

I have always wondered whether asking for chickens was Roger's clever way to make it appear like he was not seeking a handout from his younger brother. If it was, I wasn't fooled for one moment. Kenny, meanwhile, came to me with dozens of schemes to make a quick buck. He was like Ralph Kramden from *The Honeymooners*. Not one idea made any money, or sense.

The amounts to satisfy their needs, at least for the short term, were manageable, never larger than two thousand dollars, which I could easily produce from the cash in my safe. Or I simply wrote a check. Either way, it's not as if I missed the money.

My accountant, Don Gold, didn't quite see it that way.

"If you give away two thousand dollars a hundred times," Don said, "that's a lot of money."

Mike Trainer was more emphatic. "Ray, when you start saying no to these people, when you start being an asshole, that's when you will be happy," he said. He was right. He later came up with the ingenious concept of hiring family members and friends as independent contractors in training camp, allowing me to deduct their expenses from my income.

On the other hand, what was I supposed to do? If I turned them down, I would come across as the black man who made it big in whitey's world and then forgot where he came from and the people who helped him get there. Giving them money was also a heck of a lot easier than squabbling. Rewarded for my fighting skills, I still did whatever I could to avoid any conflicts outside the ring. The memories of my parents' brawls were never far beneath the surface.

On occasion, I handed over more money than they wanted, and sometimes when they did not want any at all. If someone needed a few bucks for gas, I would pull out a Ben Franklin without a second thought. When Kenny mentioned he was going shopping for a new suit, I would tell him to buy whatever he preferred, money being no object. He might spend close to a grand. One time, I went to visit my sisters without notice and took them to Saks Fifth Avenue, and gave each a five-thousand-dollar limit.

I could never be the asshole Mike suggested, except once. It happened when Roger walked into my office. I knew what he wanted and did not let him get the words out before I flashed him the same cold stare we got whenever we disappointed our father. He could see I was in no mood to make another contribution to the Roger Leonard Emergency Fund. His face turning red, he ran off without saying good-bye.

I bought homes and cars for my brothers and sisters, and for countless others. When a group went to dinner, whether there were five, ten, or twenty of us, I picked up the check. Everyone expected it. Helping to sort out the multitude of gifts was Mike's trusted assistant, Caren Kinder. Caren was my gatekeeper for decades, protecting me to no end. She was invaluable in determining what I needed to know and when I needed to know it.

More distressing than the loss of cash was the loss of closeness. No one bothered to ask: "Ray, how are *you*?" They came to me to fix their problems, never to hear about mine.

I wanted to shout: "You guys do not get it, do you? I'm in great pain, too, and my pain is just as important as your pain." After they left, their needs met, I closed the iron gates and felt alone.

Looking back and trying to make sense of this period from their perspective, I wonder if being alone was simply the price I was meant to pay for my success. They put me on a pedestal as well, and I felt just as lousy then as I did when they came for money. When the family gathered for dinner and I was running late, my mom would say, "We can't eat till Ray gets here." Momma would not have waited for any of her other kids, but since I was Sugar Ray Leonard, I was to be treated differently. It was never what I wanted. I was suspicious enough already of people's motives in the outside world, not knowing if they liked me for who I was or because of my popularity. At home, I figured I would be loved for simply being myself, a son and a brother. That's not what happened, and it was my loss. It's hard to blame them too much. After all, it was up to me to let them know how I felt, and I didn't. I couldn't.

I couldn't because of the pressure I felt living up to the image I had worked tirelessly to create. I was incredibly blessed, especially for a young black man from Palmer Park, Maryland. How could I then tell my family, or anyone, of that pain—that darkness—inside me? So I did what I always did. I buried it, which made me feel even worse.

To be fair, none of us, and that included me, had the slightest experience dealing with sudden, unimaginable success. White folks from the middle and upper classes coped much better whenever one of their own struck it rich. Money wasn't a strange, new object to them as it was for poor folk.

There were problems I couldn't fix with money, such as Roger's addiction to drugs, which dated back to the early 1970s.

Heroin was his drug of choice. Perhaps I could have made a difference if I had paid more attention to him, but there was only one person I paid attention to, and his initials were SRL. Instead of love, I gave Roger money, even if we both knew where it was going. I'm ashamed to admit I was worse than his dealer.

Similar to my friend Derrik Holmes, Roger, who turned pro in 1978 as a light middleweight, was loaded with natural ability. There is no question in my mind, and I don't believe there is in his, that if he had been able to conquer his demons, he, too, would have been a world champion. Roger was clever, elusive, fearless. His opinions regarding the strengths and weaknesses of my opponents were invaluable. There was little my brother could not do, except stay clean.

"You can't be a part-time fighter," I often told him. "You will never make it that way."

He didn't learn. Roger registered sixteen victories and only one defeat before he, like Derrik, quit for good in 1982. Unlike Derrik, he never fought for a title, and he has only one person to blame.

In the early eighties, Roger enrolled in a rehab center in Atlanta but was back on drugs within a week of his release. I went to see him in rehab, but I was high myself and in no position to offer any advice. I was incredibly embarrassed and hoped he didn't notice. It was not until about a year later, when he checked into a center on his own in D.C., that he made progress. He dropped by my house to inform me of his plans.

"Don't tell anyone, Ray, but I'm going in," he said.

I handed him a one-hundred-dollar bill, which he spent on heroin, though it was the last time he did any drugs. He's been clean for almost thirty years and today counsels others not to make the choices he made.

Roger wasn't my only sibling addicted to heroin. So was my sister

Sharon. I was quite upset but there was little I could do—until I got word while training for my fight with Johnny Gant that one of my sparring partners, Henry Bunch, had supplied her with drugs.

I decided to teach Bunch a lesson. I extended the rounds of sparring from three minutes to five and, ultimately, seven, for the sole reason that I could hurt him over and over. He was busted up pretty good by the time we were done. Many years later, I found out Bunch had not given her drugs. I felt awful.

A few weeks after the Price fight, I started to train in earnest for Benitez. He was sure to be my stiffest challenge to date. When summing up the 1970s and 1980s, boxing experts routinely cite Duran, Hearns, Hagler, and me among the era's best fighters, yet too often fail to include Benitez. He is overlooked because he was never in another memorable match after he fought me. Nor did he possess the charisma I displayed nor was he as intimidating as the other three. That doesn't mean Benitez wasn't truly gifted. He just happened to be born at the wrong time.

The youngest of three brothers who fought professionally, he was only seven years old when he made his debut in the Puerto Rican Golden Gloves. At thirteen, he won the national AAU title, and two years later, knocked out Hiram Santiago in the first round of his first pro fight.

At seventeen, Benitez shocked veteran Antonio "Kid Pambele" Cervantes to capture the WBA junior welterweight crown and become the youngest boxing champion in history. *Seventeen!* When I was seventeen, I was three long years away from competing in the Olympics. At twenty, he won the WBC welterweight championship by beating Carlos

Palomino. He knocked out Randy Shields in six rounds. I couldn't put Shields away in ten, and was fortunate to earn the decision. In thirty-nine fights, a draw vs. Harold Weston was the only blemish on his record.

Outside the ropes was an entirely different matter, and that's where he was vulnerable. His weakness? The same as many fighters: the opposite sex. His father, Gregorio, became so annoyed with Wilfred's lack of discipline that he predicted that it would likely cost him his belt.

"Both my wife and I are very disgusted with Wilfred," the elder Benitez said. "Even if they gave me $200,000 to work in the corner, I would not . . . he has not listened to anything I have told him . . . he would rather be out somewhere—anywhere—than in the gym. I have told him many times that Leonard will be in top shape and in top form, and that Leonard will beat him if he doesn't train."

Gregorio, who managed his son before he sold his interest to Jim Jacobs, the noted boxing film collector, later claimed he was merely trying to motivate him ("If I say he is going to win, then he no work"), although that type of psychological ploy wasn't something my father would ever have needed to motivate me. As much as I adored women, I knew my priorities, which was why Juanita spent very little time at our training camps and why, with one exception, the two of us did not have sex in the months leading up to a big fight. Ali couldn't say I was a "bad nigger" anymore.

I didn't pay attention to anything Gregorio Benitez said. I always felt that the write-ups in the papers did nothing to enlighten me about a fighter's strengths or weaknesses. I saw what I needed to see on film, and it was not just their footwork and punching tendencies that provided important clues. It was the words they chose and the tone they adopted in interviews. Was there the slightest sign of fear in their voice, or in their eyes, and if so, how could I take advantage of it? It was risky, however, to frame too much of any strategy on these celluloid images. How Benitez fought Palomino would no doubt be different from how he would cope with my habits. I didn't move my feet the way Cervantes did or attack like Weston. No two fighters are the same.

In breaking down Benitez from head to toe, his assets were impossible to overlook. What impressed me the most was how elusive he was, moving his head at the last possible instant to avoid direct contact. He was a very effective counterpuncher with each hand, which prevented his foes from being too aggressive, and switched easily between a right-handed and southpaw stance. When pinned against the ropes, he was extremely dangerous, and though he was not regarded as a knockout puncher, he placed his shots well. The final blow receives most of the attention from boxing fans, but it's usually the accumulation of punches that sends a fighter to the deck. Benitez, from what I heard, was also in excellent condition. Perhaps the master psychologist Papa Benitez knew what he was doing after all.

Nonetheless, I knew there was a way to beat him. There was a way to beat everybody.

One clue I picked up on film was that Benitez didn't like his opponents dictating the fight to him. If he was not in control, he became a little unsure of himself. Benitez was able to regain the upper hand— he survived three knockdowns against Bruce Curry during their 1977 bout in winning a split decision—but I planned to keep him on the defensive the whole night. I would attack from every conceivable angle, changing speeds the same way a pitcher does on the mound. Exploiting a small advantage in reach, I would use the left jab to score points and wear him down. He also had a tendency to dip his head as he threw his left, leaving him open to my uppercut. In my favor, too, was the fact that I'd fought eight times already in 1979, while Benitez had been out of the ring since March, when he beat Weston in their rematch.

As for my own work in the gym, my sparring partners got the better of me during the first week or two. That was not unusual. Once the rust was gone, I took command and put the hurt on them. I was serious when I sparred. A lot of fighters don't mind if others hit the bags or make loud noises in the background while they're in the ring. Not me. In order to totally concentrate, I needed everyone else to stop what they were doing. Sparring is not just to develop the muscles; sparring is to develop the mind.

The fight being held in Vegas, I'd have another key advantage over Benitez: Vegas was my home away from home, where I had already fought four times and felt at ease among the high rollers and celebrities. Benitez, despite his Playboy reputation, had never been on a stage quite like this and was likely to get distracted, if only slightly, and fights are often lost when one of the competitors is not completely focused on the man who will come at him from the other corner determined to beat his brains in. You can't wait until the day of the fight to enter that zone. You must be in it for days, if not weeks. It's no different, really, from the leading man who must memorize his lines in rehearsal and get into character before the cameras roll.

Another place I felt at home was on national television, and the fight was to be broadcast by ABC and Howard Cosell. Beginning with the Games in Montreal and my pro debut against Vega, I was on TV regularly. Benitez was not.

Then there was Caesars. It was boxing's new mecca, replacing Madison Square Garden in New York, which had held that honor for most of the twentieth century. By the late 1970s, Caesars was where the money was and where boxing was much more than a sport. It was a spectacle, with the boxers' names on the marquee in giant black letters, like Frank Sinatra and Sammy Davis Jr.

Nothing compared to Caesars: the aroma of cigars and booze, the parking lot packed with Ferraris and Rolls-Royces, the sexy outfits and fancy jewelry the gorgeous women wore at ringside, the organized-crime figures you could spot from a mile away, the Hollywood celebs who showed up to be seen. I wouldn't choose to fight anywhere else.

As November 30 approached, the atmosphere, however, was different from how it normally was in the days leading to a championship fight. There was a real battle going on in Iran, as fifty-three innocent Americans were being held hostage by followers of the country's new leader, the Ayatollah Khomeini. The hostages were on everybody's minds.

Closer to home, just two days before I took on Benitez, a fighter named Willie Classen passed away from injuries sustained in a November 23 bout against Wilford Scypion at the Garden.

Given the awful beating Classen was taking, many felt the referee should have stopped the fight long before Classen was knocked out in the tenth round. Although I wasn't familiar with Classen, whenever a member of our small fraternity is killed in action, I feel a deep sense of loss, as do many of my colleagues. We are aware of the great danger every time we step inside the ropes, but that doesn't lessen our shock and grief. Yet I could not afford to mourn the unfortunate death of Willie Classen. Not then. Not during the few hours that remained before I would enter the arena to risk my own hide. If I did, and I lost my focus, I could end up just like him.

By then I was already in the last stage of the change in personality I underwent before every critical match. As fight night neared, I became high-strung, rude, snapping at people for no apparent reason. Not having sex for months didn't exactly lighten the mood. To their credit, the boys gave me a lot of leeway and didn't take it personally. I was aware of my behavior, but it was more important to preserve the level of aggression I would rely on in the ring. Unless I brought out the savage in me at the right moment, I'd be doomed, and once I adopted that mind-set, I could be as mean as any brawler, especially when I was in trouble, as I was against Marcos Geraldo and would be against Tommy Hearns. I hated to lose more than anything.

Of course, in the weeks prior to any fight, it was difficult, and unwise, to maintain the edge every second. If I did, I would burn out just as I did in the gym while I prepared for Johnny Gant. Only, any loss of motivation against Benitez would be much more dangerous. I would not be able to take a week off and escape to rustic Vermont to clear my head. Gant, with all due respect, was no Benitez.

I would need to find a distraction. The answer was television. Situation comedies and action-adventure films often took my attention, if only for an hour or two, away from Wilfred Benitez. As the years went by, I turned into a VHS junkie, buying practically every tape in the store. I would slide a tape into the machine, and if it didn't instantly produce a new world, much like the comic book heroes of my youth, I'd put in another until I found the appropriate diversion. After a short respite, I returned to the task at hand, visualizing how I'd break down the other man's spirit and defenses and win the fight.

On the day before the Benitez bout, I went for a three-mile run at six

A.M. Jake and Angelo were not crazy about the idea, but running calmed me down. As I kept telling everyone, the fight was for "all the marbles."

Win, and I would be the new champion. Lose, and I would be what my critics had said all along—overrated, made-for-TV, style with no substance.

The latest question from the doubters was how I might fare if the fight lasted the full fifteen rounds. I had yet to go past ten, while Benitez went fifteen in five fights, including the previous two. No matter. I was in tremendous shape and knew when to conserve energy and pace myself. Moving up from a scheduled six to eight to ten to twelve rounds was not a hard transition to make earlier in my career. Why should fifteen, if it went that long, be any tougher? I sparred five-minute rounds in camp instead of three to build stamina. That was the only adjustment.

I was installed as a 3–1 favorite, almost unprecedented for a challenger, although I never paid much attention to the odds. The odds don't mean a damn thing when the bell rings.

Yet, as prepared as I was, one authority in the boxing business outside my circle believed I needed some last-minute advice. I was in my room around nine P.M., going through my normal visualization about what I anticipated for the fight, when the phone rang. It was Muhammad Ali.

I couldn't believe it. Ali was calling *me.*

After I got over the shock, I listened intently. It was partly due to the suggestions Ali made in his dressing room at Yankee Stadium in 1976 that I didn't sign with an established promoter. I was sure he'd come up with another gem. I wasn't disappointed.

"Don't do any showboating," he warned. "The judges won't like it."

I had to chuckle. Ali's warnings were akin to Richard Nixon giving a lecture on how to run a clean White House. Nobody clowned around like Muhammad Ali, who threw away more rounds than many fighters won. But he made a good point. The last thing the Vegas judges wanted to watch was another lounge act; there were plenty on the Strip already. They wanted to see punches that connected. They wanted to see a fighter serious about his craft. Considering the likelihood of an extremely competitive fight, I knew one or two points could make the difference.

I thanked Ali and went to sleep—well, I tried to. I never got much rest the night before a fight, and this being my first title fight, I got less than usual.

Around midnight, I jumped out of bed and went to the bathroom to look in the mirror. For ten minutes I did some shadowboxing. The exercise was geared more to checking out my mental state: Was I willing to put everything on the line? The answer was a resounding yes. I slipped back under the covers.

About a half hour later, I got up again and went through the same drill, the punches harder, the dancing faster, the eyes wider.

I got up three or four more times until, around four A.M., I finally went to sleep.

Benitez and I walked toward the center of the ring to receive the traditional prefight instructions from referee Carlos Padilla. Any assumption on my part that Benitez would be overwhelmed by the moment was immediately put aside.

He stared me down as we used to stare at each other in the hood, where most street fights wouldn't begin for maybe thirty or forty minutes while each man, his fists defiantly raised, attempted to scare off the other. Forcing someone to give up in our unwritten code generated more respect among the group than beating the living daylights out of him. Benitez was trying to establish a tone so that I would be more wary of him once the bell rang. Prizefighters since John L. Sullivan in the late 1800s had played these mind games all the time. In this case, there was reason to believe it might work. As we stood only inches apart, I was the one who appeared tentative.

I needed to recover, and fast. When I retreated to the corner, I told myself, here was the championship fight I had yearned for since committing my heart and soul to this life three years earlier. I thought for the longest time that I would never want anything as much as I wanted the gold medal. Yet as the ring started to clear at Caesars, so did my mind, giving way to the will that defined me as a fighter, and a man.

In these final moments, I never felt more alive and more authentic. It was as if I entered a room where no one else was permitted to go, where there was no confusion and no fear, where I felt happy and at peace despite taking part in a sport that required merciless brutality. In a strange way that made sense to me, I found boxing's warlike nature serene, almost beautiful, and it was why I made my comebacks years later against my better judgment and the counsel of others. I never did it for the money; because of Mike Trainer's shrewd investments, I was set for life. I didn't do it for the fame, either; there'd be an endless supply of that as well. I returned to the ring to experience the pure, almost indescribable sensation I could not attain anywhere else. I miss it terribly.

The bell rang. I was determined to show Benitez who was in control from the outset. His cocky stare was soon replaced by a look of genuine concern. He was in for the fight of his life. I landed the left jab and right hand, which created an opening for the hook. I won the first two rounds easily.

In the third, I nailed Benitez with a left, which promptly sent him to the canvas. Perhaps I gave the champ too much credit. Perhaps this evening, similar to many others in my undefeated career, was destined to be a short one. Whenever I put another man down, I finished him off.

Not this man. Benitez rose and took a standing eight-count. He was not seriously injured, and when he came out for round four, I felt like I was chasing a ghost. He slipped one punch after another. I was known as the dancer with the slick moves, but facing him was like looking in a mirror, and I did not appreciate what I was seeing. I never missed so many punches, and that takes a heavy toll, as an exhausted George Foreman discovered against Ali in Zaire. You spend more energy hitting air than hitting flesh, and it begins to wear on your confidence. Why am I not landing punches? What is wrong with me?

It became apparent that this was going to be a *long* night. Which meant that both of us, with our experience, instinctively sensed the need to pace ourselves. At various intervals, we took about twenty seconds off to step back and, standing almost flat-footed, allow time to go by without initiating any rough exchanges on the inside. Similar respites take place in every fight that doesn't end in the early going, and you can see it in the eyes of each man, who, with legs burning and lungs on the verge of exploding, relays a signal to the other without saying a word. The restless spectators, frustrated by the lack of sustained action, might not approve, but they can't relate to the pressures and demands we face every moment in the tiny space called a ring. Nobody, not even Joe Frazier, has been able to maintain a frantic pace for three full minutes round after round.

In the sixth round, our foreheads accidentally cracked together, although I was fortunate to fare better in the exchange. Blood poured down his face, while there was only a small welt on my forehead. The danger was that the blood would flow into his eyes and impair his vision, which had stopped countless fights in the past. The sport is filled with exceptional boxers who did not reach their potential because they cut too easily. Yet I did not try too aggressively to take advantage of the bleeding. I knew he could still counter and score points if I was sloppy. Benitez also injured his left thumb, and no fighter at this level is skillful enough to prevail with only one good hand. But he carried on, and actually got stronger, landing a number of solid shots over the next few rounds. My respect for him grew with every blow.

Part of the reason for my uneven performance was my fault, a stubbornness in continuing to depend on the right hand even after Angelo urged me to use the more effective jab. I suppose my ego, often a fighter's worst enemy, did not quite believe he could be in front of me one second, ready to be hit with a hard right, and gone the very next. This being my first title appearance, I sought the glory of a dazzling knockout. There was nothing glamorous about winning on points.

The main reason was Benitez. I wasn't the only boxer who could dig deep inside himself. In the ninth, after he landed a few well-timed licks, I retaliated with my most lethal combinations of the evening, sending him into the ropes. Still, he refused to go down. The critics were wrong about him, just as they were wrong about me. He was a warrior. I rocked him with a strong left hook and two overhand rights in round eleven, knocking out his mouthpiece, but not him. His father must have been proud. The fatigue was setting in, though, as I was in uncharted territory, past the tenth round, for the first time. My arms were spent. My head was pounding. My lungs were gasping for air. Maybe I couldn't go the distance.

It was not during the actual fighting that I felt the worst of it. I was too busy searching for an opening or attempting to avoid his combinations. It was during the breaks between rounds. That's how it always was. Resting in the corner for the one minute that never seemed to last long enough, I'd catch a glimpse of the man in the opposite corner and sometimes ask myself: *Why should I put my body through another three minutes of torture?*

It didn't matter one bit whether I was in control of the fight. My body wouldn't know the difference. No wonder some fighters surrender on their stools. They assess their predicament and decide that giving up is better than absorbing the pain guaranteed to come again if they answer the bell.

"Don't go to sleep on me now," Angelo warned after round eleven.

I didn't. I got back into the zone. To me, giving up was far worse than any amount of pain. My body would heal a lot faster than my pride.

Benitez remained sharp in rounds twelve and thirteen and took the fourteenth, perhaps his finest of the night, to give him hope of retaining the title with a strong fifteenth. He was as sure of himself as he was in the prefight stare, grinning when we met in the middle of the ring for the touching of the gloves to kick off the last three minutes.

I could not believe he was still on his feet, and while I was convinced I was leading on points, I couldn't be convinced enough. Judges were known to render stranger verdicts, as they already had on the undercard by awarding middleweight champion Vito Antuofermo, a 4–1 underdog, a draw against Marvin Hagler. There's no question Hagler was robbed. It's no mystery he never again trusted judges in Las Vegas. I would have felt the same way.

"This fight is very, very close," Angelo told me in the corner. "You got to fight like an animal."

Which was exactly what I tried to do, as did Benitez, the two of us giving the fans the best stretch of fierce toe-to-toe action in the entire fight.

I landed a hard left and soon followed with a right to the jaw. Later in the round came three left hooks, and with less than a minute to go, Benitez was too worn out to slip away once more. He was mine. At last.

A stinging left put him on the canvas. He rose quickly, as he did in the third, and grinned, but he was hurt. He was hurt bad. After Benitez took the mandatory eight-count, I went in for the kill. That is what fighters are taught to do from their first day in the gym, and I was no exception.

I never got the chance. Padilla ended it for me with only six seconds left, and it was the right call. Benitez was helpless.

The next thing I remember, I was standing on the second strand of ropes, my arms raised triumphantly in the air. I wasn't filled with the odd range of emotions I felt when I was on the podium in Montreal. I was ecstatic. The win, making me the new WBC welterweight champion, represented a beginning, not an end. The future was limitless.

After celebrating with Jake, Janks, Angelo, and my brothers, I was met near the center of the ring by Benitez. We hugged.

Some might wonder how two men who for forty-five minutes tried to destroy each other could embrace so soon after their battle was over, but it was precisely because we faced each other in combat that we needed to share this moment. Only the two of us—not our handlers or our loved ones—could relate to the sacrifices we made, physically, mentally, and spiritually. For months, the opponent was the enemy, the major obstacle standing in the path of greater earnings and greater fame. Yet, as most of us who fight for a living come to recognize, some sooner than others, the opponent is also a partner on the same journey.

Moments later, I climbed outside the ropes to do an interview with Howard Cosell. I paid my respects to the Classen family and praised Benitez. I then spoke about my performance.

"Don't be cocky," Howard teased, punching me lightly on the chin. There was no danger of that happening. Not after the punishment I took from Benitez, to date, the worst of my career.

For a fighter not recognized for his power, he fooled me. My face was swollen around the cheekbones and there were large welts under both eyes. I was nauseous, dehydrated, and my right hand was throbbing, as if someone had injected a needle into my knuckles. I spoke to the reporters afterward, with Benitez at my side, but instead of attending a celebration, I went to the hospital for X-rays of my hand, which proved negative. By around eleven P.M., I was back in my suite at Caesars, soothing the aches and pains in a tub of hot water. I lay there for an hour, at least, and could have stayed longer. I was in no mood to see a soul.

Soaking in the bath, stealing an occasional glance at the ugly face in the mirror, I asked myself the same questions most fighters do once every battle is over, win or lose: Was it really worth it? Were the rewards, as lucrative as they might be, worth getting beaten up, not to mention the hits one must endure day after day in the gym? And what about the chances of permanent brain damage? Fighters generally bury those fears, but I had met enough who took too many blows to the head and by their late thirties or early forties were never the same again. Would that be my pitiful fate as well? Would I have to depend on another person for the most menial tasks?

The questions were more relevant than ever. With the $1 million from the Benitez fight, after doling out a substantial portion to the government and my handlers, there was still plenty in the bank for me to walk away for good and live comfortably for the rest of my life. It was tempting.

"Ray, you are the world champion now. You have nothing left to prove," Mike Trainer said at the hospital. "This is a brutal way to make a living. Isn't it wonderful to know that you do not have to ever fight again if you don't want to?" Mike meant every word. He could never bear to see me get hit. He stayed in the dressing room until each fight was over.

But who was I kidding? I wasn't going to walk away.

Not after climbing to the top of my profession at the age of twenty-three. Not with more lucrative paydays in the years ahead. Not with there being no welterweight alive who could take me down.

And not as long as everyone in my circle kept urging me to continue—and why wouldn't they? Even if they harbored serious doubts about the condition I was in, mentally or physically, which I know they did, especially in the weeks leading up to the Hagler bout in 1987, what would possibly compel them to speak their minds? A fear for my safety? Please. They cared about me, but they cared more for their own welfare, and no one else could provide for them and their families as I could.

Every fighter is aware, or should be, of how damaging it is to be surrounded by a group of yes-men who won't pose the questions that have to be asked. The danger, of course, is that the boxer, oblivious, will take on the next assignment and the one after that, and who will ever know which blows were the ones that made him an invalid for the rest of his life? For Muhammad Ali, was it Joe Frazier who gave him Parkinson's? Earnie Shavers? Leon Spinks? Larry Holmes? Ken Norton? Who?

If I said, at the age of fifty-four, that I was thinking about coming out of retirement to fight Manny Pacquiao or Floyd Mayweather Jr., some of the boys would say, "Go for it." I'm half serious.

More than anything else, I wanted to be remembered as one of the immortals in boxing history, not just among my generation. I knew that defeating Benitez was not going to put me in that category. That goal is what inspired me to go running at five o'clock each morning, and to hit the bags until my hands could take no more. The fans had barely finished filing out of Caesars when the speculation began over who would be my next big opponent. The most likely candidates were Roberto Duran and Pipino Cuevas.

That day would arrive soon enough, but on this day, I paused to reflect on what I had just accomplished. I was now the champ, and no two words mean more to a fighter. For the rest of my life, no matter how I would fare in future contests as my skills deteriorated, I'd be called "the champ." Not "the champion," mind you—"the *champ*." It had to do with respect, as my father preached. "If a man doesn't have respect," he said, "he doesn't have his soul."

B enitez and I never met again in the ring. I would see him at other fights throughout the 1980s, but it wasn't until about a decade ago, when I paid him a visit in Puerto Rico while I was promoting an ESPN boxing show, that the two of us got a chance to spend some quality time together. It was a day I will never forget.

I picked up his mother first in San Juan, and we drove for more than an hour before arriving at a convalescent home in the suburbs. The facility resembled many of these places, the odor of sickness and death in every corridor. We reached a room that was almost dark, its lone inhabitant sitting in a rocking chair, his face and stomach bloated, his eyes staring blankly into space.

"Wilfred," his mother, Clara, said, "do you know who this is?"

"No," he said, examining me from head to toe, "but I know he beat me."

I forced a smile. I was devastated. It was one thing to meet fighters from earlier eras and see the harm our sport can inflict. It was quite another to witness the effects on someone from my era. In his early forties, his mind was essentially gone, the heavy price for sixty-two fights in a career that lasted way too long, until 1990. The official diagnosis was traumatic encephalopathy, a disease caused by a series of concussions. I couldn't help but think it could have been me in that rocking chair. Benitez squandered his entire fortune, and that could have happened to me, too, as it did to many fighters who made sketchy investments or were ripped off by those they should never have trusted. He didn't have a Mike Trainer to protect him. Few did.

Benitez and I were brought to another room, where, to my surprise, a screen had been set up to show our 1979 fight to about two dozen people. I was ambivalent about the idea, to say the least. Benitez would not remember the night, and if he did, why, in his helpless state, should he be subjected again to his most famous defeat?

The room got dark and, together again, we went back in time. I sat on a sofa, Benitez in his chair next to me, his eyes glued to the screen.

Nothing was said by either of us during the first fourteen rounds. I had not seen the footage in years, but I couldn't wait for it to be over. I started to fantasize about an alternative outcome, for this day only, in which Benitez would retain his title and everyone in the room would toast their native son.

It then hit me: Showing the fight was, on the contrary, an excellent idea. I could spot a spark in his eyes. He was back where he belonged, in the ring instead of in a chair. He was young and healthy again.

After we watched Padilla stop the fight in the fifteenth round, Benitez finally opened his mouth. He remembered.

"Su . . . gar, Su . . . gar," he said slowly, almost in a whisper. "I want . . . you to know . . . that I no train for that fight."

"Good," I said. "Thank you."

We laughed and hugged again.

Soon I was gone, grateful to be in one piece.

5

Manos de Piedra

With the belt in my possession, the time had come to claim another title: husband.

For years, it was the one title I did not actively pursue, and, if anything, I did my best—and behaved my worst—to avoid. After becoming a father in late 1973 at the age of seventeen, the last thing I craved was more responsibility, especially with all the freedoms I earned with my fists. Juanita, to her credit, was incredibly patient, never once in the six years since Ray Jr. was born pressuring me to get married. Because she believed in the special bond between us, Juanita was certain the day would come eventually, which it did, on January 19, 1980, her twenty-third birthday, in front of a packed crowd (typical me, always thinking of the gate) of about seven hundred guests at the First Baptist Church of Highland Park in Landover. Later, at the reception, there was an even bigger gathering, including a fair number who were not invited but were allowed in by one of my brothers or my close friend Joe Broddie. Things got so out of control, people banging on the doors, that Juanita stood up on a table to act as the traffic cop, motioning who could stay and who had to leave. I tried to talk her down, but it did no good. Nothing, though, could spoil the festive mood. With Ray Jr. as the ring bearer and Juanita as gorgeous as a bride could possibly be, we made for quite a threesome.

So what made me tie the knot? The simple answer is, I thought marriage was the right thing to do, which doesn't make me sound like the most romantic guy in the world, does it? Looking back, that was one of the many warning signs I missed. I first mentioned the idea to her before the Benitez fight and suggested we have the ceremony in Vegas. Not surprisingly, she felt getting married in a Vegas chapel was pretty cheesy, and I couldn't blame her, which led to the date in January.

Another sign I missed was how I chose to spend my last evening as a single man: with another woman, naturally, at a bachelor party the boys put together. I didn't know the girl and I never saw her again, but that wasn't the point. The point was that marriage, no matter how sacred a commitment, was not about to change my life. I promised myself I would still go to the coolest clubs and sleep with the hottest girls. I was Sugar Ray Leonard.

I probably got an hour or two of sleep at most before the big day—Juanita's big day, that is—and had a horrible hangover throughout the entire ceremony. Even so, I was convinced we would be together forever, which was why I rejected the suggestion when Mike Trainer first brought up the *P* word—*prenup*.

"It will protect your assets," he said, "if, God forbid, you two ever divorce."

"Mike," I interrupted, "Juanita and I will never divorce."

Mike would not let the issue die, however, and in the end, Juanita agreed to sign the prenup. She believed that no matter what happened between us, I would take care of her for the rest of her life.

After the ceremony, we flew to L.A. for our honeymoon—if you can call it that. I spent more time on the set than I did in our suite, leaving about seven A.M. each day to film a commercial and not returning until around nine at night. Juanita did not complain. It wasn't the honeymoon she was hoping for, but she had, at last, landed her man. She was Mrs. Ray Leonard.

In the weeks that followed I kept my vows—the ones to myself, not Juanita. Believe me, I wasn't proud of my actions. Every time I walked through the front door, almost like an enlisted serviceman home for a short leave, I was overcome with guilt about being absent so often. As usual, I did the only thing I knew how to do when I hurt the people I loved: I tried to buy their love back. Toys for Ray Jr., more expensive toys (cars, jewelry) for Juanita—whatever was necessary to compensate for my neglect and create a peaceful home. I engaged in my typical self-deception. Since I took care of their every need, I told myself, Juanita should be happy regardless of how much time we spent apart. She was richer than a black girl from Palmer Park could ever expect to be. The days of working at a gas station were long gone. If Juanita complained, she wasn't vocal enough to make me want to change my ways. Until it was too late.

Little Ray didn't complain, either, though our relationship was affected forever, and no amount of bribery could make up for my failings as a father. The gift he wanted most, my time, was the one gift I didn't give him. I rarely attended any of his sporting events, and if he needed something, I handed a few bucks to Craig Jones, my personal assistant, to pick it up. Craig was around the house more than I was. Years later, when Ray was in his early teens, he asked Craig for a ride to the park.

"Why don't you ask your father for a ride?" I said.

"I just did," Ray Jr. responded.

I felt like bursting into tears, but I didn't. I buried the pain with all the rest.

I loved my wife and son, but when I returned after an extended absence, I still had my Superman cape on. I was Sugar Ray and they wanted to be with Ray. After being told day after day on the road that I could do no wrong, it took a while to let go of that adulation. When Juanita and I went on a "date" to dinner or the movies, four or five of my boys routinely tagged along. It was never just the two of us.

Meanwhile, to my siblings and friends, I was still Ray the bank. If anything, with the $1 million I collected from the Benitez fight, and the guarantee of larger paydays—the dollar figures regularly appeared in the papers—I was approached more than ever to bail them out of their latest crises. I wrote the checks and didn't ask questions. Saying no was not an option.

I n late March, after four months off, the longest break since my pro debut in 1977, I returned to the ring to face England's Davey Boy Green at the Capital Centre in Landover.

Green was not a complete fighter by any means. His "conquests" included victories over household names George McGurk and Giuseppe Minotti, and that was fine with me. After the battle with Benitez, there was nothing wrong with accepting an easy payday of approximately $1.5 million. Nonetheless, I never took an opponent lightly, and that included

Davey Boy Green. In 1977, Green had been in position to pull the upset over Palomino and capture the WBC crown, until he walked into a left hook in the eleventh round. I could easily make the same mistake.

I could not have been too preoccupied with Green. Because if I had been preparing for Benitez or Duran or Hearns or Hagler, I would never have sat in the arena less than two hours before my own fight to watch one of the preliminaries, even if it did feature my brother Roger against my old rival Johnny Gant. The boys would have barricaded the dressing room door to make sure I stayed in the zone.

Nearly fifteen months since losing to me, Gant, thirty-one, was, for that era, ancient in boxing years. His chance at glory gone for good, he was simply trying to pick up a few bucks and avoid any lasting damage before he put away his gloves forever. So it goes for almost every prizefighter once the inevitable decline begins, typically in his early thirties. It rarely ends well.

Only, Gant wasn't ready to exit the stage just yet. Over the first three rounds, he pushed Roger around. I couldn't believe it.

I got out of my seat and headed for the corner.

"What the fuck are you doing?" I told Roger. "You can beat this guy. Now get off your ass and get it done! You're losing the fight. Throw your right hand."

Roger didn't listen.

In the fifth, Johnny landed a solid right cross to the chin. Roger was soon on the canvas. My brother and I got into our share of scrapes, but seeing him in trouble and being unable to do a damn thing about it was the most helpless feeling in the world. I screamed and punched the air as I stood on top of my chair, which made a few members of my team quite nervous. I could have fallen and gotten hurt, though there were two large men whose job was to make certain that didn't happen. Fortunately,

Roger gained control of the fight in time to escape with the decision. For Johnny, at least he was out of Leonards.

Next came my chance to cap off the evening. Given the level of competition, I wasn't as motivated as usual as I listened to the referee's instructions. I got pumped up in a hurry, though, thanks to Green's worst move of the night. He got right in my face and bumped me.

"Davey, what was that all about?" I asked him a few years later.

"I was trying to intimidate you," he said.

"*Intimidate* me? All you did, Davey, was piss me off."

I didn't want to just beat Davey Boy Green. I wanted to teach him a lesson.

I did just that, controlling the tempo over the first three rounds while he barely touched me. Yet I, too, learned a lesson and still tremble when I think about it.

During my previous twenty-six professional bouts, I was lucky. My opponents hit me and I hit them back, and when our business was done, we hugged, spoke to the press, got our money, and moved on to train for the next encounter. We endured our share of aches and pains, some worse than others, but they would always heal within a few days. Not once was anyone seriously injured. Not once did I see what the sport could do to a man.

Until Green fell to the floor in the fourth round. It was one punch that did it and it was perhaps the most beautiful punch I ever threw, a short left hook coming from the body and rising to strike him flush in the right temple. Whenever I connected with such power and precision, a tingling sensation similar to an electric shock traveled directly from my hand to my shoulder. It was a tremendous feeling, and one every fighter experiences when he lands the perfect shot. The world has no choice but to stop and acknowledge his work. I raised my hands and stood in admiration, as any artist would. Davey Boy Green was not going to get up before the count reached ten. No one would.

Referee Arthur Mercante got it started.

"One . . . two . . . three . . . four . . . five . . . six . . ." He abruptly stopped, signaling that the bout was over. Green was out cold.

I went immediately from admiration to fear. *Get up, Davey Boy*, I kept telling myself. *Get up! Get up! Get up now!* Seconds went by that felt like hours, my thoughts racing to the worst of possibilities.

Green slowly came to and was placed delicately on a stool near the corner. I felt a huge sense of relief, and all I could think about as I walked down the aisle was how close I had come to killing another human being. Retaining the welterweight crown was the furthest thing from my mind.

Little did I know that as I approached the dressing room, another man had gone down, and it was Angelo Dundee. Thirty years later, the details remain sketchy, but this much is clear: The blow was delivered by my longtime trainer from Palmer Park, Pepe Correa.

Pepe claims he was walking away from the ring when Angelo told him to get out of the way and used the *N* word. Pepe, younger and in better shape than Angelo, popped him with a left. Angelo's eyes rolled back, his head hitting the floor. He was out. Fortunately, he regained consciousness before too long. In his book Angelo says he still doesn't know why he was hit, and doesn't admit to using the *N* word. When I heard the news, I got worried that one of Angelo's friends might try to seek revenge against Pepe.

"Angie, don't let anything happen to him," I pleaded.

Apparently, I wasn't the only one who was worried. Pepe told me that another member of my team called him to suggest he get out of town. He didn't take his advice. Instead, he said he contacted a friend in the Mob and the matter was resolved. In any case, Pepe was wrong to hit Angelo no matter what Angelo might or might not have said to him.

A fter defeating Davey Boy Green, it became more apparent that my next fight would be against Roberto Duran.

If a deal could get done, that is, and that was no guarantee. Which was why we floated the idea of taking on Pipino Cuevas, who held the WBA welterweight crown, with the survivor becoming the division's undisputed champion. We saw it as a chance to gain leverage in any talks with Duran's people.

The problem for Cuevas was that he was not the draw Duran was, and if there is one rule in the sport that trumps the others it is this: Follow the money. Another factor was the pressure placed on the boxing authorities by officials representing the government in Panama. As a result, Cuevas was soon out of the discussion.

As usual, I stayed away from the negotiations, leaving them in the capable hands of Mike Trainer. Mike had come a long way since the fall of 1976, when he was the first to admit he knew little about the boxing world. Four years later, there was very little Mike did *not* know. The move to sign with him was proving more beneficial as the stakes continued to rise. I was not beholden to Don King or any other big-time promoter.

It made no difference that Mike and I rarely talked about our wives or our parents or our children. Or that we didn't share our deepest fears.

Every so often, usually over a beer or two, the conversation might start to veer in the direction of greater intimacy until one or both of us, sensing the dangerous ground we were entering, would quickly guide it back toward less revealing topics. It was the only way our arrangement could work. Getting closer on a personal level would have risked consequences to our professional relationship that we could not afford. What if I had let him down as a friend, or vice versa? More important than friendship was the respect I received from Mike, and it went back to when he launched Sugar Ray Leonard, Inc. Mike invited me to his home in suburban Bethesda for dinner. I had never been to dinner at a white person's house and couldn't figure out why I was there. It did not hit me until much later: Mike wanted me to understand that his wife and children were behind us 100 percent.

The most telling moment of the evening came after the soup was served. I took one spoonful and that was enough.

"Ray, is something wrong with the soup?" Mike asked.

"It's cold," I replied.

Mike explained that it was gazpacho, and that it was supposed to be cold, but he spoke to me without any hint of condescension. Not for one moment did I feel I was an uncivilized black man ignorant in the customs of a superior class.

He never looked at a person's color, only his character. Too bad the same cannot be said for the friends and family members who constantly urged me to dump him over the years.

"Ray, he's a white man," I was told, as if that fact had somehow escaped me. "He doesn't know what it's like to be a nigger, and you're a nigger."

"Hey, you don't have to remind me who I am," I shot back.

Besides, white wasn't the color on their minds. Green was, and they blamed Mike when they felt they weren't receiving their fair share. They figured I would never deprive them, so it must be the white manager in charge of the purse strings.

During the two decades Mike and I spent as business associates, we never signed a contract. A handshake was good enough.

I was the champion in the ring, and in the box office, which meant that we could set the parameters for the Duran negotiations. At the same time, Mike recognized that Bob Arum, an expert in closed-circuit television, could be very valuable to the bottom line. How these two strong-willed men, along with Don King, who enjoyed a tight relationship with Duran's people in Panama, joined forces was a textbook example of the behind-the-scenes intrigue that could occur only in boxing. You could not make this stuff up.

In April 1980, Mike, Janks Morton, and Arum were sitting in the VIP lounge of Braniff Airways at JFK Airport, waiting to board a flight to Panama to meet with Carlos Eleta, Duran's manager, when, out of nowhere, Don King appeared. King had not been invited, but the man knew everyone. King, for the most part, ignored Arum. They got along as well as Ali and Frazier.

"You sure you're doing the right thing?" King said to Arum at one point.

"What are you talking about?" Arum responded.

"I don't think the people are going to be real happy seeing you down there."

King went on to warn Arum that he might be at risk when he walked off the plane because he was interfering with the fight. Mike assumed he was kidding, but with King, one never knew. By the look on Arum's face, he wasn't sure, either.

After a certain point, Mike couldn't tolerate their juvenile behavior any longer.

"I made a deal for this fight and we're going to sign it, with or without the two of you," he said.

Arum and King got the message and agreed to be co-promoters. The deal was unprecedented. I was guaranteed a minimum of $7.5 million, with a chance to earn a few more million, depending on the closed-circuit revenue, while Duran would receive $1.5 million. By contrast, Ali and Frazier made $2.5 million apiece for their "Fight of the Century" in 1971. The Duran bout was slated for June 20.

As for the venue, we settled on the city where I became famous, Montreal. Next to fighting in D.C. or Vegas, there wasn't a place I'd feel more comfortable. I was treated well by the Canadians in 1976 and there was no reason to think I would not be given the same warm reception north of the border again.

When it came to Duran, there was nothing warm about him.

His nickname was "Manos de Piedra" ("Hands of Stone"), and with good reason. He did not defeat his opponents. He demolished them, his lone setback coming in a 1972 decision against Esteban DeJesus, which Duran avenged twice, with knockouts in 1974 and 1978. One story goes that after his defeat, he pounded the walls in his hotel bathroom till his hands were filled with blood. I wouldn't be shocked if that was true. Another nickname given to him was "El Animal." He deserved that one as well.

Take his lightweight title duel in June 1972 against the champion from Scotland, Ken Buchanan. Duran, only twenty-one, piled up a ton of points during the first twelve rounds and was nine minutes away from winning the belt. He needed only to keep Buchanan from landing a knockout blow. But that was not Roberto Duran. Duran always went for the knockout and was angry with himself, and the world, if he didn't get it. Perhaps it was his difficult upbringing—his father abandoned him when he was a kid, forcing him to drop out of school and scrounge for food on the streets—but whatever was behind that familiar rage of his, it controlled him as much as the other way around.

In the thirteenth round, as referee Johnny LoBianco attempted to pull Duran away, he nailed Buchanan. It happened to be a low blow and came after the bell. Buchanan was finished for the night. The Duran legend was just beginning.

Speaking of legends, assisting Duran in his corner were two of the fight game's most respected lifers, Ray Arcel and Freddie Brown. Arcel, eighty, worked with Hall of Famers Benny Leonard, James J. Braddock ("the Cinderella Man"), and Ezzard Charles. Brown, an ex-fighter, had been around since the twenties, serving as a cut man for Rocky Marciano, among others. No one was better. If there was an edge to be gained, physical or psychological, there was a good chance Arcel and Brown would find it. The two first hooked up with Duran in the early seventies.

By the spring of 1980, however, with Duran approaching the age of twenty-nine, there were those who thought he had lost something since relinquishing his lightweight crown to join the welterweight ranks in the late seventies. As a welterweight, the power in Duran's punches was the same. The difference was that heavier men could more easily absorb them.

I didn't buy into the perception of a less deadly Duran. He was like me and other fighters at the highest level. We may promise to give 110 percent every time, but it's almost impossible to be totally motivated if the competition doesn't match up. We are not robots. We save our best for *the* best.

I thought back to what the great comedian Jackie Gleason said to me when I ran into him two years earlier in Vegas. He could not have been more impressed with Manos de Piedra.

"I'm going to fight that guy someday," I told him.

For a change, Gleason was in no joking mood.

"Sugar, listen to me," he said. "Don't you ever . . . *ever* fight this guy. He will kill ya."

It was a lot like the day in the Olympic Village screening room when someone said Andres Aldama was going to destroy me. I wasn't afraid then and I wasn't afraid when Mr. Gleason said it.

Maybe I should have been.

The first occasion where Duran and I spent any real time together was at the April press conference to officially announce our fight. It was staged at the glamorous Waldorf-Astoria hotel in Manhattan. The top boxing writers were in attendance, geared up to begin promoting what promised to be the biggest fight since Ali vs. Frazier III five years earlier.

I looked forward to these gatherings. They gave me a chance to mingle with reporters I respected and show off my superior communication skills. I also saw an opportunity, as Ali did, to get inside my opponent's head, to win the fight before the fight. I won every time.

Well, not every time.

Early in the proceedings, Duran jabbed me softly with an oversized glove that's commonly used for promotional purposes. The photographers ate it up. For a while, I went along with the unrehearsed bit, anything for the show. Except Duran didn't know when to stop fooling around. Or he kept going just to irritate me. Either way, the playful taps got harder and harder. I gave him an angry glance. It did no good and was probably the dumbest thing I could have done. He saw that he was getting under my skin and now he would never shut up.

He called me a "motherfucker" and a "son of a bitch" and a *"marica"* (Spanish for "homosexual") and told me to kiss his balls. No one had ever spoken to me like that, not even in the hood. For the longest time I stood there like a statue, though it ran counter to every impulse in my body. I should have insulted him back and put my head squarely in his face. It was not as if I didn't know the language of the gutter as thoroughly as he did. But with Mike Trainer's mantra—"always smile for the cameras"— echoing in my ears, I was the perfect gentleman, until I could take the abuse no longer.

I told the press I would "kill" Duran in June. The words were out of my mouth before I realized what I was saying. I was never so cocky before a fight, and because it wasn't my natural behavior, I didn't hit the proper notes. I came across more frightened than fearless.

The trick to Ali's prefight bragging, besides the fact that he usually backed it up, was how he injected humor into each situation with his silly playacting and clever rhyming. He could make the most outrageous predictions and say the most demeaning things about the proud warriors he fought and somehow seem endearing.

There was nothing endearing about me on that day at the Waldorf. Round one went to Duran.

On the plane back to D.C., instead of feeling great joy about the largest fight, and payday, of my career, I felt naked. Duran had stripped me of my manhood. I did not talk during the entire flight.

Why was Duran furious with me? What did I ever do to the guy? Nothing, except perhaps have the nerve to enjoy the fame and fortune he believed should have been his all along.

Duran was no different than Hagler and others I fought, falling for the portrayal of me as the TV-manufactured spoiled brat who never had to overcome adversity to make something of himself, as they did. Duran obviously had never spent a night in Palmer Park. He didn't hang by the mall and watch the drug dealers make a score. He didn't talk to the hordes of young men without work, and without hope. And he certainly did not observe the struggles in my own family, the man of the house working twelve hours a day, six days a week, his wife raising six children before leaving for a job herself every evening. All Duran saw were the fruits of my labor, not the labor itself. All he saw were the commercials on television and the size of the purses. All he saw was what he *wanted* to see, and it was not as if Duran were applying for welfare. He wore the most expensive jewelry and ate in the finest restaurants. He enjoyed the good life just as much as I did.

Besides, it wasn't my fault that Howard Cosell adopted me or that the public embraced me. It wasn't my fault that I was articulate and charismatic, the heir to Ali in an era when boxing fans preferred artistry over aggression. Did I notice that vacuum, and do everything I could to fill it? Absolutely, and there was nothing wrong with that. Many felt I was being phony. I was not. I was merely bringing out a part of myself—the part that wished to please. I could never have pulled it off if it wasn't real. I wasn't *that* good an actor. Only later, much later, when I carried the role of Sugar

Ray too far, harming those closest to me, did I feel any doubts about who I had created.

Still, I could never have made it to the top of my profession if I didn't put in the work. I worked like crazy, just as my father did, to be the best fighter I could be, and wasn't that the American way? I beat Wilfred Benitez fair and square, as I beat the men I fought before him. The title wasn't handed to me. I took it.

For years I didn't understand Duran, and the confusion was a factor in the animosity I felt toward him. I figured out Benitez. I figured out Hearns and Hagler. Understanding the essence of the opponent I was facing made it easier for me to beat the living daylights out of him, and, when the fight was over, show genuine empathy. With Duran, however, it wasn't until the last several years that I figured him out. He wasn't a madman. He only pretended to be one. He was like me, searching for a way, any way, to stand out from the rest. Boxing is a form of entertainment, and, like Hollywood, to generate the most headlines, and dollars, one must develop a strong persona. Mine was Sugar Ray, the innocent charmer. His was Hands of Stone, the macho brute. Duran and I took on these roles without hesitation, and rarely stepped out of character. At least, not until our fighting days were long gone.

In the weeks that followed the press conference, I was determined that Duran would not seize the advantage in any future head-to-head encounters. I could not have been more naïve. I was a rank amateur compared to him. Trying to match his crudeness was like trying to compete with Ali in a battle of wits. I came up short each time and it reached the stage where I dreaded the next face-off. I had to show up, however, to meet with the press. It was in the contract.

A few days before the fight, Juanita and I were taking a postdinner walk in downtown Montreal with Angelo and his wife, Helen, when we bumped into the Duran party.

Away from the cameras, perhaps I would see a composed and civil Duran, and perhaps we could both revel in the ridiculous amount of money we were due to collect for forty-five minutes, or less, of work. There must be a decent human being in there somewhere, right?

Perhaps not. There was nothing civil about him. I saw the same Duran from before, the madman.

He cursed me again and demonstrated, by a series of obscene gestures, where he planned to strike me in the fight. Why wait any longer? I was ready to rumble right there on the street—no referee, no gloves, no handlers, no rules, nothing. I wanted the immediate gratification of knocking him to the ground. Luckily for Duran, I pulled myself together.

At the weigh-in, Duran was more crass than before, though it hardly seemed possible. He gestured to Juanita that after he was done fucking with me in the ring, he was going to fuck *her*. She was outraged. I somehow kept my emotions in check again. My chance to make him pay was coming soon enough.

During those final days, I saw Duran everywhere.

I saw him when I was jogging before dawn. I saw him when I was pounding my sparring partners who wore T-shirts with his name printed on the front. I saw him when I was watching comedies on TV. I even saw him in my dreams. Never did another fighter penetrate my psychic space as much as Duran, and there was nothing I could do about it.

Each time I saw him, he was where he belonged, on the floor, and after dissecting hours of film, I knew precisely how to put him there: I would box him to death. That was the best way to get inside Duran's head. The previous fighters who adopted a similar strategy were not able to make it work because they didn't possess my fast hands and feet. Yet Edwin Viruet forced Duran to go the distance twice. Edwin Viruet!

I would shift from side to side, exploiting a five-inch reach advantage to score with the left jab, and not allow Duran to lure me inside with his assortment of dirty tricks—he utilized his head as a weapon, shoving it into an enemy's chest—or establish any rhythm with his combinations. He was the only boxer I ever saw who used his head to hit the speed bag. I would steer clear of the ropes, where others were most vulnerable against his lunging attacks, and aim for the body—to *go downstairs,* as it's called. The media, though, was off base when it described the contest as another classic duel between the slugger and the boxer. Duran was a better boxer than he was given credit for, slipping punches almost as well as Benitez. I would not make the same mistake.

As fight night edged closer, in late May and early June, my body gradually rounded into shape. Every morning at five, wearing combat boots, I jogged five miles around nearby Greenbelt Park, navigating a steep hill that we affectionately labeled Mount Motherfuck. Listening on the transistor to my favorite D.C. radio station, I was at peace, singing along, until, after a mile or two, I didn't catch a single word or note. My mind was elsewhere, on Duran. I couldn't wait to shut him up.

When I first started jogging, Roger and Kenny beat me to the finish line and wouldn't let me hear the end of it. As my legs grew stronger, I picked up the pace and flew by both of them. It was my turn to brag.

I conquered Mount Motherfuck. The *real* motherfucker would be next.

After breakfast, wonderfully prepared by my father, who I placed on the payroll, and a shower, I took tap-dancing lessons. I can't recall what I was thinking at the time, but I must have figured that dancing would give me a little more flexibility in the ring. Around noon, I began my workouts in the basement of the Sheraton in New Carrollton, a few miles from Palmer Park. Roughly two hundred spectators paying one dollar apiece cheered me on as I did some sparring, hit the bags, and jumped rope. I hung out afterward to sign autographs.

By then, I had stopped having sex with Juanita. I needed to save every ounce of energy for Duran.

There was a great deal more, no doubt, to preparing for a match than working out in the gym and watching film, and that's where things got out of control once we arrived in Montreal in early June. I take full responsibility.

A training camp must function as a single, cohesive unit, each member assigned a specific task, willing to sacrifice individual goals for the benefit of the only individual who mattered, the fighter, the one who would, presumably, keep employing them as long as the wins, and dollars, kept coming. That was not the case in this camp, and it couldn't have happened at a worse time.

The problem was one I was quite familiar with: I couldn't say no. I couldn't tell one of Kenny's friends or Roger's friends or my friends that they couldn't join us in Montreal. After all, this would be the biggest fight of my life. I might hesitate for a moment, but it was only to watch my brothers squirm.

Before I knew it, there were too many people—several dozen, at least—with too many selfish agendas. Normally, we got by at camp with three cars and a minivan. In Montreal, we rented a bus. It was like a rock tour.

Janks Morton was in charge. He tried to insulate me from the petty disputes, but the stories trickled back to me, as they always do in a small, enclosed environment, and interfered with my preparation for Duran. The last thing I needed was to hear about one of my boys asking to borrow a car or a few extra bucks. They couldn't resist the nightlife an international city such as Montreal offered. It was almost impossible to get some of them, and that included Roger and Kenny, to cover the two-hour shifts guarding my hotel suite between ten P.M. and two A.M. The clubs were still open. They were thinking about dancing instead of Duran.

The night of June 20, billed by the French Canadians as *"Le Face-à-Face Historique,"* was here at last.

I went through my last-minute preparations in the dressing room, staring, as usual, into the mirror, searching for signs of the performance to come.

What I saw was troubling. My eyes looked vacant, disinterested. I tried to ignore it. I had no choice.

I watched none of the undercard, even though Roger was fighting. Fortunately, he managed to record a split ten-round decision over Clyde Gray. In another prelim, Gaetan Hart, a lightweight, took on Cleveland Denny, which would have received no attention except for the fact that

Denny went into convulsions from the shots he took. Weeks later, Cleveland Denny was dead.

At around 10:45 P.M., while the boys escorted me toward the ring, it was clear that my eyes had told the truth again. All I could think about was how I wished that I were anywhere else in the world other than Olympic Stadium. I felt like grabbing the microphone and saying to the 46,000-plus spectators:

"Listen, would you all terribly mind if you went home and we tried this thing tomorrow or maybe next week—same time, same place?"

It was not as if I didn't want to teach this son of a bitch a lesson for how he treated me and my wife. It was just that, at that very moment, everything felt wrong, and I knew I couldn't do a damn thing about it. I believe in biorhythms, and mine were extremely low that night. Some days, you get up on the wrong side of the bed and don't feel sharp. The difference between other jobs and what I did for a living is that if a fighter is off his game, even by a slight margin, he will lose and probably get hurt. If the fight had been the next night, or any other night, I would have kicked Duran's butt. But it wasn't.

When I climbed under the ropes, the sense of impending doom became stronger. I heard a strange sound from the crowd that I hadn't heard in my entire career, except from a group of racists at the Eklund fight in Boston. I heard boos.

How could the fans be booing me, Sugar Ray Leonard, in of all places, Montreal, where I won the gold? Was it something I said, or didn't say? Not knowing how to respond, I extended my hands, as if to assure them, *Hey, I'm right here. I'm ready to fight.*

The boos did not stop.

I wish I could say that I was unfazed by the cold reception, that I was so focused on beating Duran I could block out everything else, as the truly disciplined athletes are able to do. I couldn't. I was disturbed, confused, the fans getting inside my head just as Duran did, the fight no doubt lost before it had started. It was written that Duran had become a fan favorite for speaking a sentence or two of French whenever he appeared in public. He also wore "Bonjour, Montreal" on a T-shirt during workouts and kept up the PR campaign till the end, his supporters unfurling a flag of Quebec as Duran entered the ring. That explanation has never made sense to me, though it wouldn't have hurt if I had spoken a few words of French.

So why did they boo? I'm not sure. Perhaps some of the Canadian fans, echoing my detractors in the States, felt I had become rich and famous too soon. Or perhaps there was a tendency to cheer for the underdog, which Duran was despite his résumé and reputation. The official line in Vegas was 3-2. Whatever the motivation, it added an obstacle I didn't need to deal with in these tense moments. I had enough to deal with already.

I gazed at Duran in his corner. He was glaring at me as if he were ready to bite my head off the way he bit into the steaks he enjoyed so much. Joe Frazier said it best when he was asked who Duran reminded him of.

"Charles Manson," he said.

What was Duran's problem? Here we were, the eyes of the world upon us, raking in millions for one night of work, and he was . . . glaring?

Duran should be smiling, I thought, at how fate can turn dramatically for two poor kids, one from Palmer Park, the other from Panama, who both worked hard at their trade and would never have to work again if they so desired. Only later did it occur to me that Duran knew exactly what he was doing and that I should've been glaring at him. Instead, overwhelmed by the atmosphere, I stared at the large screen above the ring. I peered into the crowd, searching for comforting faces. I was bothered by the cold, damp air. My attention was everywhere—except where it needed to be.

Week after week, I thought about hurting Duran. Now, with the devil himself finally in my sights, I was lost.

The first round set the pace for the rest of the evening. Duran was the same as always, thrusting forward, almost recklessly, ready to die in the ring. Soon came the first hard punch, and I realized that "Hands of Stone" was no exaggeration. Each well-timed shot felt like a jackhammer being drilled into my skull, my teeth knocked back so hard I had to push them into place with my glove between rounds. I found myself in the trap I was determined to avoid, the ropes, Duran landing lefts and rights to the head and body, impressing the judges and fans.

The second round was worse. Duran caught me with a hook and right hand, and though I tried to indicate otherwise, it definitely did some damage. I may have acted my way out of trouble against Geraldo, but a seasoned pro such as Duran wasn't easily fooled. The seconds couldn't go by fast enough as he tried to end the fight right then. But I survived the round, and to show Duran, the judges, and the crowd that I was not deterred, I rose from my stool a full twenty seconds before the bell rang for round three. Looking back, it wasn't the brightest idea. I could have used the extra rest.

As dangerous as Duran was, however, his best wasn't going to put me away. I, too, was ready to die in the ring, and that, unfortunately, was where I went wrong. I fought Duran toe-to-toe instead of exploiting my superior boxing skills.

Why was I so stupid? It was because I wanted to hurt Duran the way he hurt me and Juanita with his constant insults. Gaining revenge became almost as important as gaining victory, and I refused to change my tactics no matter what Angelo might have told me in the corner. I was too caught up in my own anger and pride to listen to the man who had saved Ali more than once, and could have saved me. I never gave him the chance.

As the fight wore on, it was becoming clear that Arcel had perhaps gotten inside the head of Carlos Padilla, the same ref who worked the Benitez fight. He had expressed concerns that Padilla, known for breaking up clinches between fighters prematurely, wouldn't allow Duran to fight where he was most at home, in the trenches. In any case, Padilla compensated too much in the opposite direction. For as little as he broke us up, he might as well have taken a seat in the front row.

Still, I couldn't blame Padilla. He wasn't the one who kept retreating straight back toward the ropes instead of sliding to the right as Angelo had suggested, providing Duran enough room to advance a step or two and unload at a stationary target. If I had fought a more intelligent fight, nothing Padilla did, or did not do, would have made a difference. Yet I hung in there, and by the sixth round I was giving it to Duran as hard as he was giving it to me. If he was overlooked as a boxer, the same went for me as a slugger. Ask Andy Price. Ask Davey Boy Green. Ask Roberto Duran.

I was back in the fight, and there was still a long way to go. In the next several rounds I scored repeatedly while keeping Duran in the center of the ring. I also heard a more familiar sound—applause. Fans, whatever their rooting interest may be before a bout starts, appreciate a hard-fought contest, which both Duran and I were providing. With the courage I was displaying, they could see that I was not the pampered millionaire I was made out to be. The action, though, was too much for Juanita. She fainted into the arms of my sister Sharon during the eighth round. Juanita wasn't used to seeing her husband get his face bashed in.

Despite my renewed determination, I didn't come close to hurting Duran, which I needed to do to halt the momentum he had built in the first four rounds. I missed my target over and over, and when I did land a strong combination or two, he retaliated immediately with an effective flurry of his own. No one rocked me as hard in the body as he did. If anything, the hits he took made him counter with greater fury, as if he actually *enjoyed* the pain. Time, too, was becoming a factor as the bell sounded for round eleven. Unless I seized control of the fight, the decision would go to Duran and he would be the new champ. Yet, if there was any impulse to reverse course and box my way to the finish line, it was too late. I chose the wrong strategy and I was stuck with it.

The eleventh served up some of the fiercest combat of my career, the two of us going at each other as if everything were at stake, and I suppose it was. Roger shouted from the corner, "You're the best in the world," and I tried to prove it, hitting Duran with lefts and rights, but he stood his ground again. The slugfest continued during rounds twelve, thirteen, and fourteen, setting the stage for one last duel in the fifteenth.

Angelo gave me a pep talk in the corner. I don't remember what he said. I was too busy berating myself for how I fought the first fourteen rounds.

My desire was there. Unfortunately, my power was not. During the waning seconds of the bout, Duran smirked. He was convinced the fight was his. When the bell rang, I walked toward him to touch gloves. He would have no part of it. Instead, he shouted at me in one final act of defiance:

"Fuck you!" he said. "I show you."

Needless to say, there was no postfight hug. Duran and I were anything but partners.

My fate was now in the hands of the three judges—Raymond Baldeyrou of France, Angelo Poletti of Italy, and England's Harry Gibbs.

Would they reward Duran for being the aggressor throughout the fight? Or would they abide by boxing's unwritten rule that the champ must be knocked out or decisively outpointed to be stripped of his crown, neither of which took place? Within seconds, the ring, as it always does, filled up with handlers and boxing officials as everyone awaited the verdict.

I feared the worst. I knew what I had done right and what I had done wrong and felt the aches and pains from head to toe to know what Duran had done, and it was a great deal. Yet I couldn't be certain of the outcome. Judges were human beings, with their own prejudices and flaws. They got it wrong many times.

I didn't have to wait long.

The first card announced belonged to Baldeyrou, who scored it 146–144 in favor of Duran.

Next up was Poletti, who scored it a draw. (The WBC claimed that an error in the addition changed his tally to a one-point edge for Duran.)

Only Gibbs was left.

Gibbs scored it 145–144 . . . in favor of Duran, the new welterweight champion of the world.

Duran and his corner went crazy, as well they should.

I slowly walked back to the dressing room, a loser for the first time as a professional. I got dressed and left the stadium in no time. The sooner I abandoned the scene of the crime, the better. The boys told me I fought a courageous fight, but I didn't want to hear a word. The best thing anyone could do at that moment was to be quiet.

At the hotel, a doctor came to my suite to draw blood from ruptured vessels in both ears. The pain was almost unbearable, the knots and contusions more grotesque than the injuries I sustained against Benitez. I was afraid that I'd have cauliflower ears for the rest of my life.

I flew home the next day. It was quite a contrast from the last time I left Montreal, with a medal around my neck and the world at my feet.

At National Airport in D.C., I was moved by the hundreds of fans who showed up to offer their support. Yet I couldn't wait to get home, away from any reminder of defeat.

Over the ensuing days in Maryland, I put my own emotions aside to console others. Juanita was devastated. So was Roger and the rest of my family. Before the loss to Duran, they saw only one side of the boxing business. Seeing the other terrified them. It was not until a few days later, alone in my room, that I could experience the full impact of Montreal and sort out what it might mean.

When I was about ten years old, we moved to a house in Seat Pleasant, Maryland, about twenty minutes from D.C.

The new boxing program at the Palmer Park Recreation Center was not state of the art, but it turned us into men and kept us out of trouble. I'm the one with the funny hat.

Having my family surprise me by borrowing a camper and driving to the Olympic Games in Montreal provided me with a tremendous boost.

My brothers and sisters, including Bunny, came to many of my fights, both in the amateurs and after I turned pro.

Juanita finally got her wish on January 19, 1980, when we tied the knot at a ceremony in Maryland. Ray Jr., six, was the ring bearer.

My hands hurt me throughout the 1976 Olympics, but I had spent four years focused on winning the gold medal and nothing was going to stop me.

Wilfred Benitez gave me everything I could handle in my first title fight in 1979, which was stopped by the referee with only six seconds left in the fifteenth round.

With the money I earned from my professional debut in 1977, I was able to retire my father, who had worked so hard for so many years.

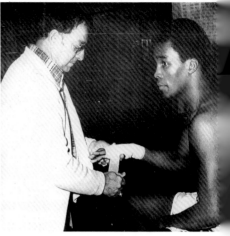

Some reporters felt I shouldn't have used the same nickname as the great Sugar Ray Robinson, but Robinson had no problem and his opinion was the only important one.

From the fall of 1976 through the Hagler fight a decade later, I was extremely fortunate to have the legendary Angelo Dundee in my corner.

In the first fight against Roberto Duran in Montreal, instead of relying on my boxing skills, I foolishly fought him toe-to-toe for fifteen rounds, and paid a heavy price.

MANNY MILLAN/GETTY IMAGES

I was a much smarter fighter in our rematch in New Orleans five months later, though that night will always be remembered for Duran's decision to quit in the eighth round.

FOCUS ON SPORT/GETTY IMAGES

I was shocked at how wonderfully Roberto Duran behaved when he did a 7UP commercial with me in the summer of 1980. His son and Ray Jr. also got along well.

I first met Muhammad Ali at a D.C. awards dinner in early 1976, and relished every opportunity to get together. He was truly The Greatest.

ASSOCIATED PRESS

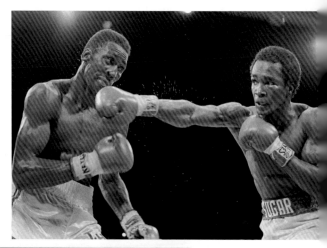

For the first several rounds of our epic 1981 fight, it was difficult to score inside against Tommy Hearns and his incredible reach, but I eventually found my range.

© BETTMANN/CORBIS

In November 1982 at a ceremony in Baltimore, Juanita was greatly relieved when I announced I was retiring due to a detached retina.

ASSOCIATED PRESS/ JOE GIZA

Before I even heard the final verdict, I felt I was already a winner in the 1987 fight against Marvin Hagler.

MANNY MILLAN/ GETTY IMAGES

I can't begin to imagine how my career and life would have turned out without my attorney Mike Trainer, who protected me in so many ways.

With Muhammad Ali nearing the end of his career, Howard Cosell needed someone to appeal to non-boxing fans and I was the lucky one he chose.

Some members of my camp were convinced Tommy Hearns was a shot fighter by the time we met again in 1989, but I knew he'd be tough and he should've gotten the decision.

ANDREW D. BERNSTEIN/GETTY IMAGES

I should have never come back to take on Hector (Macho) Camacho in 1997, but I was like too many boxers who can't stay away from the stage.

AL BELLO/GETTY IMAGES

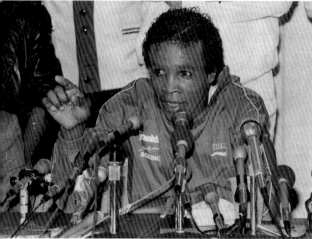

I used to think the detached retina was a curse, but it was actually a blessing as it spared me from a lot of punishment I would have received as my skills began to erode.

I can't possibly express how lucky I am to be blessed with a second chance at being a husband, with Bernadette, and a father to Daniel and Camille.

I felt a deep sense of loss, as if a part of me had been taken away for good. I was certain I would defeat every opponent until there was none left, and then retire for real, on top, undefeated like Marciano, invincible forever. As it turned out, I was not invincible.

Equally disappointing was finding out that, contrary to the image I constantly tried to convey to the press and public, I was not a model of composure who saved his best for the sport's grandest stages. The evidence was everywhere—from my juvenile responses to Duran's antics to my inability to manage my training camp to my flawed strategy in the ring. The Duran fight was bigger than the Benitez fight, much bigger, and I hadn't been ready for it.

I also needed to accept the simple fact that Roberto Duran, at least on that night, was the better man. He cut off the ring and used his expertise to outmuscle and outwit me. His heart was every bit as impressive as his hands.

I deserved credit as well. By standing my ground for fifteen rounds, I showed my critics a resilience, as Ali did against Frazier in 1971, that they didn't think was in me. I proved I could punch and take one, too. And, despite fighting Duran's fight, I came extremely close to winning. Once I got over the fog I was in during the first three or four rounds, I landed dozens of solid combinations to the head and body. If both Poletti and Gibbs had awarded me a single extra round, I would have been celebrating in Montreal, not Duran.

As the days went by, I stopped examining what went wrong and started to focus on the future:

Would I permit the defeat to weaken my confidence and perhaps define me forever? A lot of fighters were never the same after their first loss. They cashed their checks and conquered their opponents, but that intangible quality that separated them from the pack was missing.

Or would I use the defeat to spur me on to more glorious triumphs? If perfection was no longer possible, redemption was. Ali came back to defeat Frazier in their second and third duels.

The choice was mine.

6

No Más

Juanita and I flew to Honolulu in July. I needed to recuperate from the disappointment in Montreal, and the same went for her. She felt the sting of losing perhaps as much as I did, and was hoping I'd retire. We had more money in the bank than we could ever spend— the total earnings from the Duran bout would exceed $10 million—and my faculties were still intact. She was afraid, and with good cause, that I might one day end up like many in my profession who hung around a year or two too long, the next payday too tempting to turn down. Better to leave a year or two too soon.

We stayed in a plush suite with a beautiful view of the Pacific Ocean, and feasted on the finest food. Nothing was out of our price range. Roberto who?

There was no sparring in the gym. No watching reels of old fight films. And, most gratifying for her, no "dates" with any of the boys tagging along. For once, Juanita and I could act as two newlyweds in our early twenties. With Ray Jr. back in Maryland, we could enjoy a real honeymoon.

Gazing from our balcony at the most sparkling blue water I ever saw, I wondered:

Maybe Juanita was right. Maybe it was time to leave boxing. Our nest egg would not be worth a dime if I was limited, mentally or physically. And what kind of father would I be to little Ray as he grew up? There was so much I wanted to teach him. I was supposed to take care of him, not the other way around.

The money would not be anywhere near the same as I could make in the ring, but we'd survive. I could work as a boxing analyst on television, sitting in my tuxedo, hobnobbing with the network executives, watching others put their hides on the line. Come to think of it, that sounded pretty good. I'd done a few broadcasts for CBS since turning professional and got a kick out of it. I could tell the viewers how a boxer thinks and what he fears.

Another option was acting. Madison Avenue, which had shown no interest after the Olympics, now pictured me as the unique black pitchman who could appeal to whites and blacks of all classes. The paternity suit was long forgotten.

Beginning in the late 1970s, I appeared in a number of national television spots, none more popular than the campaign launched by 7UP, featuring the country's most successful young athletes, for which I was guaranteed $100,000. I fancied myself to be a fine actor, but Ray Jr. was, without a doubt, the star of the show. The spot, which lasted thirty seconds, started with us in matching white trunks hitting the speed bags, with the jingle "Feelin' 7UP" playing in the background. We shadowboxed in front of a mirror and took a long sip of the soft drink.

A few kids walked into the gym.

"Wow, is that the champ?" one asked.

"Naw, it's just my dad," Ray Jr. answered, flashing the cutest smile in the world.

My future on the small screen, despite the loss to Duran, was filled with possibilities, and there was also the big screen. I wouldn't be the first athlete to make the transition to Hollywood.

On our second day in Hawaii, I went for what I assumed would be a leisurely jog on the beach. Just because I wasn't in training didn't mean I'd let my body fall apart. I never went more than a week without engaging in some manner of exercise. That's why my weight stayed between 145 and 155 and why I didn't need to go on any rigorous program after a fight was made. I ran again the next day, and the day after that. During each run, and along the strip of shops and restaurants in lively Waikiki Beach, I was greeted by tourists telling me that I deserved the decision against Duran, and that if I'd fought my fight, it would have been no contest. I thanked them for their kind words and hurried back to our suite to see Juanita and resume our long-overdue holiday.

One afternoon, on day five or six, I left Juanita on the beach for a few minutes and went upstairs to our suite. When I got there, the large mirror in the bathroom caught my attention. I approached it, taking in my reflection. Without thinking, I began to shadowbox, slowly at first. I watched my fists reach for their target. I watched my muscles tighten with each punch I threw. I watched my feet dance in circles. I sensed sweat across my brow, on my upper lip. Closing my eyes, I felt my hands go faster and faster. I opened my eyes. They were alive in a way they never were in Montreal. I was Sugar Ray. They wanted another crack at Duran. They wanted the crown that had been taken away. The aches and pains from the beating I absorbed were long gone. So were the beatings I gave myself, day after day, for fighting him toe-to-toe. I put an end to any thoughts of retirement and plotted a course for revenge.

"You might not like what I'm going to say," I told Juanita that evening, "but you know that I want to fight Duran again, don't you?"

Of course, Juanita knew. She always knew. She knew *before* I knew. If I was deceiving myself by the jogs on the beach, I was not fooling her. The disappointment was all over her face, the tears forming before I could finish my sentence.

As usual, I was too self-absorbed to console her. My mind was already on Duran, not her. Nor did she try to talk me out of it. She'd been around me long enough to know there was nothing she or anyone else could do when I made up my mind. I was as stubborn as my mother.

The next person I told was Mike Trainer.

"Mike, I want to fight Duran again," I said. "I can beat him. I'll fight my fight this time. He won't know what hit him."

Mike did not get too excited. That wasn't his personality. He suggested I relax and enjoy my time off.

"Call me when you get home," he said. "We can talk about it then."

I called back several days later. Once I decided to seek a rematch, Juanita and I cut our trip short and flew to Maryland. The vacation was over.

What enticed me to commit every ounce of my being into a second fight with the dangerous Duran?

Money was one reason. Money always was, given my upbringing. I could never put enough away. I would also need to make more deposits in Ray the bank, as the pleas for a "loan" weren't about to go away. Everyone knew how much I made in the Duran fight. It didn't matter that I lost. Giving them handouts to cope with the latest emergency still beat a confrontation.

But money was not the overriding reason. If I never fought again, if my final appearance in the ring turned out to be my only loss as a professional, I would soon be forgotten, or, worse, ridiculed for walking away at the age of twenty-four. I'd never be able to live with myself.

Mike was fully on board with the idea of a rematch, as were Janks, Angelo, and the rest of my team. Why wouldn't they be? Another big fight meant another big check for everyone. There was only one valuable member who was opposed to a second Duran bout, and that was Dave Jacobs.

By this stage, Jake had become quite bitter. He felt overshadowed by Angelo and it was easy to see why. Angelo received more credit for my growth as a professional, and more money. His name appeared in every newspaper and magazine article about me while few reporters gave Jake the due he deserved. From the day I walked into the Palmer Park Recreation Center as a scrawny, shy kid with the silly John L. Sullivan pose until the Olympics six years later, nobody worked with me as diligently as Dave Jacobs did. Without his guidance and dedication, there would have been no gold medal and no pro career. I would have retired at the ripe old age of fourteen.

During the first few years after I turned pro, Jake didn't come to me with any concerns over money, or his reduced authority, though I had heard from others in the camp how he felt. I decided to say nothing about it, hoping that time, and the success of the whole team, would make him reflect on his good fortune. Most trainers spent a lifetime in hot, smelly gymnasiums without grooming a champion or earning any real money. If he learned to accept his role, Jake would make a bundle.

I was wrong.

While I empathized with his anger, he failed to grasp the big picture. Angelo raised my stature beyond any level Jake could ever help me attain. Jake was a good trainer, but he was a novice in the high-stakes world of professional boxing, and with the clock ticking, as it does for every fighter, I could not afford for him to learn on the job. Mike Trainer was a novice, too, but he learned fast. Dave Jacobs was no Mike Trainer.

After the Benitez fight, Jake approached me with his complaints. We agreed to give Jake enough to keep him around though it seemed just a matter of time before his discontent would resurface.

I went to see him shortly after I got back from Hawaii. Once we met in person, I figured, he would not be able to resist the chance for payback against Duran, whom he disliked nearly as much as I did. He knew what I did wrong in Montreal and would make sure it didn't happen again.

Our meeting did not go well.

"The system will not let you win," Jake insisted.

By the "system," I presumed he was referring to the boxing establishment, which did not approve of the way Mike Trainer did business, by shutting out the middlemen who were normally given a healthy percentage of the profits for doing, in many cases, absolutely nothing. In Jake's opinion, that was why I had been denied the victory the first time and why the result would be the same if the second fight also went the distance. I could see his point, but I did not go to his house to engage in a long debate over the amount of corruption in professional boxing.

"I don't give a shit about the system, Jake," I said. "All I care about is that I know I can beat Duran and I want you to help me."

"Son, you beat him the first time," he pleaded, "and they still didn't give you the decision."

Jake started to cry but the tears didn't make him any less adamant. He would not be a party to a rematch with Duran—not without a tune-up or two, and that was not going to happen.

I got up and walked toward the door.

"Jake, I'm going to win this fight with or without you," I said. I drove away, saddened at losing the support of a man who had meant so much to me.

Once Jake was off the team, I didn't look back. I only looked forward, to Duran. When asked by the reporters about Jake's departure, I was quoted as saying there was, thankfully, "one less check" to write. Sounds very insensitive, doesn't it? That's because I was furious, and when I set out to hurt someone's feelings, I can attack with words as mightily as I can with punches, and I rarely miss my target.

To this day, I am convinced the system had nothing to do with Jake's decision to bolt. He was seething, understandably, over his lack of authority. He had been demoted to third string behind Angelo *and* Janks, and this was his way to prove he didn't need me. I brought him back for the Hagler fight in 1987 and several others, but our relationship was never the same after the breakup.

* * *

The task for Mike Trainer was to get a deal done with Duran's people as fast as possible. The rush was not due to any impatience on our part, although I was getting a little sick of being introduced as the *former* welterweight champion of the world. I still don't like hearing that word today when I give motivational speeches around the country. I prefer to be called, simply, the champ.

Contrary to what fans might have assumed, once I dealt with the initial disappointment of losing to Duran, I wasn't in a constant state of despair. The urgency stemmed from the belief that the sooner we fought him, the better our chances of winning. Returning to Panama after the fight, Duran was greeted as a greater hero than ever. I was invited to attend the celebration but declined. I was not about to watch Roberto Duran show off the championship belt, *my* belt, as thousands of his countrymen cheered. For him the party never ended and that was a problem. In no time, Duran, who gained a lot of weight between fights, was at 180 pounds and climbing. If he were a stock, I would have purchased a thousand shares. Losing the necessary fat to slim down to the 147-pound welterweight limit would clearly affect his stamina.

Mike's job was tougher than it was the first time. The leverage we enjoyed as the champ during the negotiations for the duel in Montreal firmly belonged to Duran's promoter, Don King, and you could bet King was not going to waste it. The man never left a dime on the bargaining table.

But Mike was no pushover, either. He used his power—I was still the bigger draw in the all-important area of closed-circuit TV—to secure for me a guaranteed $7 million, only $1 million less than Duran's purse. Better yet, the match was to be staged at the Superdome in New

Orleans on November 25, just five months after our meeting in Montreal. Rematches between the top fighters have been known to take much longer to arrange. In the late twenties, for example, a full year passed between the two Jack Dempsey vs. Gene Tunney fights. Whoever wins the original bout might squeeze in an extra payday or two against unranked opponents who pose no viable threat. The public might not approve but it's a privilege the champ has earned and a reason why winning the first time is critical. You call the shots.

First things first. Before Duran and I met in the ring, we met, of all places, on a set to tape a commercial for 7UP.

I thought it was the most ridiculous idea ever when Mike informed me of the company's suggestion. Duran and I in the same spot, with no one around to keep us from killing each other? The animosity between us was not contrived. It was real and it wasn't going away anytime soon. And with 7UP's representatives asking for Ray Jr. to appear in the commercial again, I was not about to tolerate Duran making obscene gestures in front of my six-year-old. He insulted my wife whenever he saw her. Why would I expect him to be any less vulgar toward my son?

The money was good, so I went along, although I issued a strong warning to Mike.

"If Duran does anything crazy at all," I said, "we will be out of there so fast, you won't believe it."

There was nothing to worry about. Duran, who looked as if he hadn't missed too many meals, could not have been more professional and polite during the entire shoot. He treated Ray Jr. as if he were his own son, who also appeared in the commercial. The boys got along superbly.

I was confused: *Who* was the wild man I saw in Montreal? Was it an act? Was I now seeing the real Duran?

* * *

As I worked out and dissected footage of the first fight, my conclu-
sions came swiftly, and decisively: I'd better make dramatic changes
or history would repeat itself in New Orleans. More would be on the line
than at any point in my career. A second loss to Duran might shatter my
self-esteem, and box office appeal. Juanita wouldn't have to *ask* me to
retire.

For starters, I could not afford to be overwhelmed again by the spectacle. By the time my attention was where it should've been in Montreal,
on Duran, it was too late. He'd already seized control of the fight with
his aggression in the first few rounds. In the minds of the judges, I was
constantly on the defensive, and that was no way to retain my crown. No
matter how effective I might be in countering his vicious attacks, and
connecting with my own, for the duration of the fight, the initial impression was almost impossible to override.

Another change I set out to make was to do what Ronald Reagan
promised the American people he would do to the federal government
if he was elected president in November—trim the fat from my bloated
entourage. No longer would I give in to the pleas of my brothers for their
homeys to be part of camp in Maryland and hit the road with us for the
final weeks, especially with the fight being staged in the Big Easy. The
boys would have held a Mardi Gras celebration of their own, and guess
who would have paid the bill.

To be fair, I could have said no to any one of them at any moment,
but I didn't, and the reason was because surrounding myself with as
many people as possible fed an already oversized ego. I believed the

clippings about my invincibility and wanted everybody to share in the glory of my next, most impressive conquest. If I could have afforded it, I would have put the entire population of Palmer Park on a caravan of buses to Canada. As I prepared for New Orleans, humbled at last, it was important to remember the most recent clippings, which weren't nearly as flattering—DURAN BEATS LEONARD! I cut my entourage from several dozen to roughly half that size, leaving behind, as they say in government, any nonessential personnel. The Gipper would have been pleased.

A more disciplined mental approach and leaner team weren't sufficient. The most pivotal changes needed to take place *inside* the ropes. In Montreal, I proved to the critics that I would not back off for an instant. There was no reason to prove it again. I was desperate for a real victory, not a moral one.

I would fight my fight, not Duran's. That didn't mean I would run in circles for the entire night to stay out of his reach. That's not how the challenger seizes the crown from the champion. It meant I'd maneuver from side to side and not back up in a straight line. The objective was to keep the action toward the center of the canvas, which I did not do often enough the first time, and if I did catch myself on the ropes, I'd spin off.

I also worked on refining my uppercuts. The way Duran went after me at close range, he left himself exposed to that particular weapon. I was glad to find out that the ring at the Superdome—21 feet by 21 feet—would be larger than the one in Olympic Stadium. The more room, the easier I could operate on the perimeter. I sparred fewer rounds per workout than I had in the past, and took a day off here and there. There was no point in peaking too soon and burning out.

Another critical adjustment was to be ready for Duran's dirty tactics, which was why sparring partners proficient in mauling were brought to camp. Leading the group was Dale Staley, the James Dean look-alike I beat as an amateur in the early 1970s. Staley was proud of his reputation, referring to himself as "the American Assassin." He was disqualified *twice* for biting his opponent. Although I didn't necessarily agree with his style of combat, with my career in the balance, I was not about to seize the moral high ground. I would have put Andre the Giant on the payroll if he could help me neutralize Duran. Staley, who idolized Duran, got the best of me for a while, but once I figured out his unorthodox moves, I slapped him around, fighting dirty for probably the first time. I must admit it felt quite satisfying to take him down at his own game.

Several days before the rematch, Mike Trainer, believing I needed more instruction in spinning off the ropes, suggested that Angelo and Janks conduct a closed workout with me. No one respected Mike's intelligence more than I did. Yet my first thought was: What does a white attorney from Bethesda know about prizefighting? Plenty, it turned out. He knew a great deal about psychology as well, selling the whole idea to Angelo by making it appear to be a publicity stunt. Mike knew Angelo wouldn't be able to resist the extra attention once we told the press they couldn't attend, and he was right. Then, as long as we were in the ring, Mike asked him to show me a few techniques. The key was to make the initial move the moment I sensed the bottom strand of the ropes brushing against my calf. I also worked on pushing Duran off me whenever he tried to use his head as a weapon.

There was one more significant change in my approach to the

rematch and it didn't come from Angelo or Janks or Mike. The source was Roger.

"Ray, you got to embarrass Duran," he told me. "When you do, he will lose trust in himself and you will have him. Duran has to always be the macho man. Make fun of him, and he will not know how to handle it."

I didn't pay much attention to his suggestion. I loved Roger but he was a drug addict who threw away a promising career. Make fun of Duran? The man was a killer. The fact that Roger suggested the idea proved he was almost as crazy as Duran. Yet over the next few days, I saw my brother try out a series of unusual moves in the ring, including the bolo punch first made famous decades earlier by welterweight champion Kid Gavilan. Before too long, I found myself experimenting with similar playful gestures. Roger had clearly gotten inside my head. I was not sure that was a good thing.

In mid-November, I flew to Louisiana. I was fit, physically and mentally, although there were still moments of concern.

What if a smaller entourage and smarter strategy did not lead to a victory on November 25? What if the truth was that Duran was better than me? What would happen then? I shared these thoughts with no one. I couldn't afford for them to get back to anybody in Duran's camp. Still, the doubts were there. They always were. Which may be why I violated one of my most cherished rules about a week before the fight. I told Juanita, who was staying in a separate room, that I wanted to make love.

"We can't do that, Ray," she pleaded. "You'll need all your strength for Duran. We never have sex this close to a fight. You know that."

"Of course, I know," I protested, "but it has been many weeks since we were together."

We went back and forth for a few more minutes before she gave in. That night remains the only time before a big fight that I ever had sex within days of the opening bell.

In New Orleans, members of my team did not bump into Duran and his people as often as we did in Montreal, but nobody was complaining. Whenever we did run into him, he was the same madman as before. It was as if the 7UP commercial had never taken place.

There was one major difference: I was not rattled. I was ready.

F inally, November 25 was here. I woke up feeling the exact opposite of how I felt on that dreary day in Montreal. My biorhythms were in perfect order. I could not wait for showtime.

The next encouraging sign came at the morning weigh-in when I tipped the scales at 146 pounds on the nose. For the first fight, I weighed about a pound less and felt thin. Fans may wonder: What is the big deal about a pound or two? It can be a huge deal. The extra muscle tissue, in the upper body especially, would provide me with the armor I would need to absorb his attacks, not to mention the boost in confidence.

Nothing, though, lifted my spirits as much as the rendition of "America the Beautiful" before the fight. Normally, I don't pay attention during the national anthem or any other prefight rituals. I'm completely in the zone and have no desire to come out. This was an exception. It was the first and only time I met Ray Charles, my namesake.

How his appearance was kept a secret from me, and who invited him, I have no idea. All I recall are the chills that came over my entire body as Mr. Charles, in a blue shirt and blue blazer and wearing his familiar sunglasses, sang with remarkable passion, as if any word might be his last. I bounced up and down and could not stop smiling. I stole a glance at Duran, who was not moved one bit. He seemed removed, as I had been in Montreal, perhaps wishing he were somewhere else. The scowl was gone. For once, he did not look like Charles Manson.

You are now in America! I thought to myself. This was Team USA vs. Panama.

After Mr. Charles belted his final notes and the spectators gave him a rousing ovation, he slowly walked over to me. We embraced. I leaned my head toward his shoulder. He kissed me on the back of the neck.

"I love you, son," he said.

"I love you, too," I told him.

He had one more thing to say:

"Kick his ass!"

I knew right then Duran was mine.

I went to my corner and got serious. Everything about me that night was serious. I wore black trunks and black shoes and black socks. The gold lettering on my robe, which was also black, spelled out "Leonard," nothing else. I would have put on black gloves if they had let me.

It was not the time for any more showbiz. There was a title to win back.

"How do I look?" I had asked Mike in the dressing room before the fight. I knew he would tell it to me straight.

"You look like a mix of the Grim Reaper and an assassin," he said.

Exactly.

Almost immediately, Duran knew, Cosell knew, and the thousands of fans in the Superdome and the millions tuning in on closed-circuit knew: I was not the same man I was in Montreal. I wasn't standing still. I was dancing and jabbing, and Duran did not seem energized by every blow he absorbed. It was my turn to get inside *his* head. Aggressive as usual, he got me toward the ropes, but I spun away and connected with a hard right, and landed a solid combination before the bell. Round two offered more of the same. The strong start ensured I wouldn't have to claw from behind as I did the first time.

"He's gone," I said in the corner after the second round. "Duran is gone."

My only concern was a sagging spot I discovered near the middle of the canvas, where either Duran or I might easily lose our balance at any moment and leave ourselves wide open. It was too late to do anything except be very careful.

During the next three rounds Duran scored well, but there was no cause for alarm. My initial strategy was to maintain a safe distance, although as the bout wore on, I realized I could penetrate his defenses and pull back without risking significant damage. He, too, was not the same man from five months before. When he went after me in the midsection, I countered with uppercuts. I also noticed something I had never seen in my prior twenty-eight fights. Duran was staring at my feet, trying to time my rhythm.

Nonetheless, as the bell sounded for round seven, Duran was not close to being seriously hurt. The fight was up for grabs. I assumed I was ahead, but not by nearly enough, and there were nine rounds to go! One good poke, and the fight could turn in his direction. He was still Roberto Duran.

I then recalled the words of the renowned psychologist Dr. Roger Leonard:

"Ray, you got to *embarrass* Duran."

What did I have to lose? If it didn't work, I'd know soon enough.

In the seventh, I dropped my hands to the side and stuck my chin out, inviting Duran to hit me. I didn't choreograph any of these moves in advance, but after I could see his frustration, I kept improvising. I did the Ali shuffle. I was performing more than I was punching.

Midway through the round, I wound up my right arm several times as if I were about to throw the bolo punch I played around with during camp. I faked Duran out, firing a straight left jab instead.

The jab did not hurt him. But the reaction to the jab did. It hurt him badly.

The fans were laughing. Duran could take punishment, perhaps more than anyone in my era, or any era. What he could not take was being made to look like a fool. That went against the manly Latin American image he spent a lifetime building.

Still, it was only one more round in the books, and I knew he would be out for blood in the eighth. No more showboating, I told myself. The judges would not think too kindly of me if these theatrics went on for long, and the fight was too tight to throw away a single point.

Angelo didn't approve of my strategy, either.

"You don't need to do that," he said. "You're about to be the welter-weight champion of the world."

I looked over at Duran's corner. His eyes were vacant. He seemed more out of it than he was before the fight.

In the eighth, I continued to have my way with Duran. Then, with about thirty seconds remaining in the round, it happened.

Duran threw his arm up and walked slowly toward his corner.

Thinking it was simply another trick, I punched him in the belly. He flinched and motioned to indicate that he was done for the night. With sixteen seconds to go, the ref, Octavio Meyran, made it official: The fight was over.

From that moment on, the evening of November 25, 1980, in New Orleans, Louisiana, ceased to be about me and regaining my title. I took on a supporting role in a more complicated drama, in which an icon to an entire continent became, in one sudden, unfortunate act, an object of derision for the rest of his life. Forgotten were the victories, the devastating knockdowns, the hands of stone.

It wasn't losing the fight. Great fighters lose fights all the time. It was *how* Duran lost.

He quit, and that is the one thing you simply cannot do as a fighter. You can be lazy. You can be overweight. You can be dirty. You can fight past your prime. But you cannot give up. You can never give up.

Of all the people in the fight game, Roberto Duran was the last one you could imagine walking away. He fought with more courage than ten men combined and pain never seemed to bother him. If anything, pain made him fight harder.

Yet there he was, not bloodied, not battered, surrendering his title, and dignity, in front of the world. And while there is some question as to whether Duran ever actually uttered the famous words *"no más,"* the point was the same. He quit.

I felt sorry for him. I really did. For months, since he'd insulted me at the Waldorf, I'd wanted to hurt him. But once the second fight was over, I could hate him no more.

Moments later, we hugged. Yes, hugged, Duran and I, the enemy a partner at last.

I was asked by the press afterward, and on countless occasions in the three decades since, why Duran gave up. The fact is that I was as surprised as anyone, and my only explanation is the same one offered by the writers at ringside, that Duran felt humiliated by my antics and did not pause to consider the consequences. I certainly never bought his explanation, that he suffered from stomach cramps resulting from the three steaks he ate in the hours leading up to the bout. Before our third fight, in December 1989, Duran, if I'm not mistaken, promised he would tell the real story behind *no más*, win or lose. After I won by decision, he didn't, of course, and that's because there was no other story. There never will be.

There were some who claimed the fight in New Orleans was a fix, that Duran lost on purpose to set up a rubber match. Nothing could be further from the truth. Any chance for a third bout in the near future was eliminated the instant Duran walked to his corner, and it was a shame because I could have earned another $10 million, at least.

What disturbs me much more is the lack of respect I received for regaining the title. I was given more credit for losing courageously in Montreal than for winning cleverly in New Orleans. It was almost as if I hadn't been in the same ring with Duran. Yet I set the tone of the fight just as he set the tone the first time.

Was there a part of me that wanted to see Duran on the deck, writhing in total agony? You bet there was, but what I did was much more satisfying than putting him away.

For me, another image that stands out from that night is not something I saw in the ring. It is what I saw in the van about to transport Duran and his entourage back to their hotel while I went to meet with the press. It was chilling. Duran sat in the passenger seat. I waved, and he waved back, but he was a million miles away.

What was he thinking? Did he grasp the significance of what he had just done? Did he realize he would never be seen the same way again? In an instant, the van was gone.

The word was that Duran partied well into the night in New Orleans. That might be the case, but knowing the soul of a prizefighter as I do, there isn't enough alcohol or women on the planet to take away the pain of losing, especially the way he lost. To this day, I still agonize over each of my three defeats, and I never surrendered like Duran. I can't imagine how much *no más* must continue to haunt him.

My dealings with Duran between New Orleans and our third fight were limited, although there are two brief exchanges I will never forget.

The first would come on November 10, 1983, at Caesars. Retired at the time, due to the detached retina, I was on the HBO broadcast team covering the Duran-Hagler bout, which Hagler won in a narrow fifteen-round decision. After the fight ended, Duran walked over to me at ringside, and reached between the ropes.

"You box him, you beat him," he said.

For Duran to offer any advice to his most despised rival, the man responsible for causing him a lifetime of shame, blew me away. I would have expected him to root for Hagler over me every time.

The other memorable comment would come in 1989 when the third fight was announced at a hotel in Las Vegas. I had not spoken to Duran since the night he fought Hagler. While we were waiting backstage to meet with the reporters, Duran gave me a warm embrace.

"Thank you, my friend," he said. "Thank you."

I was shocked again. The Duran I knew from our battles in 1980 would not have said thank you if I had saved him from drowning. It turned out I *was* saving him. He was having severe financial problems.

His eyes were no longer filled with hatred. They were sad.

7

The Showdown

The plane ride from New Orleans to Washington was similar to the trip in the van after winning the gold medal. I could not wait to get home to be with my family and closest friends. The only blemish on my record was avenged, seen for what it really was, an aberration, an off night in a magnificent career, with more heroic conquests to come. I vanquished the great Duran. I was the champ again, not the "former" champ.

When I stopped celebrating, I settled back into the life—rather, the two separate lives—I lived before the fight.

At home, once I took my cape off, I was Ray, a father and a husband, my priorities in the right order. I was the same innocent kid from Palmer Park, except with money and fame. Time came to a halt. I was in no rush to go anywhere or do anything.

Away from home, Sugar Ray took over, as always. Wherever I went, whether in public appearances or intimate gatherings, Sugar Ray was the main event. He never shared top billing with anybody. He would not stand for it. In looking back, I could do what I did for many years, and that is to blame my boys for putting me on a pedestal. The truth is that I was the one to blame. I wanted to hear how special I was all the time and that's why I surrounded myself with the people I knew would tell me just that. Between fights, with no spectators to cheer me on, and no reporters to write flattering columns, the boys were where I went for applause, for validation. They never let me down.

On March 28, 1981, I took on a fighter named Larry Bonds. Bonds was put out there as an easy payday before my next major challenge, in the fall, presumably against Tommy "the Hitman" Hearns.

I deserved a breather. All fighters do after waging war, as I did against Duran—two wars, to be precise. With the belt in my possession, I could afford to gather my senses, and dollars, and face an overmatched adversary such as Bonds. It was also reasonable to assume that the fans need breathers, too. Give them too many so-called Fights of the Year in, well, a matter of *months,* and you'd dilute the impact of each one. Sooner or later, they would feel cheated, and wouldn't pay to watch the contest on closed circuit. I wouldn't blame them. It is better to stretch these history-making events out as far as possible, slowly building the level of anticipation until it reaches a feverish pitch, to where people feel they can't miss out.

The fight was arranged in a hurry, my opponent apparently not finding out until about a month before. For Bonds, fighting was almost a hobby, his last ring appearance coming in April 1980 when he knocked out Costello (no relation to Don) King. Prior to that, his most recent bout was in September 1979. Bonds drifted from one menial job to another, working in construction, as a bouncer, and collecting rubbish. In the newspaper stories before our bout, he was described as "the Fighting Garbage Man."

Bonds, however, was no bum. Ranked fifteenth by *The Ring*, he was a respectable 29-3. He possessed long arms, covered himself extremely well in the trenches, and blocked a lot of shots. He was a southpaw, which required me to make some adjustments, as lefties present the exact reverse angles on where to attack and defend. I sure couldn't take Bonds lightly, not with the Hearns match on the horizon. Bonds, though, wasn't ready for his close-up. During a prefight press conference, he asked me to sign some of my glossy eight-by-ten photographs. Can you imagine Duran, Hearns, or Hagler ever requesting my John Hancock? The only souvenir they would want was my scalp.

The fight itself, staged before twenty thousand at the Carrier Dome in Syracuse, New York, was no contest from the opening bell. I backed Bonds against the ropes and he had nowhere to go. Late in the fourth round, I sent him to the canvas with a right uppercut. Game, set, and match, I assumed, as did the crowd. But Bonds bravely hung around until the tenth, when he became a little cocky for his own good, reminiscent of Davey Boy Green in Maryland. I nailed him with five straight punches to put him back on the floor. Bonds foolishly rose at the count of six. Here was a case where the fighter should perhaps have shown *less* heart.

I kept firing away until the referee, Arthur Mercante, mercifully stopped the mismatch, Bonds fortunate to leave the ring on his own power.

Three months later, at the Astrodome in Houston, I fought Ayub Kalule.

Unlike Bonds, Kalule was no breather. A converted southpaw born in Uganda, he was the World Boxing Association's junior middleweight champion, undefeated in thirty-six bouts, and had never been knocked down.

I was motivated, and not just because I could add another title. Tommy Hearns was on the undercard, taking on Pablo Baez. Being in the same building offered Tommy and me the chance to build the interest for our fight, set for September 16, at a site yet to be determined. As long as we both took care of business, nothing would get in our way. Tommy did his part first, staggering Baez with his signature right midway in round four. The referee stopped the bout thirty seconds later. Tommy used very little energy. I would not be as fortunate.

I looked good when I arrived in the ring, wearing a black robe with yellow serpents on each sleeve and black trunks with a yellow cobra head on my left leg.

The cobra wasn't for Tommy, who was also known as "the Motor City Cobra." The cobra was for a Ugandan witch doctor who had been flown to Houston as a publicity stunt. Ugandan witch doctors are not too thrilled with the color black or snakes. Only in boxing.

I looked good in the fight as well, landing one jab after another in the first two rounds. I hoped to end the bout as convincingly as Tommy did and let the hype begin for September.

In the third, however, I bruised a knuckle in the middle finger of my hand when I struck Kalule with a left to the head, forcing me to rely more on the right. Still, I kept scoring well with both hands, mostly hits to the midsection. Somehow Kalule survived solid rights in the fourth and fifth and scored decently himself over the next several rounds. Maybe the witch doctor had put a spell on me after all. Late in the ninth round, I finally got to Kalule with two hard rights, a short left, and another right. Timbbberrr!

Kalule rose but was in a daze. With the round about to end, the bell would have saved him. Only, he didn't know it. After taking the mandatory eight-count from the referee, Carlos Berrocal, Kalule indicated he had enough. It was a smart move. I would have gone right after him in the tenth and might have hurt him badly. He could now safely return to his home in Denmark with an extra $150,000 in the bank.

I wish I had been as bright as he was. When the fight was over, I pretended I was Olga Korbut, launching a front flip near my corner. If the jump had been spontaneous, that would be one thing, but I had actually thought of the stunt the night before in my suite, figuring I would need an encore after another stellar performance in the ring.

Needless to say, I should have spent more time contemplating what to do *during* the fight. What I came up with turned out to be dramatic, all right—more than the audience ever knew.

The moment my feet were off the ground, I realized the degree of difficulty was higher than I had anticipated, and that's because I wore a protective cup, which restricted my ability to bend in the air and execute the necessary turn. I landed awkwardly, and was lucky I didn't hurt myself. I can't begin to imagine how embarrassed I would have been: "Leonard knocks out Kalule . . . then himself." I think the East German judge got it right when he gave me a 3.5.

With Kalule out of the way, the conversation at the press conference in Houston shifted, naturally, to the upcoming duel with Tommy. I started to wage the fight before the fight, the one to seize the mental edge. There was no time to waste. I hoped to avoid a repeat of what occurred when Duran gained the upper hand at the Waldorf.

"I hope one day they give a medical examination to Tommy Hearns,"

I said. "If you do an autopsy of his skull, you'll find he has no brain up there."

The reporters jumped on that comment, as I knew they would. Only years later, long after I retired for the last time, did I recognize its sheer cruelty. It was comparable to the nastiest things Ali said about his opponents, primarily Frazier, whom he portrayed as an Uncle Tom before their first fight, and a gorilla before their third.

It would be easy to say that I was merely trying to pump up interest in the fight. Easy and wrong. The truth is that there were times, and that was clearly one of them, when I was simply sick of having to live up to the image of the smiling, charming, safe Sugar Ray. It took too much energy. Everyone wants to be a smart-ass at one point or another. I was no exception.

I took several weeks off before I began to prepare for Tommy. The crack I made about his intelligence was not only mean, it was inaccurate. Tommy was very smart where it mattered most, in the ring, and he teamed with one of the craftiest trainers in boxing, Emanuel Steward. I knew Manny well from the days I spent as an amateur working out at his Kronk Gym in Detroit. Referring to me as "Superbad" for my speed and combinations, the other fighters treated me as if I were one of their own, and I was always grateful. This also meant Manny understood my strengths and weaknesses as well as anyone, and that included Angelo and Janks. He would have his fighter fully prepared for any game plan my team might devise.

I first realized how tough Tommy would be when I attended his fight against Cuevas at the Joe Louis Arena in Detroit in August 1980.

Tommy belted Cuevas, a monster puncher in his own right, at will, feeding off the excitement of his beloved fans. The bout was over in just under six minutes. I knew Tommy was good. I didn't know he was *that* good.

He had yet to leave the ring and was already lobbying for his next fight. "Come on, Sugar, let's do it," he said, pointing his finger at me.

The people in the nearby rows said the same thing. All I could do was smile and wave. I couldn't make any promises until I avenged my loss to Duran, and that was far from automatic.

I respected Tommy Hearns but I did not fear him. I did not fear anyone.

In my opinion, and I wasn't alone, there were doubts about his stamina. Of his thirty-two fights, thirty ended by a knockout, the first fourteen, from November 1977 until January 1979, decided before the fifth round. Conversely, ten of my first fourteen went past the fourth, five lasting the distance. If I had beaten my opponents as swiftly as Tommy did, I could have spared myself a lot of sleepless nights. The next ten were no less taxing, six going at least seven rounds.

In retrospect, though, I wouldn't have changed a thing. With every strong test against accomplished foes such as Marcos Geraldo, Adolfo Viruet, and Ayub Kalule, I learned to be a better fighter. I learned to dig deeper when I thought there might be nothing left. If the path had been too easy, I might not have gained the confidence to win the title on my first shot, knocking out Benitez in the final round when the outcome was still very much in doubt. I proved I could cope with any predicament. In my lone setback, I battled Duran to the end, growing stronger as the night wore on. No one doubted *my* stamina.

In late July, I began to train in Phoenix, moving later to

Los Angeles, and, finally, to Vegas, with the fight set for my familiar venue, Caesars Palace.

I was rusty in the beginning of camp, my sparring partners repeatedly connecting with lefts and rights to the head and body. I wasn't worried. As usual, it took a week or two for me to develop my rhythm.

Though Tommy looked like an ice cream cone at six feet one with only a thirty-inch waist, nobody in the welterweight division, or perhaps the entire sport, possessed a right like his. It made no difference that many of his opponents were not big-name fighters. They were professionals, each one punch away from pulling off the upset. At the same time, he wasn't as one-dimensional as it was assumed from the destruction he caused. His remarkable seventy-eight-inch reach, longer than some of the premier heavyweights in history, allowed Tommy to keep other men at bay. Just as the press failed to respect Duran's boxing abilities, they made the same error with Tommy. Of his 155 amateur victories, nearly all were by decision. The Hitman did not become the Hitman until he turned pro.

Once he acquired his reputation as a knockout artist, the adulation was not far behind. Boxing fans have forever been infatuated with fighters who could annihilate the opposition with a single blow. Many live vicariously through their heroes in the ring, and nothing is as heroic as one human being sending another to the floor, the bloodier the better. On many occasions, after my own battles and the ones I did commentary for on television, I'd scan the crowd and catch people attempting to copy the shots they just saw. A young fighter such as Tommy, only twenty-two, was most appealing. His followers could climb on board early, and hold on for what they believed would be a long ride. The fact that he lived in Detroit, the home of Joe Louis, might have also contributed to his swift rise.

* * *

When I wasn't in the gym, I watched film, breaking down frame after frame to identify Tommy's weaknesses. He had his share. Every fighter does.

One was that he didn't know how to force a clinch. He never needed to; his fights were over too fast and he was always on the offense. Being aware of when and how to stop the action, if briefly, during crucial moments of a bout can't be overstated. The extra three seconds can be just enough time to clear the senses. That's why trainer Ray Arcel had been concerned with referee Carlos Padilla in the first Duran fight. Any clinches would be to my benefit. They would disrupt the mauling tactics Duran thrived on.

Tommy was also susceptible to body shots. The way to beat him, I deduced from the films, was to chop him down like a tree by going to the midsection as often as possible. He, like Benitez, would become increasingly frustrated with the fact that he was forced to respond to the action instead of dictating it, and the left hand would get lower and lower. Before he knew it, the fight would be well into the late rounds, and he would be running out of answers. It took him twelve rounds in April to beat Randy Shields, and Shields was not in the division's upper echelon. Another disadvantage would be that the pressure on fight night would be unlike anything Tommy had ever faced. There is no way to know what that pressure will feel like until you walk down the aisle, and by then there is nothing you can do about it.

Everything was proceeding according to plan until, about two weeks before the bout, one of my sparring partners, Odell Hadley, accidentally struck me on my left eye with his elbow. Odell was a lanky, six-feet-two middleweight who would go on to compile a fairly decent record during the eighties. He was brought into camp, like several others who were tall, because his style and build resembled Tommy's, especially in how he threw his left jab. The objective, with daily repetition, was to develop the muscle memory so that I would instinctively avoid Tommy's jab, which was like a twelve-gauge shotgun that never stopped firing. It was a shot that blinded you for an instant, setting up his money punch, the right, though with Tommy, the left was a potent weapon on its own.

I didn't blame Odell. He was doing his job. By the next morning, my eye started to swell, and there was talk about possibly postponing the fight. Trying to beat Tommy Hearns would be hard enough, let alone with an eye that was less than 100 percent.

There would be no postponement. I was determined to fight on September 16 as long as I could breathe. To be ready for battle is not simply a matter of running five miles a day, hitting the bags, jumping rope, and sparring. It is about transporting one's mind to a place in which no thoughts except those related to winning the fight must be allowed to enter. Going to that place, as painful as it is, is necessary, and the thought of leaving it and trying to pick up a few weeks, or perhaps months, later where I had left off was out of the question. That was why I was always opposed to any postponements, even in the twilight of my career, when the injuries were more severe. By early September, in preparing for Tommy, I was *there*, whatever *there* meant. I couldn't start over.

My assistant, Craig Jones, asked me before one fight: "Boss, where the fuck are you?"

"Somewhere you'll never go," I told him. "Somewhere you don't *want* to go."

Fortunately, the shiner I received from Hadley's elbow went away quickly, and after a short time off I was back on schedule.

My feelings toward Tommy were nothing like the animosity I felt toward Duran, which was to my advantage. With Duran, my emotions steered me to a fight strategy doomed from the beginning. There was no chance of that happening against Tommy. My motivation came more from a desire to elevate my standing in the sport, in the era that I occupied, and in history, than to bring down another man. I respected and liked Tommy. That didn't mean I would take it easy on him if the opportunity presented itself. I didn't take it easy on anyone. The beast in me, never far below the surface, would emerge at the appropriate times. It meant I wasn't consumed with anger, as many fighters feel they need to be, no matter whom they face.

There was one person on the Hearns team who did make me angry. That was Dave Jacobs.

Jake and I had not spoken since he told me the system would prevent me from avenging the loss to Duran. I could forgive him for that. What I could not forgive him for was lending his support to Tommy.

What kind of man could do that? How could it be that everything Jake and I went through over the years—the sparring and strategy sessions, the hours of watching films, the pep talks over the phone, etc.— now meant so little to him? I was sure of one thing: If Emanuel Steward believed that putting Jake on the payroll might give Tommy an edge, he did not know me as well as he thought. Jake joining Tommy's camp only made me more determined.

Several days before the fight, a surprise visitor showed up to watch me spar in Las Vegas. Dozens of fans flocked to his side. It was Ali.

While I watched him clown around, as only he could, it hit me:

Muhammad Ali is at my camp! I have made it now! All the money and fame in the world could not provide the validation I received from his presence. Looking back, it was almost as if the torch were being officially passed, with Ali's last fight, against Trevor Berbick in the Bahamas, only three months away. I don't believe we spoke that day. There was no need. He was there for me and that was enough.

On the evening of September 15, with the fight less than twenty-four hours away, I went to sleep confident that I had done everything in my power to be ready for Tommy Hearns. But did I? And, if not, what did I miss and would it cost me the crown?

As usual, there was only one way to find out. I got up and went into the bathroom to look in the mirror. I checked the muscles in my arms and legs. They were bulging. I checked the speed of my flurries. They were fast. I began the final check, the one to tell me if I would be Sugar Ray or Ray.

I got the answer I was praying for. My eyes were wide and clear.

When Tommy took off his robe and stepped onto the scale at Caesars for the weigh-in on the morning of the fight, I was stunned. He looked like a famine victim from Africa. Officially, he came in at 145, two full pounds under the welterweight limit. I felt the difference against Duran in Montreal, and I was convinced the lesser weight would make Tommy weaker as well.

I am going to kick his ass, I thought. I glanced at Angelo and Janks. I could tell they felt the same way.

After the weigh-in, I went upstairs to my hotel suite for a meal and some rest. The main event was only hours away.

I did a lot of thinking in those hours. The fight was billed in the press as "the showdown," which made sense given that Tommy, who held the WBA crown, and I, the WBC belt, were each attempting to become the undisputed welterweight champion of the world. But when I considered what the confrontation truly symbolized for me, I came up with another word, and had it stitched on the back of the robe I would wear into the ring. The word was *deliverance*. In the dictionary, the definition is "liberation, salvation, rescue." That summed it up.

Taking on Tommy Hearns was my chance to acquire the respect that I was being denied by a number of the veteran boxing writers who still saw me as a fighter created by television who had yet to defeat a star opponent. In their view, Benitez was not in that class. Duran was, but they argued that the outcome in New Orleans was more about him surrendering than my causing him to surrender. Conversely, they saw Tommy, with his devastating power, as a legitimate fighter who earned his way to the top without being coddled by Cosell. The commercials I appeared in reinforced this point of view. I sold soda. Real fighters didn't sell soda.

Some even framed the duel as a clash between the boxer who abandoned his roots to prosper in the white culture (me) and the one who stayed true to his heritage (Tommy). I didn't get riled up at the time, recognizing that these reporters were no different from the promoters, manufacturing a conflict to drum up more interest in an event. Years later, I came to realize how absurd their argument was, and how much it disturbed me. It wasn't just during the buildup for the Hearns bout when I heard such nonsense. At various times in my career, I was criticized for trying to act white, for "selling out."

What was my crime? It was that I had the nerve to be well-spoken, which went against the perception of the illiterate black fighter. The fact is that I never thought of *trying* to act white, whatever that meant. I was simply interested in bettering myself, inside as well as outside the ropes. A boxer's career is not long, and I wanted to be certain I'd still make a decent living when I put the gloves away for good. Besides, I grew up in Palmer Park, trained in Watts and Detroit, and spent plenty of time in Harlem. I felt as comfortable in the projects as I did in the boardrooms. I cared about the injustices committed against my race, even if I did not speak out publicly, as Ali and football star Jim Brown did. I donated my share to black causes. I just didn't need to have my picture in the paper to prove it.

About eight or nine hours after the weigh-in, I was stunned again. The Tommy Hearns I saw when I entered the ring around 7:30 P.M. was not the same fighter from the morning. He looked as if somebody had pumped him up with air. He clearly had spent the whole afternoon hydrating himself. Any illusions of an early knockout on my part were put aside. Caught off guard, I needed to do something, and quickly. Tommy was on his way toward the center of the ring. It came to me just in time.

I bounced up and down as the ref, Davey Pearl, issued his instructions. By not staying flat on my feet, Tommy was unable to fully appreciate the height difference between us, which was at least three inches. It was no secret that he was taller, but I hoped to put a little doubt in his mind. Despite our God-given talents, we were also human, and that meant being prone to insecurities like anybody else, especially as we prepared to enter a place in which there would be no escape from the

182 THE BIG FIGHT

opponent, and ourselves. I retreated to my corner, confident that I'd gotten inside Tommy's head once more.

Another thought occurred to me during those final critical seconds. It came as I scanned the seats at ringside. I noticed the usual entertainment stars who loved the fights, as well as other high rollers, among the nearly twenty-four thousand spectators squeezed into a temporary outdoor stadium adjacent to the hotel's parking lot. With the revenue from pay-per-view television and the closed-circuit distribution, the fight would gross more than $35 million, a record at the time for a sporting event.

The person, however, who captured my attention was Muhammad Ali, wearing a tie and jacket, in the third row. I decided that, for this one night, I would be Ali—at least, a facsimile of Ali. There could be only one Ali. Why Ali? With his bravado and footwork, he blended the ideal skills to outfox Tommy Hearns. If I could channel "the Greatest" for the next hour or maybe less, I would be the undisputed champ.

I rose from my stool, said a prayer, and took a deep breath.

The bell sounded.

During the opening three minutes, the "showdown" was a standoff, both of us getting acclimated to the opponent and the surroundings. The temperature in Vegas was a serious factor, having been in the 100s all week long and still in the low 90s when the fight got under way, which made pacing oneself more crucial than usual. No matter how good the shape Tommy and I were in, neither of us could sustain a maximum effort under these conditions for the whole night.

Speaking of hot, that's what Tommy was because of what I did after I heard the bell ending round one. I told myself I was going to be Ali and I meant it. I touched Tommy lightly on the side of the head with my right hand.

"I gotcha, sucker," I said.

He responded with his own right, which was quite a bit harder than mine. It was the exact reaction I was aiming for. Tommy deserved the round. He landed more punches. Yet sometimes you don't need to capture a round to advance your cause. This was one of those times. When a fighter is angry, and Tommy was no exception, he doesn't think clearly, as I learned the hard way in Montreal. The more I could take him out of his rhythm, the more he might leave himself open to my attacks.

Tommy was not the only one who was upset. So was Roger, who began to shout from the corner after Tommy's retaliatory strike. I love Roger with all my heart, and I know he was only trying to stick up for his "little" brother, but he was also high as a kite.

"Get him out of here!" Janks yelled.

My brother Kenny replaced Roger. Kenny was more subdued than Roger. Who wasn't? It was the right move. I had enough to worry about.

Round two was similar to the first, with no serious blows exchanged. While Tommy landed his jab effectively, I was trying to figure out how to penetrate his defenses to operate on his body, and to do it from close range. If I tried to attack consistently from a long distance, I might wind up like Pipino Cuevas. Exploiting his four-inch reach advantage, Tommy would be able to throw lefts from his favorite angles, and those jabs, besides scoring points, would do damage. He was awarded the second round as well, which meant I faced another early deficit, as I did in the first Duran fight. I was also worried about my eye, still not healed from the errant Odell Hadley elbow. The belts from Tommy weren't helping.

"You've got to get closer to him," Angelo pleaded. "You've got to start fighting."

Easy for Angelo to say. Trying to get close to Tommy Hearns carried its own risks. I wasn't fighting Davey Boy Green or Larry Bonds or Ayub Kalule. I was fighting the Hitman, and he wasn't called the Hitman for nothing. I had no choice. Either I hit *him* or I'd return to Palmer Park with another defeat. The first few days after losing to Duran were perhaps the worst days of my life, and I'd die before I went through that again.

While I was more aggressive over the next couple of rounds, I didn't come close to putting Tommy in trouble. On the other hand, although he landed plenty of good shots, he didn't come close, either. Seeing my head snap back on several occasions, many of the fans at Caesars, and no doubt on the closed-circuit telecast, thought he had scored more frequently, but some of the blows were glancing, not direct. Either way, the judges were impressed, giving Tommy valuable points.

With five rounds in the books, a third of the fight, I needed to make something happen. In round six, I did.

The left hook was the one. Coming with about a minute remaining in the round, it snapped Tommy's head back. He was hurt.

I went for the kill, firing lefts and rights to the head and rib cage as fast as possible. I wanted the fight to be over. My eye was not getting any better, and sooner or later he might land that devastating right of his.

Unfortunately, I got too excited. If I had slowed down and shortened my punches, I might have put him away. No one had hit the Hitman like this before.

I could not wait for round seven. I was sure Tommy had not yet recovered. I was right. He wasn't the same fighter from the first five rounds. Working inside repeatedly, I threw more left hooks to his defenseless jaw. My arms were weary, yet I told myself to keep punching no matter how exhausted I got. Tommy was ready to fall. Maybe so, but I couldn't finish him off. He staggered back to his corner, but had survived.

In the eighth, Tommy regained his footing, and by the ninth he was all over the ring, keeping me off balance with his flickering jab and remarkable reach. In a reversal of roles, I was stalking *him* as he conducted a boxing clinic, reverting back to his days as an amateur. When I saw this pattern develop, I should have resorted more to my own jab. I had a pretty good one. But I didn't. Instead, spoiled by my success in rounds six and seven, I kept waiting for the decisive blow to put him down. I kept waiting . . . and waiting.

His strategy paid off. Though he wasn't inflicting much punishment, he was winning rounds and the rounds were winding down. My eye was getting worse, and by the eleventh or twelfth, my vision was down to 50 percent of normal, perhaps less. Given my inability to clearly see every punch he threw, I was risking a heck of a lot more than a belt. But I'd never quit before in the ring and I wasn't about to start now. I saw what quitting did to Duran's reputation. The fight was slipping away and I had no answers. My mind told me: *You need to throw more punches!* My body didn't listen. People admire our bulging muscles and

lean waistlines and automatically assume that we have superhuman pow-
ers. We don't. We break down like everyone else. Our bodies can't always
do whatever our minds command.

As the twelfth round got under way, the doubts about Tommy's
stamina seemed laughable. He couldn't have looked any fresher. All he
had to do was keep boxing for another twelve minutes, and the WBA
and WBC crowns would be his. While I got in the best licks, primarily in
rounds six and seven, it didn't matter.

Then it came, the spark I needed, from the voice of Angelo Dundee.
Angelo did not make the contribution we assumed he would after coming aboard in 1976, leading to the bitter run-ins with Mike Trainer and
the restructuring of his contract a few years later. But, at roughly 8:30
P.M. on Wednesday, September 16, 1981, Angelo came to my rescue, just
as he had saved Ali against Cooper and Liston in the early 1960s, and for
that I will always be grateful.

"You're blowing it now, son," he said. "You're blowing it."

The way Angelo said it was as important as what he said, with the
perfect mixture of urgency, encouragement, and affection. Angelo was
no Knute Rockne, but, with the exception of the Dick Eklund fight,
he knew precisely how to get through to me at the most pivotal
moments, and no moment in the fight, or in my career, was more pivotal
than this.

As I relaxed on the stool, my eye nearly closed, I realized how right
he was. I *was* blowing it. A punch or two away from putting Tommy out
in the sixth or seventh rounds, I was on the verge of losing my crown,
of being what some of the writers said I still was, a made-for-TV fighter
who was no match for the real thing, Tommy Hearns. I decided to attack

Tommy with everything I had no matter how close I might get to his right hand. If I was going down, I was going down as a warrior.

Midway through the thirteenth round, I got my chance, unleashing a right that hit him squarely in the head. His head snapped back as it had in the sixth, Tommy staggering along the ropes. He was hurt worse than before. I proceeded to throw about twenty-five punches in a row, hitting Tommy everywhere, and hard. I couldn't have stopped even if I had wanted to, the exhilaration as each shot met its target the most wonderful feeling in the world. I fed off the roar of the fans, and the sight of my opponent in trouble, ready to be destroyed. And to think there were people who had questioned if I could be ferocious enough when it was necessary. How wrong they were. I loved to hit other men. I loved to see them crumble.

Tommy fell into the ropes and was practically on the canvas, though referee Davey Pearl did not rule it a knockdown, and then told Tommy to "get up" instead of asking him if he *could* get up. Pearl's response was a prime example of how the men wearing trunks are not the only ones in the ring who can let the pressure of a championship fight cloud their judgment.

No matter. Once Tommy was back on his feet, I pummeled him with another barrage. He fell again, his battered body draped over the lower strand of the ropes.

This time, the countdown began. After getting up, Tommy was ready to go again, but was saved by the bell. He might have bought himself a chance to regroup over those last thirty seconds if he had known how to clinch. That's what I would have done.

I nearly ran from my corner for the start of round fourteen. Tommy escaped in rounds six and seven from a certain knockout, in part due to my negligence. He wasn't going to escape this time.

A right to the head. A hook to the body. Four more rights to the head. The great Tommy Hearns was a punching bag.

Again, I couldn't stop. Thankfully, with a minute and fifteen seconds to go in the round, Davey Pearl stopped it for me.

I wasn't much better off than Tommy was. When Janks and my brothers lifted me in the air, I slumped into their arms and almost collapsed onto the canvas. I had nothing left. Everything went into those last two rounds. Everything and more.

Tommy and I hugged. We had never been enemies in the first place, despite the insensitive things I said about him.

About an hour later, in meeting with the reporters, we came across as the best of friends, and why wouldn't we be? We gave the world quite a show, and made millions doing it. No matter who prevailed, we were both set for life, and, still in our twenties, there was every reason to think he and I would soon see each other again in the ring to make more history, and money. The public would demand a rematch, and we would be happy to give it to them.

For me, the satisfaction was not just beating Tommy and winning the crown. It was the way I beat him. The experts said I could win only by decision. Knocking him out, with my eye nearly shut and after my opponent, by all accounts, had been in control of the fight, proved I was truly one of the greats. Hearns was a giant, and I slayed him.

Thirty years later, the fight remains my defining moment as a fighter. I was at the peak of my abilities, and so was Tommy. I've run into him many times over the years, usually at a fight in Vegas, and the affection between us remains genuine. Which is why it deeply saddens me to see him go through rough financial times and it is painful when I have to tell him that we're not living in the 1980s anymore.

"Let's do something together," Tommy suggested last year. "We can both go around the country doing exhibitions. The people love us."

"The people love us, Tommy," I said, "but they don't want to see two old guys in the ring with gloves and headgear on. I don't want to get hit by you and I don't think you want to get hit by me. Let's leave the past where it belongs."

And what a past it was.

8

Seeing a New Future

I thought I knew what fame was before the fight with Tommy. It was nothing compared to how I was treated after the fight. I traveled to the White House to visit President Reagan and to Hollywood to mingle with celebrities. I appeared on the talk shows and was named the *Sports Illustrated* Sportsman of the Year. I was Sugar Ray Leonard 24/7, and loved every minute of it. Ray was never around. I didn't need him. He would have just gotten in the way.

Another reward was the attention I received from members of the opposite sex.

It had been like that since my early years as a pro, when, once a month, I used to walk into Odell's, a black nightclub in downtown Baltimore, and the girls would scream as if I were a rock star. I'd take the hottest ones I could find to the local Holiday Inn, sharing them with the rest of the boys. Then came the unforgettable trip to Baton Rouge after the Geraldo fight. Once I beat Tommy, however, the amount of women we met, and the caliber of those women, rose to a whole new level. They were faster, looser, better dressed. I got an inkling of how Hugh Hefner must have felt.

Much of the credit, I suppose, goes to James Anderson, who had come aboard as my bodyguard. From his years with Ali, he knew everybody, including the sort of women who hung around boxers, and not because they came to watch us beat each other up. These women were groupies, and every sport has them—women who gravitate to the company of rich, famous, and well-built men, if you know what I mean, for adventures in bed that they would never get from their boyfriends back home. James kept a book—and yes, it was black—filled with the names and numbers of the most attractive women, black and white, in cities from coast to coast. A few days prior to our arrival in a certain destination, usually L.A. or Vegas, he would call them. James was a better recruiter than Joe Paterno.

"Do you want to meet the Sugar Man?" he would ask. They always said yes.

"Great, and bring some friends with you."

At the hotel, after exchanging small talk, the evening began. I didn't know their names. I didn't care. We weren't there to make friends. The first choice was mine.

"James, the one in the red dress," I'd say, and, presto, the woman and I would retreat to my bedroom, leaving the boys to fight over the rest. From what they told me, they did just fine. As much as they wanted to, the boys could not accommodate everyone, the rejects told their services were no longer required. A few didn't take the dismissal very well, waiting outside in the hallway for another chance. It wasn't a matter of money; these women weren't getting paid. They just wanted to be with the champ.

I messed around back in Maryland as well. The only difference there was that being that close to my wife and child, the guilt got to me at times. It must not have been that bad. It didn't stop me. Nothing did.

The nights were not the problem. When I was in the middle of the act, I had the time of my life. I didn't think about Juanita or little Ray. These women treated me as if I were a god, and I can't think of many men who would have resisted. Only after the sex was over, my needs satisfied, did I remember I was a married man breaking my vows once again. It would be three or four in the morning, I'd be in the arms of a stranger who was sound asleep, and all I could think about was that I had to get home before daylight arrived. When I saw the light, I would cry, and not because I was afraid of how Juanita might react. I could usually talk myself out of any trouble or I would buy her an expensive gift if talking didn't work. All would be forgiven . . . until the next time, and there would always be a next time. The reason I cried was because in the light, no longer protected by the darkness, I saw the ugly reality of who I had become.

I couldn't have engaged in such despicable behavior without a little help, and I am not referring to James Anderson or any of the boys. I am referring to the presence of alcohol, and eventually cocaine, which began to take over my life during the early eighties. There I go again, searching for a convenient scapegoat. If it wasn't my evil twin, Sugar Ray, the booze or drugs had to be responsible for my transgressions. The fact is that I put those substances into my body, me, Ray Charles Leonard, not some character I invented.

An early indication that something was wrong came in the winter of 1982 while I was training for Bruce Finch, my first fight after Hearns.

Finch was like Larry Bonds, a routine payday before I took on another highly touted contender. As a matter of fact, Finch had *lost* to Bonds in 1977, a knockout victim in the fifth round. No wonder I found it difficult to get fired up in training camp. Still, I wasn't too worried, and neither was anyone on my team. Once I got back into the rhythm of running and hitting sparring partners, there was no question that I'd be prepared for the fight, slated for February 15 in Reno, Nevada. I was a champion, and that's what champions did.

Not this champion. I looked for any excuse to take a break, such as the time Juanita and I got into another heated argument only days before the fight. I don't remember what it was about, though I'm sure she accused me of sleeping with another woman and I'm sure she was right. Our disputes were rarely about anything else. Instead of calling a friend, which would have been the mature thing to do, I hung out in my hotel suite with four bottles of vodka. Vodka is no friend. Vodka never tells you the truth.

Drinking the first minibar bottle, I thought: *What the fuck are you doing? You have a fight in a couple of days and you never drink this close to a fight.* Finch, if flawed, was still a professional boxer capable of landing a knockout punch. Drinking the second, I stopped worrying about Finch. On the third and fourth bottles, I forgot why I started to drink in the first place. Little did I realize that these desperate escapes into alcohol, and, later, cocaine, would soon become an almost daily occurrence, and that they weren't really escapes at all. I was not free. Furthest thing from it.

Then came the fight itself, before about seven thousand fans at the Centennial Coliseum in Reno. For the record, I sent Finch to the deck twice in the second round, and again in the third. He got up each time, but referee Mills Lane saw enough, stopping the fight with about a minute to go in the third. To the reporters and fans, the night went as expected, a simple title defense against an ex–club fighter clearly out of his league.

The victory was anything but simple. Finch connected in the second with a combination that made me realize I was in a fight. I was alert enough to keep the damage hidden, but that was why I pursued him aggressively from then on. I wanted to finish it as quickly as possible before Finch, and the crowd, discovered I wasn't at my best.

The problem wasn't physical. It was mental. I was thinking about everything except how to take out Bruce Finch. I had assumed any troubles in motivation would vanish the minute the bell sounded. They always had before, even when the competition was weak. Except that in those days I was on a mission to win a title, each conquest bringing me closer. Now, with the belts secured, Duran and Hearns vanquished, the passion for boxing was almost gone. Another sign came after the fight, when I saw Finch and his family in tears. I told them I was sorry. Fighters do not apologize. We may embrace our opponents. We may applaud them for their courage. We do not apologize.

In the van on our way back to the hotel, the strangest thing happened. No one spoke. Normally, Janks or Angelo or one of the boys or my father would compliment me on a punch I threw or a move I made. This time, nothing I did deserved any praise. I felt as if I were going to a funeral. I should have been mad at myself. Instead, I was mad at them. I spent the rest of the evening in my room alone, sulking, acting like a child. It wasn't the first time.

Over the next few days I gave some thought to retiring but I wasn't serious. At twenty-five, I was entering the prime of my career and I wasn't about to stop being Sugar Ray Leonard. I was just in a rut. I'd come out of it.

By early spring, I was training for my next opponent, Roger Stafford, the bout scheduled for May 14 in Buffalo, New York. Following Stafford, the future possibilities included WBA light welterweight champion Aaron Pryor and the man everyone was talking about, Marvelous Marvin Hagler. Some may have assumed that because Hagler was a middleweight, there was too great a discrepancy in our weight divisions, that I would not bulk up to 160, and he would not slim down to 154. Nonetheless, after I survived Hearns, it seemed almost inevitable that Hagler and I would meet someday. The public would demand it, and when it does, the authorities in boxing find a way to make the fight. The payoff would be too enormous to resist.

Stafford was no Hearns but he was no Finch, either. The previous November, he knocked Pipino Cuevas down in the second round and won a unanimous decision, which *The Ring* chose as the top upset of 1981. If I was not at my best, I could very well lose my title, and any chance for a payday with Hagler.

While training for Stafford, however, my mood was as lousy as it had been for Finch, if not worse. I usually looked forward to the sparring sessions. I loved beating up my partners and entertaining the fans, many of whom could never afford the high ticket prices for a real fight. I spent extra time deciding which colors I'd wear into the ring. I wanted everything to be perfect.

That was not the case in preparing for Stafford. I got dressed at the last minute and gave the absolute minimum effort when I worked out. It did not help that the fight was to be staged in Buffalo. Nothing against the fine citizens of Buffalo, but it is always cold there, even in late April. One weekend, I felt so empty that I went back to Maryland and consumed three or four glasses of wine at dinner with Juanita. I was trying to be a fighter and a civilian at the same time. It is not possible.

As it turned out, a cranky disposition was the least of my problems.

It started on the fourth day in Buffalo. I noticed spots out of my left eye that I'd never seen before. I didn't pay too much attention at first. Either I was more weary than I thought or I had been staring too long into the sun. I didn't tell anybody, figuring the spots would disappear. Little things like that came up all the time during training and were gone in a day or two. When I did tell a few people in camp, they told me not to worry. Everybody gets these spots, they said. I went back to working out, looking for a reason to get fired up about Roger Stafford.

Except that the spots, known more commonly as floaters, did not go away, and of greater concern was that my eyelid began to feel like a curtain that was slowly closing, my visibility becoming less clear. I didn't feel any pain in the eye, and there was no swelling, but something was obviously wrong. After I explained the situation to Julius (Juice) Gatling, one of my boys, he urged me to have the eye examined immediately. Juice was uniquely attuned to any eye difficulties, given that he had lost one of his in a car accident several years earlier. In being candid, though, he caught flack from several members of my team who were more interested in their paychecks than my well-being. Shocking, isn't it?

I visited a doctor who gave me a few eyedrops and suggested I have it checked out again after the fight. The sense of relief I felt cannot be overstated. I trained with renewed vigor when I returned to the hotel. For the first time, I was eager to face Stafford.

The excitement did not last. I saw more spots. The eyedrops were not the solution. A week before the fight, on a Friday morning, I went to see another doctor, a specialist. The news was grim.

"I'm sorry to tell you this, but you have a detached retina," he said.

"A detached retina? How serious is that?" I said.

"Very serious," he said.

"Should I go on with the fight?" I asked. He said he wouldn't if it were him. I respected his view but decided to seek a second opinion.

The original idea was to go on Monday to the Wilmer Eye Institute at Johns Hopkins University in Baltimore, but waiting an entire weekend for more details would drive me crazy. Instead, we made plans for me, Janks, and my father to fly from Buffalo to Washington on Saturday morning. Before we could leave, I had to pretend that everything was normal. It was one of the hardest acting jobs I ever had to do.

When I returned to the hotel gym, there were tons of people waiting for me, including the mayor and several local TV crews. They expected the usual show—shadowboxing, jumping rope, hitting the bags, etc. I gave it to them. What else could I do? While I was performing, I felt horrible. These nice people were getting pumped up about the kind of event that rarely comes to Buffalo, telling me over and over how much the city adored me. I was almost certain there would be no fight and I couldn't clue them in.

During the flight, I stared out the window for the longest time.

Suddenly, shockingly, my father and I talked. We never talked. We exchanged meaningless sentences. But now we were engaging in an actual conversation about issues that mattered—his fears and my fears, and how he would pray for my recovery. He cried. I couldn't remember the last time I saw him cry.

Around five P.M., after hooking up with Juanita and Mike Trainer at the airport in D.C., we found ourselves in the office of Dr. Ronald Michels, who had operated on heavyweight Earnie Shavers for a similar ailment. I was scared and I wasn't the only one.

Dr. Michels asked me to read the eye chart. It was as if I were back in elementary school. I recited each letter correctly except for one on the bottom row.

I looked around the room. Everyone was smiling. How bad could my eye be if I could see that far away?

The next part of the examination was to dilate the pupil. I lay down on a table as Dr. Michels shone a light and did an inspection of my retina. After he finished, he paused. I could tell by the expression on his face that what he was about to tell me would not be what I wanted to hear. "There is definitely a partial detachment," he said. "And you don't have much time. If you don't take care of this in the next week or so, you could go blind in that eye."

There, he said it, the *B* word, the word that had been in the back of my mind from the moment I noticed the very first floater. Now it was out there, no longer just a fear, and there was nowhere to hide. It was as if he had said "You have a tumor." Yet I maintained my composure. I always did, at least in public. That was not the case with Juanita. She began to sob. We excused ourselves and went into another office. She cried louder and louder. There was nothing I could say to wipe away her tears.

Not everyone in our group, however, was as mindful of my welfare. After the doctor said I'd need an operation, Janks Morton had the nerve to ask: "Can he fight and come back later for the surgery?" We all looked at Janks as if he were out of his mind. I did not ask him then, or ever, how he could have been so insensitive, though I never forgot what he said.

Dr. Michels told me I could come back in a few days to have the surgery, which I was inclined to do. I was a fighter and I needed time to get in the zone. I was then reminded of how much of a fighter Juanita Wilkinson was, and always had been. The tears gone, she was stronger than anyone on my team.

"No," she insisted. "We will stay here tonight and have the surgery tomorrow." I was in no position to argue. Tomorrow it was.

It was during these exchanges, and they were frequent, when Juanita's love and concern for my well-being made me cherish her more than words can describe. And when I reflect on the pain I caused her by chasing after women who could never match her kindness, the guilt becomes almost more than I can withstand. Juanita didn't leave my sight the whole night, sleeping on a cot next to me.

I got almost no sleep. The nurses barged into the room four or five times to check my temperature and administer blood tests. They weren't the only visitors. The story that I was at Johns Hopkins had been all over the news. As a result, until close to midnight, strangers kept popping in, wishing me well. I appreciated their concern, though I would have preferred a little privacy. It wasn't until the morning that I received the proper security.

The biggest reason for my lack of sleep was the fear that I could not bury with my usual resolve. Of all the parts that made me a champion, I relied on my eyes the most, and now they were the ones that were letting me down. I had thought I was invincible. I wasn't, and it wasn't my future as a boxer I was most worried about. It was my ability to see, period, out of my left eye. What if something went wrong on the operating table? What if the detachment was greater than they thought? This wasn't a fight. I couldn't talk to Angelo and go over any adjustments in the corner. If anybody was "blowing it," it would not be me. Yes, I'd still have one good eye left, but that's no way to go through life. I'd never be the same again.

I took time that evening to compose in my head the statement I would make to the press once I came to after the operation. Here, thankfully, was one aspect of this awful ordeal I could control. For a change, however, the precise words did not come. Each time I attempted to put a positive spin on the situation—*the operation was a success, my eye will be 100 percent,* etc.—I had to stop and start over. My first impulse, as usual, was to think about my image and make people feel good, but there was no guarantee the surgery would go well. After three or four attempts, I gave up and dozed off. I was given anesthesia in the morning and the next thing I remember, I was in the recovery room with a black patch over my eye.

The operation lasted about two hours and did go well, thank God, although it would be weeks, if not months, before the doctors would know if I'd make a complete recovery. I was fortunate that the tear occurred at the bottom of the eye and that just under 50 percent of the retina had separated.

I couldn't wait that long. Once everyone left my room upstairs except for Juanita, I did what I was specifically told not to do. I ripped the patch off. I didn't see much, only a glimmer of light, but I saw enough. I was not blind in my left eye. That night, I slept like a baby. Over the next several days, I received thousands of letters and calls, including one from President Reagan. I do not remember what the president said, but he was very friendly. I spent about a week in the hospital, Juanita taking care of everything. She fed me. She bathed me. She walked me to the bathroom. When I woke up in the middle of the night in pain, she gave me my pills. She was an angel.

On May 16, wearing the patch, I left the hospital and returned to my house in the D.C. suburb of Mitchellville to begin pondering my next move. Nothing was certain anymore.

It was one thing to *think* about retirement, which I did routinely— after Benitez, the first Duran fight, and Finch. I was the one in control, assessing how much more punishment my body was willing to take, and nobody except my wife was privy to those thoughts. It was quite another to have events control me, to be forced, perhaps, at the ridiculously young age of twenty-six to leave the only career I had ever known. And to do what, exactly? Commercials? Commentary? I wasn't sure. I decided to give myself six months to figure things out.

Many fans and members of the boxing community didn't need six months to render their verdict: I should quit immediately. In their view, I risked permanent damage to my eye and had absolutely nothing left to prove.

If I did return to the ring, it would reveal, as the noted *Washington Post* columnist Shirley Povich put it, "a foolish pluck that would also invite the suspicion he wants more money than his monthly printouts show him to own, in the millions." Although I respected this opinion, I wasn't going to make a rash decision with countless ramifications, and not just for me and my loved ones. The end of my boxing career would mean the end of lucrative paydays for the rest of Team Leonard.

On May 27, I met with reporters for the first time since the operation. Wearing a pair of glasses I borrowed from Roger, I was not my normal confident self. I told them about ripping the eye patch off in my room, and addressed speculation that the injury took place during the Hearns fight. I traced it instead to the workout when I was struck by Odell Hadley's elbow. Only much later did it occur to me that the damage I sustained in the Geraldo fight in May 1979 was the more likely cause. Either way, it made no difference. What mattered was whether my eye would heal.

The conference was soon over, the beast fed for another day. The reporters would devote their precious column inches to other men now, fighters they were sure would be back in action.

Boxing didn't stop when Joe Louis retired or Muhammad Ali retired, and it wasn't about to stop with Sugar Ray Leonard on the sidelines.

A writer asked me if I would miss the sport during the next six months.

"Time will tell," I said.

I didn't miss it at first. I enjoyed being back home with Juanita and Ray Jr., now eight. We watched television, went bowling, did a lot of things normal families do. I was also grateful to be spared Mount Motherfuck and the other rigors of training. It felt no different from the breaks I regularly took after every fight. Three months went by between Bonds and Kalule, five between Hearns and Finch. Long gone were the days of fighting once a month. Plus, with the endorsement opportunities and the chance to do more boxing analysis on television, there would be plenty to keep me busy.

Yet as the days turned into weeks, the weeks into months, I was overcome with more and more anxiety. Whenever I had felt those emotions before, and it was fairly often, I headed to the gym. There was nothing like pounding the bags, or some poor soul's face, to flush the anger out of my system. Without the gym, I needed a new haven.

It didn't take me long to find one.

I don't recall where I was or who I was with when I did cocaine for the first time that summer. I was wary, I must admit, knowing how much drugs messed up Roger, as well as my sister Sharon. Yet I wasn't weak like they were. If I could handle Benitez, Duran, and Hearns, I could certainly handle a little white powder. Besides, during my trips to California, the people I did coke with did not work on the streets, as did the drug dealers back in Palmer Park. They lived in mansions with swimming pools. They were some of the most high-profile stars in music and movies, people of stature. If they thought cocaine was cool, who was I to argue? Wherever I went, cocaine was on the table, as if it were part of the furniture. I was surprised when it *wasn't* there.

The high I got from cocaine was incredible. I tried pot a few times as a teenager, but it made me paranoid, and I was too serious about boxing to mess around for long. Coke made me feel like I did in the ring, in complete control. I became funny, engaging, articulate. Coke made the anxieties go away. I was Sugar Ray again.

Except that they kept coming back, over and over. Which meant I needed more coke. Lots more.

Fortunately, due to my celebrity status, I didn't have to buy my own. The high rollers I hung with were thrilled to share with the champ, coke being another symbol of their vast wealth and power. As time went on, though, and my appetite grew, I couldn't wait for the next party in Bel Air or the next visit to a swanky club in West Hollywood. I paid for the stuff myself, doling out one thousand dollars here, two thousand dollars there, which seemed a bargain for the buzz cocaine gave me. Only, those dollars began adding up in a hurry. One friend I used as a supplier estimates that I spent a quarter of a million dollars per year on coke, and I bet he's not far off. The stuff he bought was high quality, though he admitted to me last year, as I had suspected, that he cut some of it for what he termed "a handler's fee." There was nothing I could have done. I was not about to ask a stranger working the streets to take his place.

I kept my habit a secret, but always worried that people would find out. Each time I visited Dr. Michels for a checkup, I wondered: If you do cocaine, can your pupils still dilate? If he did observe a difference, he never said anything. Nor did anybody else. Yet they had to know.

One time, a member of my team tried to convince me to stop taking drugs by appealing to another vice of mine, and smartly picked a time when he knew I couldn't walk away. We were thirty-five thousand feet in the air, flying to somewhere I don't remember.

"Ray, did you happen to know that cocaine kills your sex drive?" the person said.

I appreciated the effort. I knew, however, that there was no validity to that statement, not for me. Cocaine, if anything, increased my interest in sex.

What about Mike Trainer? If he was my protector, it's natural to ask: Why didn't he protect me from my most dangerous enemy . . . myself? It's because that's never what our relationship was about. He kept track of my business affairs but did not interfere in my personal matters, unless I sought his advice, which was rare. Even if Mike had spoken up forcefully, I was not in the frame of mind to listen. The spell drugs and alcohol cast over me was overwhelming and, like most victims of substance abuse, I was the last to recognize it.

"You need to see somebody," Juanita told me one morning after another night I couldn't remember. "You're an alcoholic, Ray."

No way, I told her. The impression I had of alcoholics came from the movies—dirty, down-and-out bums thrown out of bars, not famous prizefighters worth millions. Not Sugar Ray Leonard. She was right, of course, but to admit to being an alcoholic was something I could not do. Not in 1982. I did instead what any alcoholic would do when he or she gets angry. I drank some more.

The public, thank goodness, had no clue as to who I had become. They still saw me as the kid who took the gold in Montreal, and the three of us as the all-American family they wanted us to be. It's strange to believe that so many fans would be fooled, but it was a role my wife and I knew how to play. We were experts. When a TV crew or magazine reporter came to the house for a puff piece, we posed for cute pictures and said all the right things. The moment they left, we returned to being as dysfunctional as ever.

I assumed nothing could take me down, and that included the

authorities, although there were some awfully close calls over the years.

After one nasty fight with Juanita, I took off in my Jeep and was driving on Route 1 just outside D.C. when a pickup truck hit me as I was trying to make a left turn. The car was totaled, the wheel bent up, and I briefly lost consciousness. I was fortunate to escape with only a bruised sternum and cuts on my face and wrist. While I was being treated in the hospital, a friend who assisted with my security found out where the vehicle was impounded, and supposedly conducted a thorough search before the cops could to make certain there was no coke on the seat or in the glove compartment. There wasn't. He later claimed that he proceeded to pay the orderlies in the hospital a couple of hundred bucks apiece to hand him the sample of blood taken from me after the crash, which surely contained traces of alcohol. To show how messed up I was, when he explained what he had done, it did not occur to me how close I had come to getting into serious trouble.

The other harrowing moment that stands out came as I was about to board the *Queen Elizabeth II* for a cruise to England in the late summer of 1982. I had agreed to appear in a documentary film to be shot on the ship. The way I was acting, leaving the country was the best move I could make.

When I was about ten or fifteen yards from being searched by customs at the gate, I suddenly remembered the cocaine in my pocket and started to panic. How would I talk my way out of this one? Thinking fast, I slipped the cocaine to Ollie Dunlap, my administrative assistant. I figured it would be easier to get Ollie out of jail than me. I didn't tell him what was in the aluminum foil, though by the expression on his face

I could tell that he had a pretty good idea. He broke into a cold sweat and kept his hand clenched until we passed through customs. Once I was safely in my cabin, I got the cocaine back and never carried it in public again. I apologized to Ollie. I could have ruined his life. It was bad enough that I was ruining my own.

The cruise on the *Queen Elizabeth II* was memorable for another reason besides almost going to jail.

The crew filming the documentary asked me to spar a few rounds with a fellow named Steve Sinclair, who had a job on the ship's crew. Why not? After all, what could some lowly sailor do to me? I'd throw a few innocent body shots, slip a few from him, and the crew would have the footage they required. Yet before I knew it, with several hundred tourists assembled in the ship's ballroom, Sinclair, an ex-fighter who weighed about 190, landed a hard blow, to my injured eye, no less, which I didn't exactly appreciate during an "exhibition." Ollie told me later that my eyes got that intense, almost deranged look he knew only too well. I promptly tagged Steve with a belt to the body. There was nothing innocent about it. Down he went. He wasn't badly hurt, thank goodness, and collected himself to finish the show. Needless to say, he didn't throw any more hard blows.

It was not until the session was done that it hit me: *What the hell is wrong with you? You are the welterweight champion of the freaking universe and you just knocked down a sailor who works on the* Queen Elizabeth II. *You could have hurt him bad!* Maybe it was my head, not my eye, that needed to be examined. As for the eye, I was relieved that the punch did no apparent damage, though putting gloves on only a few months after surgery must rank among my dumbest decisions, and the list is long. At the same time, the applause felt wonderful. I missed fighting more than I was willing to admit.

W hile the leaves began to change colors, one reporter after another wanted to know if I'd ever fight again.

As usual, I was vague enough to give off signals in both directions, which indicated how confused I was. Juanita, my mom, and what seemed to be the entire free world, judging from the mail I received, felt the same as they did in the spring when I had the operation. With my finances and faculties in order, why should I take the risk? I understood where they were coming from, and at times agreed with them. Other times, I felt that at my age there was still so much for me to accomplish. The end of my career would come soon enough.

In October, I flew to Brockton, Massachusetts, to tape an interview with Marvin Hagler for HBO. I had begun to do quite a bit of work for the cable network, which was becoming a more prominent player in boxing. When we sat down in his backyard, I was impressed by the tranquillity of the surroundings and what they said about the man himself. He was at peace. He did not need the spotlight to make him whole.

As Hagler and I talked, I could not help but wonder: Why was I asking the questions instead of answering them?

Dr. Michels had assured me that I would not be risking any greater damage to my eye than normal if I decided to compete again. I could call Mike Trainer and he'd initiate talks with Hagler, Pryor, or anyone else and put together an attractive matchup in no time. As for the public, they might question my wisdom at first, but would eventually welcome me back with open arms. In any case, interviewing Hagler was tougher than I imagined. During a break, I drank about two or three Long Island Iced Teas, my favorite alcoholic beverage. I went back to finish the interview, but the TV exec at HBO took one look and had me drink a few cups of coffee. He always knew what to do whenever I lost my bearings. Once, in a production meeting for an upcoming telecast, I took out a vial of coke and a spoon and had a hit right there at the conference table. He just kept talking as if nothing happened.

As the weeks went by, I changed my mind every day, if not every hour. The only firm decision I made was that I'd make a formal announcement about my plans on November 9 at the Baltimore Civic Center in a program entitled "An Evening with Sugar Ray." I could never do anything quietly, could I? I invited family and friends, including Howard Cosell, who kindly agreed to be master of ceremonies. We sold tickets at two dollars apiece, the proceeds going to a fund to provide summer jobs for kids in Baltimore. The night promised to have all the excitement of a title fight . . . except for the fight itself.

About a week before the announcement, I made the decision: I would retire. I could not imagine going against my fans. I wanted more than anything to please them while I was in the ring, and the same desire carried over to *leaving* the ring. If I resumed my career, I'd be violating the trust they had placed in me since the Olympics, when, of everyone in the fight game, I was the lucky one chosen to succeed Ali. By yielding to common sense, I'd demonstrate that their faith in me was well deserved, that I was, indeed, the rare prizefighter to exit the stage at the proper time. I revealed my feelings in a *Sports Illustrated* cover piece, set to hit the newsstands a few days after the ceremony in Baltimore. The byline said it all: "by Ray Charles Leonard, as told to

Pat Putnam," the magazine's boxing writer. I was Ray now. Sugar Ray belonged in the past.

When the night arrived, the suspense in Baltimore was exactly the mood I was looking for. Nobody, not even Juanita or Mike or my parents, knew for sure what I would tell the crowd. The trouble was, neither did I.

I thought I knew. Why else would I have agreed to the *SI* interview? Yet while I waited in the dressing room, as the crowd, which included Ali and Hagler, took their seats, I began to have second thoughts. There was only one way to regain control.

"Give me my medicine," I told Kenny and Joe Broddie, who carried it with them.

That's what I called coke, as if it were a prescription to make me feel better, which I suppose it did. I took a few hits but I still wasn't relaxed. I took a few more. The extra hits did the trick. The boys checked the outside of my nostrils to make certain there was no residue of powder. Imagine if I had missed a spot and it was caught on camera. I could have retired and been arrested on the same night.

Howard seized the microphone in the makeshift ring that had been set up and the event got under way. While the approximately seventy-five hundred fans in attendance saw highlights of my greatest fights, I couldn't help but think back to my first pro bout against Luis Vega, staged in this very same arena five years earlier. A lot had happened in those five years. I had grown from a boxer into a fighter, a boy into a man. My mind continued to wander as Ali entertained the crowd. It was only six years since Charlie Brotman and I visited with him in his dressing room at Yankee Stadium before the Norton fight. It was a lifetime ago.

I could delay the announcement no longer. I took the stage. I reminded myself to speak slowly, assuming that the cocaine would speed up my normal delivery. I paused after every few words.

Staring at Hagler, I was tempted to tell the audience I was ready to take him on. I never ran from a challenge in my life. Knowing my flair for the dramatic, many expected me to do just that, including Marvin, the dollar signs no doubt already flashing in his mind. But I couldn't. The commitment wasn't there. That's when I knew it was over.

"A fight with this champion," I said, "would be one of the greatest in boxing history. This is the only man that could make it possible . . . but, unfortunately, it will never happen."

Someone in the crowd called out: "Does that mean you won't fight anyone?"

"That's it," I said. "That's it."

The crowd reaction was mixed, most relieved that I was putting my health first, others disappointed about the battles that would never take place.

Hagler was more than disappointed. He was disgusted. Convinced that he was asked to be at the ceremony because I planned to announce my intention to fight him, he felt used. That wasn't the truth. I wanted him there *in case* I decided I was coming back. I didn't know what I'd say till I said it.

After being among the last to leave the arena, about a dozen of us drove to a cozy restaurant in the Little Italy section of Baltimore to celebrate.

Celebrate what? As one person after another came over to congratulate me, I smiled and kept pretending everything was wonderful. It was not. I was dying inside, just as I was on the podium in Montreal after I won the gold. The finality of it all hit me with the force of a Hearns right hand, and there would be no turning back. The public would not permit it. Before long, I was wasted.

9

"I Am Back"

Without me in the picture, there were still titles to be taken, money to be made.

The WBA and WBC crowns, which I vacated, were seized in 1983 by Donald Curry and Milton McCrory while Hearns moved up to the light-middleweight ranks to capture his own title, outdueling another former adversary of mine, Wilfred Benitez, in fifteen rounds. Hagler, meanwhile, as ferocious as ever, knocked out Tony Sibson in the sixth round, Wilford Scypion in the fourth. Even Duran, now in his early thirties, was back in decent form, on a mission to make everybody forget New Orleans. All the great fighters from my era were doing what they did best.

Almost all. I was in a much different fight and losing badly, the plunges into alcohol and coke more frequent, and dangerous, than before. With my departure from the sport official, gone was any possibility of an imminent return to the world I relied on to avoid the pain. Without any warning, I'd be reminded of the two men who sexually abused me. Or the memory of my parents cursing one another, screaming, wailing, and out of control, would suddenly overwhelm me.

I carried on as best I could, the commentary I did for HBO, as well as CBS, giving me a chance to spend time in an environment I cherished, and with people I admired. It became tough, though, come fight night, when the old jitters reappeared, except that I would be putting on my tuxedo instead of my trunks, and it would not matter what I saw in my bathroom mirror. Yet once the bell rang, I was relieved to be sitting in the front row, where left hooks were not allowed. I clearly had made the right decision.

At home, carrying on wasn't as easy. Spending time with Juanita made me realize that we should have never been married in the first place, and that was entirely because of me, not her. I wasn't ready to fully commit in January 1980, when we tied the knot, and I wasn't ready three years later. We were too young when we fell in love, me only sixteen, Juanita fifteen, knowing almost nothing about the world and ourselves. Only a year later, we were parents, of which we knew even less. Then came the Games in Montreal and my pro career and the train that could not stop, the train I did not want to stop. I wasn't equipped to handle the demands of both fame and matrimony. One had to lose out, and one did.

Juanita did everything she could to keep us together. She even snorted cocaine with me. She felt that if she could be as cool as the women I partied with, I would not need to party with them any longer. She and I once did coke from midnight until around eight or nine the next morning. We did so much her nose began to bleed.

"That's it," Juanita said. "I will never do any coke again." She never did. I wish I could have been as strong as she was. She wasn't anything like those other women and stopped trying to be. She was better. I was also ashamed to have her see me in that condition. I was used to doing coke with people I barely knew. I didn't care what they thought. But I had known Juanita since before there was a Sugar Ray, and never wanted her to think any less of me.

If that was my goal, I failed miserably, and it wasn't just the nights when I was away. The nights I was at home were often worse.

I would stumble into bed, drunk or high or both, and demand sex, and if Juanita didn't give it to me, I'd accuse her of having boyfriends she didn't have. To her credit, she didn't back down. She would search the house for my cocaine and flush a gram or two down the toilet. That's when we'd have our loudest arguments. We made Cicero and Getha Leonard look like Ozzie and Harriet.

Soon, a full year had passed since retirement number two. On the actual anniversary, in fact, I was in Las Vegas to do the commentary for the Duran-Hagler fight. Marvin was a heavy favorite, as Duran, despite impressive wins earlier in 1983 against Cuevas and Davey Moore, was considered past his prime. Nonetheless, he put forth a tremendous effort, almost pulling off the upset, and that's when he told me how I could succeed against Hagler by boxing him. They were the first kind words Duran had said to me since we taped the 7UP commercial in the summer of 1980. I found it amusing that the other boxers felt much more at ease talking to me after I was no longer a threat. That was not a problem for me. I could have a friendly chat with my opponent in the weeks leading to a fight and still want to kick his ass once the bell rang.

Several hours after the fight, in my hotel suite, I paused to reflect on what Duran said to me and I got excited. Come to think of it, I always got excited after watching Hagler in action. I realized that he was not as invincible as the media made him out to be. He was as flawed as the rest of us, and I knew exactly how to take advantage of those flaws. I'd box him just as Duran had suggested. That's what he did for fifteen rounds. But when the sun came up the next morning, the excitement was gone. If there was a way to outmaneuver Hagler, someone else would have to try. I was not ready to face anyone, let alone the best pound-for-pound fighter on the planet.

Nonetheless, I continued to work out two or three times a week. Which is why when Kenny and his good friend J. D. Brown asked me to take part in an exhibition entitled "Holiday Salute to the Armed Forces," which they were planning for Andrews Air Force Base outside D.C. on December 10, I agreed without hesitation. In addition to supporting Kenny, I'd be able to do two things I loved: boxing and performing in front of the public. I saw the evening as nothing more than that, an exhibition.

I couldn't show up, however, without bringing my A game—well, at least the closest I could come to one after not boxing at all for twenty-two long months. I'd be taking on professional fighters, not a sailor on the *QEII*, and if I wasn't sharp, physically and mentally, it would become obvious in a hurry. I could get hurt. Worse, I could get humiliated. If I no longer had my career, I did have my reputation. Almost every day for over a month I trained, not for a Duran or a Hearns, perhaps, but enough to hold my own against the two fighters I would be facing at Andrews for three rounds apiece, Odell Leonard and Herman Epps. I was thrilled to be back in the gym, my home away from home. I wasn't thrilled to be back at Mount Motherfuck, but the grueling runs were essential. They always were. I didn't notice any profound changes right away, but as the days wore on, I began to realize how much I missed my old life. I felt like a fighter again.

I told Mike Trainer and he didn't read much into it. Mike was used to me toying with the possibility of making a return and then dropping the entire matter. I once told him to meet me in his office the following Monday morning to make plans for a comeback. When I showed up, I never brought the matter up and neither did he. Mike, if truth be told, would have been happy to see me retire as far back as the Benitez fight in 1979, and when I did finally quit, he thought I had made the correct decision. I also called Charlie Brotman to suggest he invite a group of reporters to the exhibition. I wasn't ready to announce a comeback just yet, but thought it would be convenient to have the press around in case that's what I decided.

The final test would come in the only place it could, the ring.

There was no title at stake, but I was as nervous as I could be when I stepped between the ropes inside Hangar 3 at Andrews in front of only the press, employees from the Department of Defense, and air force personnel. I was fit enough, weighing 151 pounds, but still could not tell where my mind was and would not be sure until I threw my first punch and the first punch hit me.

Within a few seconds, the answer came: I was totally into it. I was thinking my way around the ring, plotting the next move like a chess match, the way I always fought, except against Duran in Montreal. I experienced the familiar rush I got whenever I landed a good shot and could not wait to land the next one. I was moving well, too, slipping one punch after another. I was so comfortable that I took off my headgear and put it back on only after I was ordered to by the officials. I felt the same feelings I had in the workouts and knew I'd be foolish to ignore them. In the third round, I put Epps on the deck. Against Odell Leonard, I was in command from start to finish. The six rounds went by in a flash. I could have easily gone six more.

When I met with the reporters afterward, I made it official.

"Are you going to make a comeback?" they asked.

"It's not a comeback," I said. "I *am* back."

Telling Juanita was another matter entirely. Nobody was happier than she was on that evening in Baltimore. She had wanted me to retire on so many occasions, I lost count, and it was not just about getting me away from the ring and the risk I took every time the bell rang. For Juanita, retirement meant the demise of the one man who constantly got between her and her husband. She loved the life boxing gave us but she hated Sugar Ray. Unfortunately, as she soon discovered, I did not need to be an active fighter to play the part. Sugar Ray could survive on alcohol and coke and the attention he received from his boys and his fans, and no amount of fancy jewelry and luxury cars he gave his wife could begin to make up for the pain he inflicted. She was running out of hope, until the fall of 1983, when she learned she was pregnant. If Juanita could not save our marriage, perhaps a baby could. We had been trying for more than a year, Juanita even taking fertility pills. We tried despite our problems, or rather, *because* of them. I was in Vegas when she put Ray Jr. on the phone to relay the news. I was so excited I almost took the next flight home.

Now, only a few months later, before the child could be born, Juanita would have to be told that I was headed back to the world she dreaded.

I could not have picked a worse time. She was in the hospital, suffering from something called hyperemesis, an illness causing nausea and dehydration. When I arrived from the exhibition, she was sound asleep. I lay down quietly in the cot next to her bed, praying to come up with the right words when I knew there were none. I fell asleep as well.

The next morning, she could tell something was up.

"Ray, where are you going?" Juanita said.

"To talk to some reporters, that's all," I told her.

"For what?" she asked. She didn't wait for an answer. "You're going to fight again."

I couldn't lie, not this time. She expressed her disapproval, but I was soon out the door. I was not one to offer long explanations, and it wouldn't have mattered anyway. I had made up my mind.

Why *was* I coming back, and wouldn't I be going against the very fans whose opinions supposedly meant the world to me? Wouldn't they perceive me as just another hardheaded fighter who couldn't stay away, who needed the adulation—and the money—he could not obtain anywhere else? I took pride in making a clean getaway from a sport in which there are few happy endings. I would be throwing that distinction away for good.

For a change, the wishes of others did not matter. What mattered was how I felt. I never wanted to quit on that night in Baltimore. Sure, I was not at my best against Finch and I was not motivated to take on Stafford. Yet, throw a Marvin Hagler or a Tommy Hearns in front of me and I would have been out for blood. I lived for those challenges. I was out to make history and I could not do it wearing a monkey suit and a headset, watching others steal the glory.

Furthermore, in no way could I be compared to an over-the-hill Joe

Louis taking on Rocky Marciano in his prime, or an immobile Muhammad Ali attempting to wrest the crown away from a younger, more powerful Larry Holmes. Louis was thirty-seven; Ali, thirty-eight. I was twenty-seven, younger than Hagler (twenty-nine), for heaven's sake. A strong argument could be made that my best years were *ahead* of me. I was positive of one thing: Unless I returned, I would spend the rest of my life wondering how great I might have become. And as for any fears about my detached retina, if Dr. Michels wasn't concerned, neither was I and neither should anyone else be. The only questions were: Whom do I fight, and when?

Not Hagler, that's for sure. He was too big and too good. I was cocky, but not cocky enough to assume I could jump back into the ring after two years off and compete at Hagler's level, and in a higher weight class, no less. I would need a tune-up or two, at least, before taking him on or, for that matter, any of the bigger names.

We decided on Kevin Howard. Kevin who? It was a fair question. Howard had lost four of his twenty-four bouts, one of his victories, I kid you not, coming against a fighter named Richard Nixon. Only in boxing. We chose Howard because he was slow and never kept himself in the best shape. I saw the fight when he lost eleven of twelve rounds to Marlon Starling. Marlon Starling! I was guaranteed $3 million, an unprecedented total for a nontitle match against an unknown. Howard also agreed to wear thumbless gloves, for which we proposed to obtain approval from the state boxing commission. Being poked in the eye by the thumb was considered to be the leading cause of detached retinas. Howard would receive $125,000 for his night's work, by far the largest check of his career. The ten-round junior middleweight bout was set for February 25 at the Centrum in Worcester, Massachusetts.

In the gym, one of the necessary adjustments I had to make, and it sounds strange, was to program my face to learn how to take hits again. After being out for such an extended period, the first blows I absorbed hurt in ways they never hurt before. My skin texture, not accustomed to the trauma, swelled quickly. I also had to prepare myself mentally, to again summon the commitment to throw a punch and not worry about the punches coming back. For me, it was no problem. In retirement, I gained a greater appreciation of how blessed I had been to make a living in a profession I loved. I was not about to waste a second chance.

Things at home were looking up, too. I was not out getting high or drunk every night. Being in the gym, I didn't need the coke anymore. Juanita and I were very excited about the baby, due in June. It would be much different from when Ray Jr. was born. There would be no concerns about money or how my parents might feel, and everybody would be together instead of living in two separate homes. I saw it as an opportunity to atone for the mistakes I made the first time. I promised myself I would be there for our new child in ways I never was for little Ray.

It was just as we were putting our lives back together that Juanita got sick again, coming down with an ulcer in her esophagus. She couldn't digest an ounce of food. She would go into the hospital for four or five days until she could again digest properly and return home, but the problem would once more flare up and she'd be in for another four or five days. She dropped twenty-five pounds in a few months, and doctors told Juanita that if the next remedy they tried did not work, they would have to abort the baby or risk losing her. The idea, a feeding tube that went up her nose and down her throat past the ulcer, did work, thank God, and both she and the fetus were safe. I didn't think about it at the time, but the ulcer was clearly related to the stress caused by our arguments. The prospect of a new baby wasn't bringing us closer, as Juanita prayed it would. It did, for perhaps a month or two, but I became too busy being Sugar Ray again. I couldn't get rid of him.

If the ulcer was not alarming enough, Juanita then contracted a disease known as Bell's palsy. The right side of her face became paralyzed, which she did not realize until her mom asked, "Why is your face crooked?" I cried like a baby when I saw her in the hospital. With medication and treatment, it returned to normal, though stress again was the cause. Her pregnancy, except for brief intervals, was an ordeal for the whole nine months.

I tried to be there for Juanita as often as possible, but I had a fight to worry about. In early February, we moved training camp to Massachusetts for the last stretch. I was ready to entertain the fans once more with my footwork. I was ready to land jabs to set up the rights. I was ready to have my face take its licks and not flinch. I was ready for anything.

Almost anything.

On February 13, less than two weeks before the Howard fight, I was undergoing a routine examination by retinal specialist Edward Ryan of the Massachusetts Eye and Ear Infirmary when he discovered an area of retinal thinning in my right eye. *That's just wonderful,* I thought, *now my right eye is having problems.*

The good news, and believe me, I was dying for any good news, was that the solution was a relatively minor procedure called cryotherapy, in which Dr. Ryan created scar tissue and strenghtened the retina, the whole operation taking only a few minutes. I was also relieved that there was no connection with the detached retina in the left eye. The bad news was that the Howard bout would end up being postponed till May 11. I was crushed. After spending weeks attempting to convince the public I was not risking more harm to my left eye, I was forced to address questions about the right one. I gave thought to quitting on the spot, interpreting the latest setback as a sign that maybe God, sensing I didn't receive his earlier message, did not want me to fight again.

One may ask: What was so horrible about waiting an additional two and a half months? The situation, after all, could have been a lot worse. The eye would heal and I'd be able to resume training before too long.

The problem was that by this stage of my preparations, I was in the zone again. I didn't get there against Finch, nowhere near it, and wouldn't have gotten there if the Stafford bout had been held. And now that I was there, I was afraid I would not be able to find my way back.

Howard, meanwhile, decided not to waste the February 25 date, taking on Bill "Fireball" Bradley in Atlantic City. He assumed a bit of a risk but it worked out, as he put Bradley away in six rounds.

Once I received permission from the doctors, I went back to the gym, training mostly with sparring partners who could race around the ring. I wasn't worried about power. The power would return. I was concerned about speed and accuracy. Those are the attributes a boxer loses the most when he's off for too long. Ali, in his postexile years, turned into a stationary target who fought bravely with Frazier and Shavers and the other brawlers of his generation. The result is still difficult to accept.

The weeks flew by. Before I knew it, it was May 11. At last, I would be inside the ropes for the first time in twenty-seven months. Except, as I feared, I never did get back in the zone I was in prior to the postponement. It was reminiscent of the Duran fight in Montreal. My biorhythms were off. The signs came early, and often, that it was not going to be my night.

The first sign came shortly after I climbed under the ropes. I liked to get loose for a few minutes, receive the ref's instructions, stare menacingly at my opponent in a last-ditch psych job, say a prayer, and then get down to business. But after the national anthem, sung beautifully by my sister Sandy, I was forced to wait for the ring announcer to introduce Donald Curry, Aaron Pryor, and, finally, Hagler. Hagler, a Massachusetts resident, received a loud ovation. One would have thought he was fighting, not me. The delay started to get on my nerves. Normally, I would be too focused to allow such a minor intrusion to distract me while I prepared for battle.

The second sign came in my corner between the first and second rounds. The first three minutes had gone as expected. I slid cautiously from side to side, getting a feel for Howard, and a feel for the situation— the noise of the crowd, the heat from the lights, the other man anxious to send me to the deck. I was also, contrary to my statements before the fight, concerned about my left eye and what might happen if I was hit there again. Who wouldn't be?

The most unusual thing occurred during that first break: I talked. I never talked in the corner. I didn't talk when Angelo berated me during the Eklund fight. I also looked away; at what, I don't remember. The point is that I was not where I needed to be.

If that wasn't disturbing enough, Howard was proving to be a more worthy adversary than anyone in my camp had anticipated. He hit hard and I should have seen it coming from the moment I touched his shoulder during the prefight press conference. Howard's muscles were defined, cut. Whoever did the scouting report was either poorly mistaken or Howard put in more time than usual at the gym.

In the third, I clowned around a little as I did during the seventh round of the Duran rematch. I did it to fire myself up more than for the spectators, and it seemed to pay off. I was into the fight. Howard did not back off, though, gaining more respect, but I was Sugar Ray Leonard and it was only a matter of time before there was a knockdown.

It was, except for one tiny detail. Howard did not fall. I did.

It happened with about thirty seconds left in the fourth round. After I threw a careless left jab, he responded with a solid right, the punch landing squarely on my jaw. I was back on my feet immediately, but the damage had been done, to my ego, mostly. In thirty-three previous fights, no one—not Benitez, not Duran, not Hearns, *no one*—had done this to me, and to think the man to register my first official knockdown was Kevin Howard, a four-time loser, remains as hard to believe today as it was on that eerie night in Worcester.

Within seconds, once I got over the shock, I made two snap decisions: I would fight as hard as I fought in my entire life to make Howard pay for what he did, and then I'd never fight again. If Howard could put me down, imagine what Hagler could do.

There would be time to think more about my future after the fight. First I had to finish it.

Before the fifth round, I stood in my corner and waved to Juanita at ringside to assure her I was not hurt. I had been worried about her. She had been through a lot over the last six months and didn't take it too well whenever I got hit hard. There was also somebody else's welfare to consider. Her due date was only a few weeks away.

I also waved to Howard in the opposite corner. I was coming after him, and I wanted him to know it.

Howard came after me as well. Only, his brief window of opportunity was gone. I scored repeatedly to the body and moved around the ring over the next two rounds. Howard didn't come close to putting me down again.

Late in the eighth, I landed my best combinations of the night. Howard was hurt. He hung on until the bell but I pounced on him again midway through the ninth. With about thirty seconds to go in the round, the referee stopped the fight. Howard was furious and he had every right to be. Though I was connecting with one clean shot after another, he remained alert enough to force a clinch and defend himself. Howard got a bit carried away, however, later telling the press that the only reason the fight was called was because he was on his way to winning a decision. First of all, it wasn't true—I was ahead on each of the three cards—and second, I would have knocked him out if the fight had lasted much longer. To his credit, Howard apologized to me in the locker room afterward for his comments.

Typically, after a victory, I'd celebrate in one form or another. Not on this night. There was nothing to be proud of. It took me nine rounds to put away an ex–club fighter. Some tune-up. The tune-up made me look like a club fighter.

Shortly after I was interviewed in the ring by Larry Merchant from HBO, Juanita, Ray Jr., and I met for a few minutes in a vacant bathroom. I told them about the decision I reached after the knockdown, to retire once more. They seemed relieved, especially Juanita. She was getting her husband back just in time to welcome the new addition to our family.

I wasted no time in informing the writers, who praised me in the ensuing days for coming to the only sane conclusion. Those who weren't very pleased included Hagler, denied yet again a likely eight-figure payday, Kenny, and J. D. Brown. Kenny and J.D. had launched a new promotion company, and saw me as their chief attraction. When news of my announcement spread, they rushed into the interview room to find out for themselves. They didn't dare say a word to me, though the expressions on their faces said plenty: *How could you do this to us? This was our one chance to make a fortune.*

After the conference ended, the reporters rushed back to their typewriters to compose another Sugar Ray Leonard obituary. This time I meant it, though, and there wasn't the deep sadness I experienced after the event in Baltimore. It was not the public that was the driving force behind this decision. It was me. It was my inability to be the fighter I once was and was now convinced I would never be again.

I walked away with no regrets. I was great once and that was good enough. I had a long life ahead of me and I couldn't wait to get started living it.

In June, everyone gathered in Las Vegas for the Duran-Hearns match, the WBC light-middleweight title on the line. I was set to do the broadcast, but almost didn't make the trip, with Juanita's delivery date only about a week away. I left Maryland two days before the fight, and was asleep when the phone rang in the middle of the night. Juanita was in labor. I couldn't get a flight out of Vegas till six A.M., and ended up missing my son's birth by one stinking hour. I've felt awful about it ever since.

Several days later, the four of us, including our new son, Jarrel, left the hospital for our home in Potomac.

Maybe Juanita was right after all. Maybe Jarrel would save our marriage. Maybe I would become the husband and father I never was.

Maybe Ray would stick around.

10

Simply Marvelous

R ay stuck around, though not for long. I proved to be as weak
as ever, surrendering once more to the temptations of fame. I
went back to drugs. I went back to loose women. I went back
to being Sugar Ray. The next two years remain a blur, one sad, shameful
incident leading to another. I was on the run again. I did not miss fighting. I missed *preparing* to fight. I missed the zone that enabled me, if
temporarily, to escape the pain.

Being Sugar Ray came with a cost, as always. The women I attracted
were as devious as I was. Two examples stand out. I'm sure there are
many others I've conveniently chosen to forget.

One was in Alaska, of all places, where Kenny and I went to make a
personal appearance. I did tons of meet and greets in those days. It didn't
take much time and the money was good.

After business came pleasure. My brother and I scored some of the
best blow of our lives and shared it with this incredibly sexy woman. After
we gave her a clean new T-shirt to wear, she went into the bathroom to

try it on. When she returned, the T-shirt was all she had on. The action got hot and heavy until everyone went to sleep. A few hours later, when he and I woke up, the woman and the coke were gone. She was a pro and we never saw her again. On another occasion, I got up in the morning at the Alexis Park Resort Hotel in Vegas after spending the night with a girl I met at a club and discovered that my money and jewelry, estimated at about thirty-five thousand dollars, were missing. I informed hotel security, who wanted to make a full report to the police. Eager to avoid the publicity, I asked them not to bother, although the robbery somehow made it into the papers. What happens in Vegas, apparently, does not always stay in Vegas. I did learn another important lesson. From then on, whenever I had a girl, I stashed valuables in the hotel safe or under the mattress.

At home in Maryland, my judgment could be just as cloudy. One time, and I still can't believe I did this, I took the Mercedes I had purchased for Juanita and drove to another girl's apartment. Juanita says she never told little Ray about my flings but he knew. On nights I was out of town, when he heard her sobbing, he would slip under the covers to comfort her.

"Mommy, it's going to be okay," he said.

Juanita often took the kids and stayed with her mom for a day or two in nearby Largo. Yet she would always return, granting me another chance. She loved me. That was her mistake.

I went back to work as a commentator for HBO and CBS. With me gone for good, Hagler and Hearns took over the sport. Hagler put away

Mustafa Hamsho in three rounds while Hearns knocked out Fred Hutch-ings, also in three, setting the stage for their much-anticipated fight on April 15, 1985, at Caesars, the WBA, WBC, and IBF middleweight crowns on the line. I did the color for HBO and was as blown away as everyone by the ferocity of exchanges between the two, Hagler winning by a TKO in round three. Never was I as grateful to be on the other side of the ropes.

In March 1986, however, I felt the exact opposite. I was back in Vegas to see Hagler defend his crown against John "the Beast" Mugabi. I went as a fan, not as a broadcaster, sitting in the second row with Ollie Dunlap and Michael J. Fox, the actor. During the fourth or fifth round, it became apparent that Mugabi, a slugger, was giving Hagler a much tougher test than anyone had predicted. I recalled again what Duran said to me after his loss to Hagler: "You box him, you beat him." Mugabi was boxing him.

I couldn't help it. Right then and there, I began to see myself in the ring.

"Michael, I can beat this guy," I said.

"Sure, you can, Ray," he said. "Do you want another beer?"

I didn't have time to argue. From that moment on, I rooted for Hagler harder than I ever rooted for anyone. "Jab, jab, move," I shouted. "You can do it, Marvin." The last thing I wanted was for John Mugabi to do the job for me.

Hagler connected with a series of solid shots in the sixth, but could not put him away. The longer the fight went on, the more concerned I became. Finally, in round eleven, Hagler sent Mugabi to the deck. He didn't get up and that was smart of him. I was the happiest man in the arena, next to Hagler.

When I returned to the hotel, I phoned Mike Trainer. It was about two A.M. on the East Coast. He didn't sound thrilled to hear from me.

"Mike, I'm ready to take on Hagler," I said.

"Ray, have you been drinking?" Mike said.

"Yes," I conceded, "but that's not the point. I can beat him."

Mike figured I was out of my mind and once the alcohol wore off I'd drop the idea, just as I did the other times. He figured wrong. I called him back the next day, sober but determined. Mike knew that sound in my voice. He knew this was different.

I thought about the risks I would be taking, to my health and my legacy, and how returning to the ring would affect my wife and kids. The boxer is hardly the only person who must sacrifice. So must his loved ones, and my family had sacrificed plenty. Yet the more thinking I did, the more I was convinced that I was doing the right thing. I never should have retired the second time, after defeating Kevin Howard. I did it because I was frustrated with my performance in Worcester, when in actuality it was quite respectable after being away from the ring for twenty-seven months. If I had just waited a few days, maybe a few hours, I would have come to my senses and told Mike to make my next match. Once I made the announcement, I couldn't take it back.

I thought about a conversation I had with Hagler only two months before at the formal opening of Jameson's, a restaurant in Bethesda that Mike was a part-owner of. Hagler, who came with his wife, Bertha, and I got to know each other that evening, both of us getting drunk, sharing stories about our families and our fights.

For all our differences, and there were many, Hagler and I discovered that we had a lot in common, neither needing a thing from the other, which was rare in my life, and his, too, probably. Under different circumstances, if there had not been a natural tension between the two of us, each vying to be the man in our sport, he and I could have been good friends. There are truths about us, about how we tick, that only another fighter can ever begin to understand. I could relate to the lack of motivation he was expressing, having felt the same ambivalence when I trained for Finch and Stafford. People have speculated that I lured Hagler into being vulnerable on purpose, to soften him up, because I had already decided to come out of retirement. That wasn't the case, although once I did choose to return, I remembered what a relaxed Hagler had told me and looked for ways to use this information to my advantage. Who could blame me?

The question then became: How do I tell the world I am returning to the ring? A press conference? No. I was above that. I was still the champ, in my mind, and bringing the media together would have brought my stock down, making me appear desperate. Instead, I had to almost make it seem as if Hagler were the one pursuing me. If the public was opposed to my return—and, yes, what people thought of me still mattered too much for my own good—or if Hagler did not bite, I would be able to move on without sacrificing my pride.

My chance came on May 1 when James Brown, a sportscaster for one of the D.C. TV stations, asked me during a casual lunch in town and posed the same question I'd been asked a million times in the two years since the Kevin Howard bout: Would I ever consider fighting again? In the past, I'd deliver a quick and definitive no, and the interviewer would proceed to other issues. Not this time. I told J.B., as Brown was affectionately called, I wasn't interested in a comeback, but I'd be open to one fight, and one fight only, against Hagler. I meant exactly what I said. I was also savvy enough to know I'd stand a better chance of gaining the public's approval if they believed it was for one night. They had invested too much in the notion that I was different from the other fighters, in knowing my limitations. I was no different, as they would find out over and over.

The next morning, the phone did not stop ringing. The reporters wanted to determine how serious I was, and so did Pat Petronelli, Hagler's manager, who, from what I can recall, told Mike he was confident that his man would accept the challenge, although Hagler was away on a cruise in the Caribbean and couldn't be reached. Mike wasn't pleased that I did the interview, convinced that I weakened our bargaining position. He had already put out feelers to the Hagler camp before I went public. I didn't care. I wanted the word out to move the process forward as rapidly as possible. My job was done. Now it was up to Hagler.

A lot of people thought I was crazy for challenging him, including members of my own family.

"Who is your tune-up?" Roger asked.

"Hagler," I said.

"No, who is your *tune-up*?" he persisted.

"Hagler," I repeated.

The reason for not arranging a tune-up was not only to make the public feel better about my decision. I also thought I would have trouble getting motivated for a lesser opponent, just as I couldn't get fired up for Kevin Howard. As for the fact that Ali, after being in exile for three and a half years, had two tune-ups (Jerry Quarry and Oscar Bonavena) before his first bout with Frazier, the comparison was not valid. Ali was interested in a career. I was interested in a night.

No one in my inner circle tried to talk me out of taking on Hagler, and why would they? After assuming that the days of large paychecks were gone forever, here, out of nowhere, was a chance for one more. So what if I got whipped? The money would be in the bank either way. It required someone on the outside who didn't stand to profit to question my sanity.

Someone like Howard Cosell. I was walking in the Hamptons one afternoon when I heard his distinctive voice.

"Suuugggar Ray, what are you doing in my neighborhood?" Howard asked.

Howard invited me to his house for lunch and I was happy to accept. The gratitude I felt toward him went back more than a decade. I never lost sight of how important a role he played in my becoming Sugar Ray.

By this stage of his life, Howard, in his late sixties, was finished with boxing, at least at the professional level. The last straw was the mismatch in November 1982 between the champ, Larry Holmes, and Randall "Tex" Cobb. Howard was angry that the referee, Steve Crosson, had allowed the bout to continue. In 1985, he came out with his controversial book *I Never Played the Game,* in which, among other things, he blasted his former colleagues on *Monday Night Football.*

We exchanged some small talk before he got serious.

"Son," he said, "I don't want you to get hurt."

I respected Howard for being blunt. It was one of the most endearing things about him. But I could be blunt, too.

"Howard," I said, "I believe I can win this fight. They told you not to write your book, but you still wrote it and you still believe in every single word of it. Right?"

He paused. I never saw Howard Cosell pause for that long.

"I guess you got me, son," he said.

While I waited for Hagler to make his decision, I didn't waste any time. If I was to be at my best, and it would take my best to outduel a man whose last loss was in March 1976, *before* I competed in the Olympics, I'd have to train harder and smarter. In the four years since beating Finch I had fought just once, for a total of twenty-six minutes and thirty-two seconds.

A few weeks later, Hagler weighed in. During an appearance on *The Tonight Show Starring Johnny Carson,* Hagler said he was going to "sit back and lick [his] chops. And just wait." I couldn't believe it. Who did he think he was?

The wait for Hagler to decide went on . . . and on . . . and on. I found out how others, including Hagler, must have felt when I took forever to make my intentions known after the eye surgery.

What was taking him so long? The advantages of fighting me could not be any clearer:

In addition to the money, which figured to be in the $10 million range, Hagler would get his opportunity to shut up the one person responsible for the boxing world not affording him the respect he felt he deserved. He couldn't stand the fact that I kept stealing the show, with high-profile triumphs against Duran and Hearns, while he was virtually ignored when he won title bouts over Alan Minter, Fulgencio Obelmejias, and Vito Antuofermo. In his mind, I even seized too much of the spotlight at my farewell announcement in Baltimore. All anybody could talk about the next day was how smart I was to retire.

It was not till my second retirement, in 1984, and his victory over

Hearns a year later, that Hagler became the man, and now here I was trying to steal the show once more. No wonder he milked the situation for as long as he could. I would have done the same thing. Having everyone breathlessly await your every word is intoxicating, and the moment you make a decision, the attention shifts to someone else.

Day after day the speculation went on: Will he accept my challenge? Will he take on Hearns again instead? Or will he retire?

I told the reporters I would not wait forever. I was bluffing but had to say something. I began to think he might take the rematch with Tommy, which had been discussed by the two camps prior to my offer, and force me to wait for him as he had waited for me.

At last, on July 2, Hagler held a press conference. The news did not appear encouraging.

"I'm very seriously thinking about retirement from the boxing game," Hagler said. "And what I feel is that I'm going to need a little bit more time to determine what my future will be."

A little more time, Marvin? I felt like saying. *You've had two full months!* Of course, given my track record, I was hardly one to talk.

He went on to indicate that money was not everything and that his family, which included his wife and their five children, was his primary consideration. I could definitely relate, recalling how many times Juanita was hoping I would quit and the disappointment she went through every time I decided to keep fighting. He suggested that I take on "the Mugabis or the Hearnses or the [Donald] Currys" before challenging him.

What I took away most from his press conference, however, was what Hagler did *not* say. He did not say he was retiring, not yet anyway. I still felt confident that he'd accept the challenge. Try turning down

$10 million. It's not easy. Believe me, I know. I also knew instinctively what others close to me did not know, that Hagler would never forgive himself if he let the opportunity pass. No matter how justifiable his reasons for quitting might have been, he'd be accused until the day he died of ducking me, and for a fighter there is no worse shame, and that includes losing.

Still, the weeks went by with no further word from the Mysterious One. Maybe Bertha Hagler would succeed where Juanita Leonard never could.

Finally, on August 18, three and a half months after I did the interview with J. B. Hagler, through a spokesman at Top Rank, the Las Vegas–based fight promotion firm, made his decision known: He was in.

I was overjoyed, although there was still the matter of the finances to work out, and with Bob Arum, the head of Top Rank and promoter of every Hagler title defense, doing the bidding, the negotiations were bound to be contentious. It was no secret that Mike Trainer and Bob Arum did not always see eye to eye. Hagler's decision also made me anxious. I realized there would be no going back. It was one thing to talk trash in the newspapers. I was a fighter and that's what fighters did. That's how we got by in the streets. But if you talk trash in the streets and get your ass kicked, no one finds out and you often get a chance to redeem yourself. Now the whole world would find out and I'd have to live with the outcome forever, and I still wasn't sure if I could pull it off.

There was only one way to find out, and it wasn't my body that needed the most work. It was my mind. My mind let me down in the preparation for Kevin Howard, and that was why I was knocked down for the first time in my career. My mind needed to be where it had been for the second Duran fight and the Hearns battle, where the only thing that mattered in my life was winning. Once I got there, *if* I got there, nothing could stop me.

As I kept working, so did Mike Trainer and Bob Arum. Their task was just as daunting.

Dividing the pot of gold to each party's satisfaction and ironing out the other issues were not going to happen overnight. It was not until late October, after two months of spirited negotiations, that the two sides reached an agreement. Hagler, the champion, was guaranteed $11.75 million while I was to take home at least $11 million. Another key element of the deal was convincing Hagler to accept twelve rounds instead of the standard fifteen for a championship fight. Hagler wanted fifteen. The extra three rounds were crucial when he rallied to secure the decision over Duran in 1983. Yet Mike shrewdly made Hagler's people believe it was a deal breaker when it never was. I was willing to go fifteen rounds if necessary, though given my time away from the ring, the less energy I spent, physically and mentally, the better.

The fight was set for April 6 at Caesars. I couldn't have been more satisfied. Caesars was where I won my first title, against Benitez, and where I would now win my last.

April was a long way off and I was grateful. When I issued the challenge to Hagler, I was hoping to get the fight in before the end of the year. Understanding the level of commitment it would require, I didn't know how long I would be able to maintain it. But as the months dragged on, I began to see the advantages of any delays. In addition to the extra work I could get in, which I needed, the later the fight was staged, the more it would render insignificant that I had been away from the ring for so long. By April, I would be fighting for the first time in thirty-five months, while more than a year would have passed since Hagler's last bout vs. Mugabi. To me, there would be little difference in the degree of rust. The layoff also meant I had absorbed far fewer blows than Hagler in recent years, and there are only so many hits a fighter can take in his career.

On November 3, Hagler and I met in the Grand Ballroom of the Waldorf-Astoria in New York for the press conference formally announcing the fight. The Waldorf was where Duran first got inside my head before the disaster in Montreal. Six years later, a heck of a lot brighter, I had my opportunity to do the same to Hagler.

During my opening remarks, I thanked the champ for giving me a shot and walked from the podium to his seat at the right side of the head table to shake his hand. He didn't turn around. I walked back to the podium and delivered my next line with perfect comedic timing.

"Apparently, he has his fight face on," I said.

A few people chuckled but Hagler stared straight ahead as if I weren't there. That was fine with me. He'd see me soon enough.

From that day forward, everything I said to the reporters over the following five months was designed to work on Hagler's psyche. I felt it was his weakest part. I was measuring him the same way I measured fighters in the ring, looking for an opening and pouncing on it. I benefited enormously from the work I had done to prepare for the fights of his I covered on HBO. I also knew, from our talks at his house in Brockton and the restaurant in Bethesda, what motivated him and what scared him. For the press conference in Manhattan, for instance, I wore a jacket that had shoulder pads to create the illusion of being as cut and muscular as possible to show Hagler he wouldn't be able to overpower me. I'd come in at 158 or 159 pounds and look every ounce of it.

With the deal official, I finished assembling Team Leonard, which included, as usual, Angelo, Janks, Ollie, Juice, Joe, my brothers, and about a dozen others. Also among us for the first time since 1980 was my ex-trainer, Dave Jacobs.

Jake and I hadn't had spoken for years. I'd never completely forgiven him for joining the Hearns camp. Nonetheless, sincerely believing the Hagler fight, win or lose, would be my last, I was determined to bring the entire cast together for one final, magical encore. I thought back to what it used to be like in the early days before the squabbling over money, and before my troubles with drugs and alcohol. I yearned for it to be that way one last time. Was I naïve? Maybe. To conquer Hagler, though, I needed more than a strategy to mess with his psyche. I needed to dig deeply, to be brave enough to look into my own soul and rediscover the joy of what inspired me to run five miles at five o'clock every morning and take a pounding from sparring partners who were out to make a name for themselves. I needed to be a fighter again. The best way was to have the people around who made me one in the first place.

Jake, assigned to manage the sparring partners, fit right in. I knew he would. After being on the outs for six years, he welcomed the chance for another ride. The rest of Team Leonard, no matter what their own misgivings might have been, were also serious from day one. Except Leonard himself.

A few months earlier, before the agreement was signed, I went to Miami for about a week to cover a fight for HBO. While I was there, I decided to get in a couple of workout sessions during my spare time. I also squeezed in something else on this trip—a woman. But when I appeared sluggish in the gym, Ollie let me have it. There was a time for fooling around with women. This wasn't it.

"Hagler will beat the shit out of you," he said. "You've got to get your body in shape."

I don't recall what I said but I was pissed. For three days, I wouldn't let Ollie ride in the limo with us to the gym, and I told Mike I wanted him off the team. Mike ignored me, and Ollie and I were soon speaking to each other again.

Mike, too, had moments when he questioned my commitment. At one stage, he had urged me to fight sparring partners without my headgear, and to let them use ten-ounce gloves. His point was that I needed to simulate as closely as possible the conditions of an actual fight. Mike believed Sugar Ray Leonard could beat Hagler but Ray Leonard couldn't.

Ollie and Mike were not alone. Even Juanita chimed in. I arrived at our home in Potomac from a workout one afternoon with contusions and bumps everywhere. The sparring partners had been roughing me up again.

"Ray, are you upset that you said yes to fighting Hagler?" she asked.

I became defensive right away. That's what I do.

"No, no, no," I protested. "How can you ask me that?"

Juanita did not give up.

"Sweetheart, it's okay. Sometimes we say things we don't mean."

Now I was really angry. Of course I meant what I said. I wanted Hagler. I wanted Hagler more than anything in the world.

After I settled down, however, I realized Juanita was right, that when I was honest with myself, admittedly a rare development, there were times I wished I could call the whole thing off. I was grateful that Juanita spoke up, and the same went for Mike and Ollie, especially Ollie. He did it at the risk of losing his job, and there were not too many members of my circle who would take that chance. The three helped me understand that if I did not get serious, Hagler would destroy me. Before very long, it was the sparring partners who left the gym with bumps and contusions. By the end of November, I had already sparred more than a hundred rounds.

With the fight still four months away, it made no sense to maintain the same pace. A fighter who overtrains is as likely to lose as a fighter who doesn't put the work in. Besides, there was other work to do, for Hagler and me. Now that the fight was made, we had to go out and sell it. The more fans we could put in the seats for the closed-circuit telecast, the more we each stood to gain. The bout was likely to generate more revenue than any boxing event in history.

Hagler and I launched a seven-week, twelve-city tour across the country. I embraced the opportunity to meet with reporters to talk about the fight. I even wrote down my speeches and went over them on the plane. The same couldn't be said of Hagler, who dreaded the gatherings and showed up late. I thought about saying something but decided it wasn't my place. If I were the champ, I certainly would not appreciate it if I were taken to task. Yet I could not remain silent. I took him off to the side in a hotel ballroom where no one could hear us.

"Marvin, they're paying us," I said. "We're professionals, man. You can't walk in when you want. It's not cool."

He stared at me for the longest time. Maybe we wouldn't have to wait until April to see who was the better man.

"I'm sorry, Ray," he said.

I was ecstatic, but I didn't show it. I didn't want to tip him off. By apologizing, Hagler was giving me respect, and the more respect he showed, the more he'd be wary of me once we entered the ring. It was an important victory in the other fight I was waging, the one to get inside that bald head of his.

Too bad my lecture did little good. Hagler was late again, for an appearance he and I were scheduled to make with Bob Hope. He made Bob Hope wait! The president didn't make Bob Hope wait. In mid-December, the problem was finally solved. After six stops, Hagler said *no más* to the rest of the tour, skipping appearances in Detroit and Chicago. I could understand why. This was one contest in which he had no shot against me, and he knew it. I was outgoing, cracking jokes, while he couldn't wait for the ordeal to be over. In Chicago, not one to skip an opportunity, I took the stage without him, and for a brief time played both parts.

"Ray, what will your strategy be for the fight?"

"Well, Marvin, I'm glad you asked."

The audience loved it. The only thing I couldn't do was shave my head.

Hagler's departure from the tour represented another triumph. If my mere presence made him uncomfortable in front of the reporters, imagine, I thought, how uncomfortable he will feel in front of 15,000-plus spectators at Caesars Palace. He was used to big fights but he was not used to fights *this* big, while I was—the two Duran duels and the encounter with Tommy. I felt confident that Hagler, for all his bravado, would have just as much trouble coping with the whole scene as I did in Montreal against Duran.

His journey to reach the top of the boxing world was quite impressive, to say the least. Hagler, the eldest of six, dropped out of high school in Newark, New Jersey, to help support his family. In 1969, two years after riots in the city left twenty-six people dead and caused more than $10 million in property damage, the Haglers moved to join relatives in Brockton, best known as the hometown of Rocky Marciano. Within a few years, he began to carve out his own place in history, winning the national amateur middleweight title in 1973 and going unbeaten in his first twenty-six professional fights before losing a controversial decision in January 1976 to Philly fighter Bobby "Boogaloo" Watts. Hagler lost again two months later to Willie "the Worm" Monroe, another Philadelphia product. The two setbacks only made him more determined, and he didn't lose again. The lone blemish was the 1979 draw in Vegas with Antuofermo, after which he captured his next sixteen fights, defending his middleweight crown twelve times.

Hagler received a lot of credit for his rise and, in time, a lot of money, although never enough of both in his opinion, and I was the person to blame. I made $40,000 in my pro debut; he made $50. I made $1 million against Benitez; on the undercard he made $40,000 vs. Antuofermo. I understood his frustration. I would have felt the same outrage if someone was making that much more than I was. But to resent me for the discrepancy—that I could not understand. I didn't steal the money. They gave it to me because I won the gold medal and the hearts of America, and because I made money for the boxing establishment by putting people in the seats. Hagler didn't compete in the Olympics and his fights didn't generate much attention until the mid-1980s. Furthermore, by the spring of 1987, Hagler was rich and famous, set for life, and I don't recall *him* volunteering to hand over any of his hard-earned cash to the fighters toiling for the small amounts he used to make.

Hagler, who owned the WBC and WBA middleweight crowns, was upset that the WBA did not approve of me as an opponent and opted not to sanction the bout. I didn't care. I wasn't planning to stick around anyway. I was coming back for one fight, and the only reward I craved was the satisfaction of victory.

In late January, we established camp in Hilton Head, South Carolina. It was cold and I despised cold weather, but training in Maryland was out of the question. I needed a quiet spot where there would be few distractions. Another important decision we later made was to place Juanita in charge. A camp is no different from a family, with people's needs often conflicting, and despite her reservations about me fighting again, no one would look out for my welfare more than my wife. I could not afford a repeat of Montreal.

With my mind on track, my body was next. I needed to build a new one. I would have to look the part for real. I couldn't wear shoulder pads into the ring.

Day by day, it started to form—in the arms, the thighs, the biceps, everywhere. I was becoming a legitimate middleweight. It was an odd feeling to see a different person in the mirror, yet the eyes were the same, hungry, angry, alive, and that's what mattered most.

In sparring sessions I worked with fighters who were ruthless, ready to attack, attack, and attack some more, just as Hagler would. They included Johnny Walker, who could hammer away with either hand,

Robert "Boo Boo" Sawyer, and Dwayne "the Barbarian" Cooper, whose bald pate served as an appropriate target. Walker switched frequently from an orthodox to a southpaw stance, a common Hagler maneuver that required his opponents to make on-the-fly changes to cope effectively with directly opposite angles. No boxer at our level could go back and forth as seamlessly as Hagler could. He changed from one round to the next. He changed in the *middle* of a round. Each sparring partner also helped me get acquainted again with the sensation of my face getting pummeled. It was a tough enough adjustment when I came back in 1984 after a two-year break, let alone three years of boozing, snorting, and running in and out of countless bedrooms.

My strategy from the opening bell would be to disrupt Hagler's rhythm. Hagler reminded me of a truck going down a hill, building up speed and then running you over. He had a chin made of granite. In all his fights I saw in person or on film, I never saw him buckle, not once. I saw him get cut, but that only motivated Hagler to fight with more venom. Any suggestion might make a difference, however insignificant it appeared. Enter J. D. Brown to the rescue.

J.D., long over his disappointment about my retirement following the Kevin Howard fight after he and Kenny had launched their new promotion company, agreed to be a spy for us at Hagler's camp in Palm Springs, California. Spies in boxing had been around as long as punching bags, and with most sparring sessions open to the public, almost anyone could get in. For J.D. to get paid, he had to provide a picture of himself with Hagler. No problem. He dyed his hair gray, put on horn-rimmed glasses, and secured the photo and an autograph, to boot. For three solid days, J.D. watched Hagler work out. The majority of what J.D. put in his report was nothing I had not known before, but he did come up with one fascinating insight I'd use on fight night. He noticed that just before the bell would sound to begin every round, Hagler would go stand in the middle of the ring as if to declare: *This is my territory, pal. I dare you to try to take it away from me.* I decided that if I accomplished nothing else at Caesars Palace, I would reach the center of the ring before he did.

In late February, Angelo arrived in Hilton Head. Normally he didn't show up this early before a fight. Of course there was nothing normal about facing Marvin Hagler.

Angelo showed me the best angles to approach Hagler; because he wasn't a natural southpaw, I should work on avoiding his more deadly right hand. He also told me that because Hagler was stronger did not mean I couldn't push him around in a clinch. This was another way to break his rhythm, and the more frustrated he became, the more he would stray from his comfort zone.

By late March, when we left Hilton Head to spend the final week in Las Vegas, everything was coming together.

I was used to my new body, my hands and feet moving as smoothly as they did with the old one. I could not wait to disprove the critics who said the additional ten pounds would slow me down. I was nailing guys in the gym so convincingly that I was starting to believe the surest way to confuse Hagler was to do what neither he nor anyone would anticipate, and that was to fight him toe-to-toe. Given that he'd incurred a lot of scar tissue, I saw no reason why I couldn't open up old cuts. He cut easily, he told me over drinks that night at Jameson's. I didn't forget.

Was I out of my mind? Didn't I learn my lesson from fighting Duran that way in Montreal? Didn't I see what Hagler did to Tommy when he tried to slug it out with him? Apparently not.

Fortunately I woke up to reality. It occurred when I was sparring in Las Vegas a few days before the fight. Quincy Taylor, another southpaw we used, threw a left hand that rocked my socks off. I should have taken a knee. But no, not me. I was Sugar Ray. I didn't go down in the gym. I did the Ali thing, pretending that I wasn't hurt, and the audience fell for it. Quincy knew better, as did my boys. He took it easy, firing harmless shots to the body to let me recover. Quincy, who would become the middleweight champion in the mid-1990s, did not want to be known as the sparring partner who caused a delay in the Leonard-Hagler fight. Time was called and I was out of danger.

Still, the punch did damage—to the confidence of my team. I detected the change during the ride back to the hotel. No one said a word. I knew what they were thinking: *He's really gotten in over his head this time.* I had never been hit that hard this close to fight night.

I called Mike when I got back to my room. I was more determined than ever.

"These motherfuckers think I'm going to lose," I said. "I'll show them. I'm not going to let Hagler touch me."

The punch served another purpose as well. I reviewed the sequence on tape a few hours later and was relieved to see there were no glaring errors with my footwork or defense. Quincy simply caught me with a good shot when I got too careless, which can happen to anyone. Yet I could not overlook the obvious: What if Hagler did the same? Fighting toe-to-toe was now out of the question. I would do instead what Duran told me back in 1983: "You box him, you beat him." Thank God for Quincy Taylor.

The boys were not the only ones lacking confidence in my chances of pulling off the upset. So were the boxing writers, many of whom were good friends. There were too many strikes against me: a three-year layoff, a higher weight class, an opponent who had not lost in eleven years. To them, the real Sugar Ray Leonard was last seen against Hearns in 1981, and would never be seen again. Some went as far as to suggest I might get seriously hurt, which could cripple the sport's credibility for years. Of the sixty-seven writers polled before the fight in one newspaper article, sixty chose Hagler, fifty-two by knockout. Of the seven who went with me, only two (Bart Ripp from the *Albuquerque Tribune* and Michael Katz of the *New York Daily News*) predicted that I would put Hagler away. The doubters included Larry Merchant, who saw Hagler winning via a ninth-round KO.

Larry, however, was rooting for me, as were many of the writers. On the day before the fight, along with HBO's Ross Greenburg and Barry Tompkins, he watched my workout. Later after a brief conversation at the house I was renting, the three headed for the door. Larry abruptly turned around and approached me again while the other two hung back. He had one last thing to say:

"Make me a liar."

April 6 finally arrived.

After a restless night, with one trip after another to the bathroom mirror, I got up early, around seven. I can't think of a key fight—Aldama, Benitez, Duran I and II, Hearns—when I wasn't up early.

The day's first order of business was the traditional morning weigh-in at the Sports Pavilion in Caesars.

The weigh-in went unnoticed for decades, until 1964, when Ali pretended to be crazy during the one before his first title fight with Liston. From then on, with the help of television, fighters have used the stage for last-minute drama to pump up interest in the event. For my purposes, I went in with no game plan, but soon sensed another chance to get inside Hagler's head. Both he and I were asked to wait off to the side while the other stepped on the scales. I went first, Hagler patiently watching as I came in at 158 pounds. But when it was his turn to be weighed, I walked away. I was letting him know that while he was the champ, I wasn't going to give an inch. After the weigh-in, I went upstairs to my suite for the rest of the afternoon. I enjoyed my one meal of the day: chicken with tons of gravy and onions, vegetables, and corn bread.

More than a full year had gone by since I had decided to come out of retirement. A lot of people thought I was nuts and there were moments when I was one of them. I lost my focus on numerous occasions, and it showed in the gym and in my behavior. Each time, thankfully, there was someone to remind me who I used to be, and who I could be again if I put in the work, which I did. By the time we broke camp, I was ready. I didn't need the money, and I didn't need to punish my body. I had punished my body enough. I did need the challenge, and I got it, and now, in only a few hours, in a specially constructed outdoor stadium in the parking lot at Caesars, I'd find out if the work would pay off. The idea of fighting Hagler was brought up in 1981 and 1982, and again in 1984, and many experts believed that was when we should have fought, in our prime. None of that was important. We were fighting at last, and the whole world was about to tune in. They called it the "SuperFight" and that's what it was.

* * *

When the bell rang for round one, I accomplished my first goal: I beat Hagler to the center of the ring. I felt like putting up a flag.

My next goal was to win the round. That was not as crucial in other matches, when the opponents were not as imposing and there would be fourteen rounds remaining. But this being a twelve-rounder and Hagler being who he was, likely to dictate the tempo at some juncture, I needed to steal as many of the early rounds as possible, in case the long layoff took its toll.

So far so good as I slid from side to side, keeping Hagler at bay as he pursued me from one end of the twenty-square-foot ring to another. Beginning in the summer of 1986, before I knew if there would be a fight, I ran five miles a day at Mount Motherfuck, building the endurance in my legs, and they weren't letting me down. Neither was my jab. Getting the first several out of the way got rid of the nerves, and after that, they were quick, effective. The objective was to land a series of combinations in each round, usually with a right-hand lead, and then dance out of his range.

"Stick and jab," Ollie kept yelling. "Stick and jab."

As the bell rang, when I was about to throw a left, Hagler flinched and covered up. I suddenly realized the fearless Hagler was as nervous as I was. He was mine.

Round two was very similar, Hagler stalking me as I maintained a safe distance, changing directions, keeping him off balance: *"You box him, you beat him."* He was fighting orthodox instead of south-paw and I couldn't understand why. Did he really believe that he could outbox me? If he did, he would keep throwing rounds away, and with each round, each minute, I became more comfortable. Three years is a long time to be away from the ring, and it takes a while to remember where you are, who you are. Hagler switched to southpaw to start the third round. It made no difference as he continued to miss his target. In the fourth, just to irritate him, I threw a mini bolo punch, reminiscent of the one in round seven of the Duran rematch. The punch, which landed close to Hagler's groin, got a reaction from the crowd. I was getting under his skin.

"Fight like a man, bitch," Hagler said. "Fight like a man."

In the fifth, Hagler, who was about a 3½–1 favorite, turned into the Hagler everyone expected. He landed a solid combination late in the round, catching me with his best shot of the evening, a hard right upper-cut that made my knees buckle. I was in trouble, trapped in the worst possible position, the ropes, and was fortunate that the bell rang.

"Don't lay on the ropes," Angelo told me.

There was not the slightest trace of panic in Angelo's voice and demeanor, and if there had been, I might have panicked, too. When Jake, who did lose control, shouted, "Don't let him draw you into a punch-ing match," Angelo sternly told him, "Quiet, quiet," and there was not another peep from Jake. The exchange between them summed up the differences in the two men and illustrated why I made the proper choice in hiring Angelo in the fall of 1976. Jake was the right man for the gym, for the hours and hours of tedious work it takes to remain sharp and fit. Angelo was the right man for the arena, for when the pressures—and almost every fight has them—demand a steady hand.

In round six, I set out to prove that Hagler had inflicted no lasting damage in the preceding round and that I was still controlling the action. Hagler stayed aggressive but I counterpunched effectively, and, as it turned out, won the round on all three of the judges' cards. I was putting Hagler in a hole, and the fight was already half over. A lot of people assumed I would be on the canvas by this stage, if not a stretcher.

In the seventh, my legs began to go. They had carried me this far, longer, perhaps, than I had any right to expect. I would now have to rely on my will and intelligence to contend with a fresher Hagler, who pinned me against the ropes again and connected with a series of good shots.

"I want you off the ropes," Angelo said during the break. He wasn't the only one.

The eighth passed without much incident, and I was grateful. I needed to pace myself for the final four rounds. Hagler was going to throw everything he had. He had waited a long five years for the chance to shut me up and he was running out of time.

In the ninth, I fought flat-footed too much, and paid the price. I was caught by the ropes once more, Hagler firing away repeatedly, landing a series of stinging lefts and rights to my head. I saw those punches coming, yet there was little I could do about them. At no point, however, did I become discouraged. I knew I would dig deep, and that's what I did, unleashing, in rat-a-tat fashion, one punch after another to curtail his momentum. I did not win the round, according to two of the judges, or hurt Hagler, but the speed and fury of my blows fired up the fans, reminding them of the boxer I used to be. The bell rang.

"We got nine minutes," Angelo said.

Nine minutes is a lifetime in boxing. Did I have them in me?

For that matter, as round ten got under way, how much did Hagler have left in the tank? Everyone had focused on my three-year hiatus from the sport, but there were some who had observed signs of Hagler's decline in the fight with Mugabi. I did not necessarily subscribe to that point of view, although there was little doubt that Hagler was growing weary as well. He trained for about two months in Palm Springs. Would it mean the difference over the last three rounds?

Fortunately, in rounds ten and eleven I found my second wind and stopped being a stationary target. When the fighting reverted to the inside, I gave as good as I received, impressing the crowd, and the judges. I was feeling confident enough that late in the eleventh, hands by my sides, I stuck my chin out several times to taunt Hagler as I taunted Duran in New Orleans.

One round to go. I sat on my stool awaiting Angelo's final words of encouragement. He didn't let me down.

"We got three minutes," he said. "New champion! New champion!"

I jumped up and raised both gloves in the air. The fans roared. Many had not been with me at the start, but the fact that I was still standing in the ring with the invincible Hagler won them over. All I had to do was stand until the end and I'd be a winner, with the public and myself, whether the judges saw it that way or not.

I walked toward the center of the ring. I had claimed the spot since the opening round and I was not about to surrender it now. As the bell rang, I could not resist getting inside Hagler's head one last time.

"Wanna fight me now?" I said. "Wanna fight me?" They were the only words I said to him the entire fight. I started the last round as I did the first, dancing, searching for any openings to score before skirting out of his range. Hagler kept stalking, looking to land the one punch he might need to save the day.

Halfway through the round, I glanced toward my corner. Before the fight, I had instructed Ollie to shout "Thirty" whenever there were thirty seconds left in a round. I would then throw as many flurries as possible in hopes of leaving the judges with a positive impression that might help me secure the round. But in the twelfth there was no signal from Ollie, not yet, the seconds taking forever to go by. I must have glanced over two or three times until, finally, he shouted the magic word. I summoned whatever energy I had left, and it was not much, Hagler doing the same, the noise deafening, the bell coming at last.

I walked back to my corner—stumbled, was more like it—Ollie and Janks keeping me from falling to the canvas. With the ring filling up in a hurry, I found Hagler and we hugged. We were partners once more.

"You're still the champ to me," I told him.

Now it was up to the three judges, and it would not take long, both Hagler and I confident that we deserved the decision.

Before the verdict was read, the ring announcer said it was a split decision. I got a knot in my stomach.

The first card belonged to Lou Filippo, who scored the fight 115–113 in favor of Hagler. Next was Jo Jo Guerra, who gave me the nod, 118–110, generating a fair amount of criticism later, mainly because of the one-sided margin, and even I had to agree there was no way I took ten of the twelve rounds. One judge was left, Dave Moretti.

The announcer prolonged the suspense as much as possible, revealing the point totals (115–113), and, finally, the winner . . . "and new middleweight champion of . . ."

The word *new* was all I needed to hear. I climbed to the bottom strand of the ropes and raised my arms. I had done it. I had done what no one, including members of my own team, my own *family*, thought was possible. I had dethroned the mighty Marvin Hagler.

The celebration began and did not end for days, if not weeks. I don't remember if I slept that night, and if I did, it could not have been for more than an hour or two. There would be plenty of time to sleep later.

Of all the beautiful memories from that evening and the next morning, two stick out. One took place shortly after the fight. James Anderson put me on his shoulders and carried me through the front entrance of Caesars, people cheering as we went by. I could have stayed on his shoulders forever. The other occurred during breakfast. I was sitting with Juanita when John Madden, the pro football commentator, walked over to our table and sat directly across from us. Madden, who had been convinced that I would be destroyed by Hagler, looked me in the eye for at least thirty seconds without making a sound. He shook his head two or three times.

"I've never seen anything like that," he said, and walked away.

In retrospect, nearly a quarter century later, the victory in 1987 means as much to me now as it did then, maybe more. If the fight with Tommy was my greatest achievement in the ring, the fight with Hagler was my proudest. I was not at my best. I was nowhere near my best ever again after I beat Tommy. I don't care who you are. You can't take three years off in this sport, which asks for everything you have, and expect to come back and be the same. Ali couldn't. I couldn't. Yet the will deep inside me did come back, for one night, and that was enough. People have said I was lucky the fight was scheduled for twelve rounds instead of fifteen, but I prepared for twelve and I would've prepared for fifteen. Making it twelve meant the task was mentally easier. It was not why I won the fight.

Many don't believe I actually did win the fight, and there is nothing I can say to change their minds. Leading the charge is Hagler himself. He became outraged the moment the decision was announced and he has been upset about it ever since, blaming the same Vegas bias that he felt had led to the draw with Antuofermo in 1979. Hagler even claimed that when we embraced in the ring, I told him, "You won the fight." I said no such thing. Why would I? The reality is that he was devastated and needed an explanation. The one man he wanted to beat most in his life beat him.

If Hagler felt the bout was stolen from him, it begs the obvious question: Why didn't he ask for a rematch? Mike Trainer and I were open to the idea, but we never heard one word from him or his representatives. He took off for Italy and his dreams of an acting career.

I hoped Hagler and I would become friends again, just as Tommy and I did. Boxing is a business that is done with us before we realize it, when we are replaced by men younger and stronger and faster who can make more money for the people who run it, which is fine. There is still the rest of our lives to enjoy, if we're lucky, if we didn't take too many punches in the wrong places or put our money in the wrong hands. We could sit back and reflect on what the two of us did together, and that could be special, too. Yet Hagler has never been interested in a friendship with me. I took away more than his title. I took away a part of him.

I bumped into Hagler in the men's room at a club in Las Vegas about six months after our battle and tried to make polite conversation. He threw water on his face, gave me a cold stare, and walked off without responding.

"Fuck you," I said. "I don't need to be your friend."

Eventually, he would speak to me, although the resentment was still there. In September 1999, I saw him at the Mandalay Bay in Vegas after the duel between Oscar De La Hoya and Felix Trinidad, which Trinidad won in a narrow decision.

"Marvin," I said, "I can't believe Oscar lost that fight."

Hagler did not miss a beat.

"I can," he said. "You know Vegas, right?"

The upset over Hagler put me back in the spotlight—and in a way I could have never imagined. About two months after the fight, I got an urgent call around 10 on a cold, rainy night from the police asking for my help in a case involving a man who had kidnapped an eighteen-month-old girl but wouldn't tell them where he left her. He would only tell Sugar Ray Leonard, his idol. At first, I thought it was one of my boys pulling a prank. Two minutes later, I knew it was no prank—a squad car had pulled up in front of my house. An officer asked if I would go with them to the kidnapper's apartment. I was assured the police would be close enough in case he tried to harm me.

When we arrived, he was excited to see me, recalling the details of some of my biggest fights. I smiled. The idea was to humor him for as long as possible.

"That's cool man," I said. "We should have dinner and talk about this. But, first, let's go find the baby you took. Is that okay with you?"

"I'd like that a lot," he said.

He took me and the police to a nearby park where we wandered around for about ten minutes until we heard someone crying in the distance. The baby had been tied to a tree. Thank God she was not seriously hurt. The guy was immediately taken away.

I couldn't sleep when I got home. I realized there was a lot more to being famous than I thought.

11

Finding Love Again

I n the months after the Hagler fight, all it seemed anyone wanted to know was: Who is next? *Who is next?* Didn't the reporters hear me when I said the Hagler fight would be my last, win or lose? They did, but they knew me too well, and couldn't imagine that I would ride off into the sunset again at the age of thirty, fresh from pulling off the upset of the year, if not the decade. That isn't very old for a boxer, especially given my general inactivity over the previous five years, and with the potential paydays on the horizon, I stood to make another fortune. Nonetheless, on May 27, I did it again. I retired. I made a promise to the fans that I felt I had to keep. I had broken too many already.

As for the vows to my wife, they were worth the usual amount, nothing. The win over Hagler sent my ego into the stratosphere, and with no need to run five miles at Mount Motherfuck or spar for an hour in the gym, I went back to the life I'd put on hold: alcohol and women. I felt more entitled to these rewards than before, and who would deny them to me? The only good sense I showed was not doing any more coke, and that was because of James. Besides Mike and Ollie, James was probably the only member of my team who could speak his mind without fearing the consequences. He could land another job in five minutes and I'd be a fool to let him go.

"Ray, think of the harm that you would do to your kids if you were arrested for drug possession," he pointed out. "The damage would last forever."

I didn't respond, but after he took off, I went to my room and cried for an hour. I haven't done coke since.

Still, the arguments with Juanita became nastier and my conduct more inexcusable. I didn't need cocaine to be an asshole.

"That's it," she said one night in late 1987 after I told her I would not stop drinking. "I'm leaving, and the kids are going with me."

I couldn't let that happen. Even with the alcohol in my system, I came up with a plan, just as I did in the ring whenever I felt my advantage slipping away.

I retrieved the .38 automatic I kept in a little box and fired a series of shots at the TV set in the bedroom, pieces of glass scattering everywhere. If Juanita feared that I might kill myself, I was sure she'd run up the stairs and not leave my sight. She never came. The next sound I heard was the slamming of the car door. I assumed for years that she didn't hear the shots, but she heard them loud and clear. She didn't come upstairs because she was afraid I was just crazy enough to shoot her.

Yet, after a few days, Juanita was back home, granting me another chance. I blew it, of course, as I did the others, and when she again threatened to leave after the next altercation, I took a can of kerosene from the garage and poured its contents on the floor in the foyer. I was nothing if not creative.

"If you leave me, I promise I will burn this house down," I said.

She left. She knew I was bluffing. I was always bluffing.

The house smelled of kerosene for days. Yet she returned once more. Juanita was either foolish or a saint.

The night that finally ended our marriage fit the pattern perfectly: me wasted, her ranting. I demanded she hand over her wedding ring, which I then placed on my finger. As the argument grew more heated, I gave her a little shove, accidentally scraping Juanita on the forehead with the ring's large diamond. Blood trickled down the bridge of her nose. I was horrified. How could I have done this to the woman I loved? At the same time, she had pushed my buttons, but that's no excuse. I prefer to believe that was the alcoholic in me, not the real me.

Juanita did not panic. She calmly packed her bags, rounded up the boys, and loaded them into the car. I went outside to try to stop them. I didn't have a prayer.

"Leave my momma alone!" Jarrel, three, yelled. "I hate you. I hate you." His words hurt worse than any punishment I ever absorbed in the ring. Ray Jr., fourteen, also defended his mother, his eyes filled with anger.

As I stood in the dark watching them drive to the front gate, I realized the sides had been drawn. It was no longer merely a fight between husband and wife. It was three against one. I never felt so alone in my life.

Juanita didn't come back after a few days this time. She never came back.

Ray Jr. did. At first, I figured he came back for me, to prove he was on my side after all, and to see if we could establish the closeness that had always been missing from our relationship.

Once again, I was deceiving myself. Ray came back because Potomac was his home, where his friends were and where he was a star running back in high school. Although we lived in the same house, Ray and I might as well have been living in different counties for the amount of time we spent together. While he was out with his buddies, I remained in the bedroom, as if I were the victim. I cried in bed every night, and didn't wake up till ten or eleven.

And there were women. There were always women. But the women meant less to me than before, and never stayed the night. I hated the house I used to love, its large rooms and hallways empty, depressing, a prison. Without Juanita around, I did not know whom to trust. No matter how often she and I fought, she was the only person I could count on and now I couldn't anymore. It was no coincidence that once she left for good, I began to entertain the notion of returning to the ring. Where else was I to go?

In August 1988, I made it official: I was coming out of retirement for the third time, which had to be a record. If there were those who thought I was breaking a promise and risking damage to my legacy—and I was guilty on both counts—I didn't mind. I missed the ring. I missed having a place to release my anger.

My opponent would be an unknown from Canada, Donny Lalonde. I liked Lalonde from the moment I met him in Mike Trainer's office. Good-looking, with long blond hair, he seemed more like a surfer than a fighter. He held the World Boxing Council light-heavyweight title, though the fighters he beat were as anonymous as he was. At stake besides the belt would be the WBC's new super-middleweight crown at 168 pounds, meaning if I won, I'd become only the second boxer to capture world titles in five divisions, assuming that Tommy Hearns got past James Kinchen a few days before my fight. The money was irresistible: $12 million up front, with a chance for another $3 million. The bout was scheduled for November 7 at Caesars.

The only negative in returning was that I'd have to do it without Angelo. I don't recall the specifics, but I believe that Angelo was not pleased with his earnings from the Hagler fight, and refused to work for me again unless he received a formal contract. I felt bad about the break, but I trusted Mike and I was with two trainers—Jake and Janks—who had known me for almost twenty years. I appreciated Angelo's contributions, especially in the corner during the Hearns and Hagler bouts, but boxing was a business and he knew it as well as anyone.

I trained hard for Lalonde, realizing the key to winning was the same as it was against Hagler, forcing Lalonde to miss. The more he missed, the more he would doubt himself, and I'd be in command. He would also be intimidated by the atmosphere at Caesars, which he had never come close to experiencing. Still, I wasn't about to take Lalonde lightly. I made that mistake with Kevin Howard and found my ass on the canvas. Yet, once again, I had trouble getting motivated and snapped at members of my team more than usual. The difficulties in my personal life were clearly getting to me. Two weeks before the bout, I woke up in the middle of the night after a premonition—which I believe in—that I would be knocked down.

I tried to forget about it but I couldn't. As I stood in the corner on fight night awaiting the bell, I became convinced that the vision was about to come true. The only question was: Which round? The answer was the fourth, a Lalonde right on the side of my head doing the trick.

Once back on my feet, I was calm. I wasn't hurt and now I could get on with the business of winning the fight. I took a deep breath. After the first knockdown, too many fighters panic, which leads to a mistake and the next, and often conclusive, knockdown. The key is to slow down your heart rate and survive the round, which I did. Lalonde made it easier by rushing his punches. In the fifth, I measured him, scoring with shorter, crisper shots, and took over the match. There was nothing like a knockdown to get me out of a rut.

The end came in round nine. After he stung me with a right uppercut, I responded with my most fluid combinations of the night, a left hook to the jaw sending him to the deck. Lalonde got up in time, but another hook finished him off. I was not proud of my effort. At least I didn't retire, as I did minutes after the Howard bout. The next retirement, I told myself, had better be the last.

I returned to Potomac, to drinking and crying at night, sleeping in late. I still loved Juanita, and wondered if there was any chance of winning her back. I saw more women, but the idea of another serious relationship was out of the question.

Then, out of nowhere, there she was and my life would never be the same.

I met Bernadette Robi at a Luther Vandross concert at the Los Angeles Sports Arena in April 1989. She was with saxophonist Kenny G and his girlfriend, Lyndie. I did not get a chance to talk to her much that night, but a day or two later, Kenny called. He asked me about my marital status. I told him I was legally separated. "Good, because my friend Bernadette was inquiring," he said.

"Which one was Bernadette?" I said. "The girl with the curly hair?"

"That's the one," he said.

I called the same night and her machine picked up. When we finally did speak, I felt as if I had known her for years. However, I was not ready. I was nowhere near ready. We made plans to get together on three different occasions, each one in a larger group setting. I stood her up every time.

Any other woman would have decided I wasn't worth the trouble, which was what her friends told her. Not Bern. She believed in us long before there was an us. The fourth time, when I promised I'd meet her for dinner with friends, including Kenny G and the actor Dudley Moore, in Venice Beach, she took charge.

"I am picking *you* up," she said.

I was a bit taken aback, though intrigued. Women didn't pick me up. That's not how it worked. Yet we had a blast, and afterward, driving around Venice, I told her that every time we crossed a bridge, and there were quite a few, I would give her a kiss. With much reluctance, she let me get away with a few kisses.

Upon arriving at my hotel in Westwood, I invited her upstairs for a nightcap. We kissed and I squeezed her tightly. I got ready to take Bern to bed. That's what I did on first dates . . . on every date. That was not what Bern did. Her eyes were warm, but firm. There was no room for compromise.

"I have to leave," she said.

I was in shock. Who exactly was this woman who was so different from the other girls? Didn't she know who I was?

The next morning, I called to tell her how much I enjoyed myself. From then on, we saw each other whenever I came to L.A., which was often. I started to have feelings for her that I had been sure I would never have again. More than her drop-dead looks, I fell for the beauty on the inside, the sweetness, sensitivity and intelligence that made me believe in the future.

Early on in our courtship, Bern and I were invited to an event at the home of a well-known Hollywood producer. I told the boys and they were fired up, as some of the hottest celebrities in town were bound to be there.

Bern set me straight.

"Ray, I really don't think you should bring them," she said. "There will be people there who are more famous than you are and they won't have their security."

Not bring the boys? Was she out of her mind?

I brought the boys everywhere. They were not just my security; they were my security blanket. I could walk in as Sugar Ray Leonard, the part I knew better than any other, charm everyone, and the evening would be a huge success. I wasn't quite sure how Ray Leonard would fare.

Three hours before departing, I made the decision: The boys would stay home. Bern was right. I didn't need them. I could be Ray, and everything would be just fine.

Thank goodness they didn't come. When the door opened at the producer's home, standing in front of us were Ronald and Nancy Reagan. I can't imagine how the boys would have handled themselves. I was in a cold sweat myself, and I was accustomed to meeting the top people in politics and show business. Bern and I hung out for hours and I didn't feel uncomfortable for one second.

Yet the months went by, and still we did not have sex. I was becoming a little edgy, but didn't pressure her. It wouldn't have done any good. I might have ruined everything.

One day I could tell from how intensely Bern kissed me in the car that this would be the night. I showered for a half hour, perhaps longer, sprayed on too much cologne, and had two or three drinks. I was as terrified as I was at sixteen when Juanita told me she did not come over to my house to watch TV. I now knew plenty about sex, but nothing about making love. All I can say is that it was worth the wait, and it was not the act itself as much as the connection we made during and after that was so meaningful. The clearest indication came the next morning. I had a plane to catch, but didn't want to leave her side. Normally, after sleeping with someone, I was out the door before dawn. After I left, I called her from the car, and again from the airport. I told Bern how happy I was, and that I loved her. The boys were speechless.

I opened up to her, and because I did, she saw the side of me that wasn't very attractive. Just because I was in love again did not mean I would stay away from alcohol and other women. Days would go by without a single phone call, and when I did call, I would be slurring my words, inventing the latest lie. But from the sound of my voice, she always knew, just as Juanita knew, the only difference being that Bern's forgiveness wasn't for sale. Once, after she could not reach me for several hours on her birthday, she was very upset when we finally connected. I arranged for a new BMW to be delivered to her house. She sent it back.

"Ray, this car means nothing to me," Bern said. "What you're doing is damaging the relationship. Just imagine a bridge. You are chipping away at the foundation and the thing will collapse."

I apologized. Of course, no sooner was one apology offered than I'd need to make another, and another. Getting rid of my old habits wasn't going to be easy. It was the world I knew from my life as a celebrity. It took years to construct.

Over time, I slowly got rid of the other women—except Juanita. No matter how close Bern and I became, I couldn't get Juanita out of my head. She was my first love and stood by me even as I tried to destroy us and myself. When I began to destroy the kids, that she could not tolerate.

In the late fall of 1989, I had to find out once and for all.

"I'm going to see Juanita," I told Bern.

I feared Bern might end it and I wouldn't blame her. She surprised me again.

"Do what is best for your family," she said. "You owe it to them."

A few days later in Maryland, I made love to Juanita for the first time in well over a year, but there was something wrong, and I didn't know what it was until she issued an ultimatum the following morning while we were still in bed.

"Ray, I'm willing to get back together, but you have to get rid of Bernadette," Juanita said. "I can't share you with another woman again."

I didn't speak for a few minutes. I was confused. Yet as I thought about it, I saw my situation more clearly than I had in the longest time. The woman I wanted to be with was not next to me in bed. She was three thousand miles away, in California, and I could not be with her soon enough.

"I can't get rid of Bernadette," I told Juanita. "I just can't do that."

I couldn't believe what I said. I had told her the truth. I never told her the truth.

Now, for a change, I was the one walking away, and any chance of reconciling was gone forever.

The next day, I was on a plane to Los Angeles.

Getting rid of alcohol was an entirely different matter. Bern was very patient with me, but there were times when the disease threatened to do what Juanita could not—break us up.

Each morning after I woke up, there was only one way to tell how I behaved the night before. If Bern spoke to me, I knew I had survived another night. If she was in tears, I knew I had messed up. I messed up a lot.

I doubt we would have survived if not for the consoling talks Bern had with her mom, Martha. They'd dealt with the situation before, with Bern's father, Paul Robi, an original member of the Platters, the vocal group from the fifties, who also had a drinking problem.

"You're an alcoholic," Bern said. When she said it, she looked me in the eyes just as Juanita did, and I gave the same answer.

"No, I am not!" I protested.

Bern wasn't Juanita. She didn't let me live in denial. I agreed with her suggestion to see a therapist. Seeing one, I learned, was not the same as admitting a problem. That would take years.

In the spring of 1989, I went back to work. My opponent would be Tommy Hearns.

Eight years since our historic duel, we were headed to Caesars again and for more money than last time—a guaranteed $13 million for me, $11 million for Tommy. Were we, both in our thirties, the same fighters we had been in 1981? Of course not. But we were still two of the best in the world, with plenty to prove—me, that the poor performance against Lalonde was a fluke; Tommy, that he wasn't finished after his surprising loss to Iran Barkley, which was followed by a narrow decision over Kinchen. Our rematch, entitled "The War," was scheduled for June 12.

I was sure that Tommy, eroded skills or not, would be the Tommy Hearns of old. From my experience after losing to Duran, I knew there was no greater incentive for a fighter than to avenge defeat. You are willing to put your body and mind through hell, if necessary. Too bad the rest of Team Leonard did not give Tommy the same respect. The others were certain he was shot, and it affected the effort they put forth at training camp in Palm Beach, Florida. It was similar to the mood before the first Duran fight, the boys concerned more with their own needs than with mine, but with only days left before the main event, it was too late to restore order. I couldn't rely on Juanita, or Janks Morton, who had left after Lalonde, to get everyone in line. The behavior of Roger and Kenny hurt the most. As my older brothers, it was their duty to look out for me. They didn't.

I never got into my zone and there were plenty of signs, none more revealing than what took place during the morning weigh-in. It had been reported that a nineteen-year-old girl was found shot to death at Tommy's house in Southfield, Michigan, and that his brother, Henry, twenty-two, was a suspect.

"Tommy, I'm sorry," I said. "I hope everything will be okay."

That was the worst thing I could have said. Not that I didn't feel sympathy for Tommy. I did. But expressing the slightest compassion to an opponent only hours before going into combat proved I wasn't ready. Can you imagine me approaching Tommy before our first bout, or Duran or Hagler, and letting my guard down like that? I could have had one of the boys relay the same message or sent a telegram.

Further evidence came as soon as the bell rang. My eyes were filled with fear instead of confidence. The plan was to attack Tommy with a steady diet of overhand rights, just as Kinchen did. In camp, I overpowered one sparring partner after another with the right. Yet, against Tommy, every overhand right I threw was off target. There was no snap in my jabs, and the left hooks felt like lead. I was in trouble. Pepe and Jake tried to get me back on track between rounds, but there was little that could be salvaged at this stage. Not even Angelo could have saved me. I'd have to find something that worked, and fast.

In round three, I went down, a hard right nailing me on the side of the head. I got up in a hurry and was alert enough, but I wasn't facing Kevin Howard or Donny Lalonde. When Tommy Hearns went for the kill, he got his man.

Fortunately, by maintaining my distance, I hung on until the bell and recovered by the start of round four. In the fifth, it was my turn to score as I landed a hard left hook to the chin. He was hurt. If Tommy was a shot fighter, as everybody claimed, here was my opportunity to put him away. I threw more combinations and trapped him near the ropes, but I punched myself out and he survived. My window was gone. Over the next four rounds, he got in his licks and I got in mine. The fight was clearly going the distance.

Or was it? In the eleventh, Tommy connected with three straight rights and a left that sent me to the canvas again, the first time I was knocked down twice in the same fight. I hung on once more, though with only one round to go, the task confronting me was obvious: Knock Tommy out or lose.

I tried with everything I had, controlling most of the action, but Tommy had learned a lot in eight years. He finally knew how to clinch, buying himself precious seconds till the bell rang. The only uncertainty left was the margin of defeat. I braced myself for the announcement.

The judges must have been watching a different fight. It was ruled a draw. What saved me was my aggressiveness in the final round. I was stunned. Unlike Hagler, Tommy had a right to feel robbed.

He didn't. That's because he accomplished something much more important than winning the fight. He redeemed himself. For the rest of his life, he would be able to say that on June 12, 1989, he held his own against me. That was enough.

As for me, the future was uncertain, although retirement was not an option no matter how many people might have urged me to quit. I was not going out like this. My showing had nothing to do with declining abilities. The problem was my attitude, and that could be fixed.

One way to do it was by agreeing to take on Duran next. I would have no trouble getting motivated for him. After what happened in New Orleans, I assumed the two of us would never meet again. But nine years had passed since that strange night, and Duran, now thirty-eight, had done a superb job of rehabilitating himself. He had won eight of his last nine bouts, including an upset over Iran Barkley in February, which earned him the WBC middleweight title. The bout was slated for December 7 in Las Vegas, but instead of Caesars, where I had fought the previous three times, the site would be an outdoor stadium adjacent to the Mirage, the new hotel owned by multimillionaire Steve Wynn.

In the fall, I set up camp in Hilton Head. As I did for the second Duran bout, I cut back on my entourage—only, this time, those affected included Roger and Kenny. The way they fooled around in Florida meant I could no longer trust them. Breaking the news to them was one of the hardest things I have ever done. I told Roger first.

"You are my brother and I love you," I said, "but you cannot go with me to the next fight."

Roger was crushed, though his spirits brightened considerably when he took a glance at the farewell check I handed him, for $100,000. That's a lot of chickens. His take per fight was typically in the $40,000 range. Kenny was wounded, too, but I wasn't about to change my mind. My career came first.

Also let go was Dave Jacobs. Having two voices in the corner in the last fight had been one too many. I put Pepe in charge and he made me work, in the gym and on the road, building my reflexes and stamina. I was thirty-three, not twenty-three. I could not rely on speed any longer.

Walking down the aisle on an extremely cold fight night, I was well aware that a third straight lackluster effort would result in more pleas for retirement. I wasn't ready to exit the stage quite yet.

I went out and proved it, capturing every round on at least two of the three cards, except for the twelfth, when the outcome was no longer in doubt. The rigorous training had paid off. I kept sliding out of range, forcing Duran to miss an astonishing 86 percent of his punches, although he connected often enough that I needed sixty stitches to close gashes in my left eyelid, right eyebrow, and upper lip. I was a mess. I was also a winner again.

* * *

My next fight wasn't in the ring. It was in a courthouse in Rockville, Maryland.

On November 2, 1990, Juanita and I appeared in court to determine the temporary alimony and child support payments, which she was seeking to increase. I usually had a good sense of how a judge was going to rule, being wrong only in the second Hearns fight, but this time I didn't have a clue.

Before we could find out, I received word that Juanita wanted a few minutes alone with me. My attorneys were opposed, as were hers, including the celebrated Marvin Mitchelson. We overruled them. The battle was between us, not our attorneys.

I met her in a conference room. She started to cry.

"Ray, I'm scared," Juanita said.

"I'm scared, too," I said.

"I don't know what to do," she said.

Neither did I. But I had to do something.

"We've been together a long time," I said, "and our kids don't need this. You and I can work this out without any more meetings with our attorneys. How much money do you want for the divorce to go through?"

"Twenty million," Juanita said with no hesitation.

"No, Juanita, what do you *need*?" I asked.

We went back and forth for another minute or two before coming to an agreement.

A short time later, Juanita and I left the courthouse together, smiling and holding hands as the reporters and camera crews crowded around us. We'd soon no longer be husband and wife, but despite all the arguments, we loved each other and that would never change.

She got into her car. I got into mine. The following day, I flew to Los Angeles.

Bern was waiting for me.

12

Peace at Last

What else was waiting for me, I could not be sure. The smart thing to do was to leave the fight game for good. I had beaten them all—Benitez, Duran (twice), Hearns, Hagler—my position as one of the all-time greats secured forever. In addition, unlike too many of my colleagues, I was not showing any ill effects from the hits I had taken. The years I lost due to the detached retina, which I long thought of as a curse, were actually a blessing. After beating Bruce Finch in February 1982, I appeared in the ring only five times for the rest of the eighties, for a total of fifty-four rounds. If I had not suffered the eye injury, there is little doubt I would have fought twice as often, and the damage those extra blows might have caused is frightening to consider.

Naturally, I didn't do the smart thing. I rarely did.

Instead, in late November, I signed on to fight Terry Norris, the WBC super-welterweight champion. I was very excited. For the first time, I would be fighting in Madison Square Garden. I always felt I'd missed something by not competing in the Garden, where Dempsey and Louis and Marciano and Robinson and Ali had fought. At last, in the twilight of my career, I would get a chance.

As for my opponent, I wasn't too worried. Norris had definite strengths. At twenty-three, he was fearless, fast, and could attack with either hand. But taking on John Mugabi at the Sun Dome in Tampa, Florida, or Tony Montgomery at the Civic Auditorium in Santa Monica, California—they were two of his recent foes—would not be the same as a duel in the Garden against the conqueror of Duran, Hearns, and Hagler. The fight, for which I was guaranteed $4 million, was set for February 9.

In December, I began to work out across the street from the same Palmer Park gym where, twenty years before, I took up the sport. Of the three men who taught me back then, only Pepe was with me, determined that I train as diligently as I did in preparing for Duran. Keeping me on my toes was Michael Ward, nineteen, a welterweight from the D.C. area with a promising future. As the weeks went by, my body grew stronger. I had not been in this kind of shape since the Hagler fight. Poor Terry Norris would not know what hit him.

Neither would I. One day in camp, Ward dropped me with a shot to the chin. He also rocked me in the ribs. The fact that he got through my defenses was proof that my reflexes were not as sharp as I assumed.

The ribs were cracked, which meant I should have asked for an immediate postponement. I didn't. I'd required a postponement against Kevin Howard, and it disrupted my rhythm. I decided the Norris fight would take place on February 9 or not at all.

Donning a flak jacket similar to the type quarterbacks in the NFL wear, I kept training, the sparring partners instructed to avoid hitting me anywhere near the ribs. I put a sweatshirt on over the jacket to keep the press in the dark. If news of the injury leaked, the fight would be postponed for sure.

Cracked ribs or not, I figured to make short work of Norris. His day would come, just not in my era.

I was right—well, partially right. His day came sooner than I expected.

I knew it the moment I walked down the aisle, much like a frightened groom who does not want to go through with the wedding. I loved everything about fighting but fighting itself, and it is fair to suggest that, except for the Hagler bout, the passion had been mostly missing for a full decade, since I beat Hearns. Only, I was too stubborn to admit it. Instead, I kept coming back and would continue to until someone would help me see the light. That someone would be Terry Norris.

As I climbed into the ring, I was no longer in pain due to the shots I received in the dressing room. It's a shame there were no shots to alleviate the other pain I was feeling.

A few days before the fight, I was sent a cassette from Juanita, featuring a ballad from the well-known R&B singer and songwriter Peabo Bryson. I thought I was long over her, but I obviously wasn't. I knew she was dating Peabo and that sending the tape was her attempt to hurt me as badly as I had hurt her. It worked. If that wasn't bad enough, she gave the four ringside seats I had set aside for her to her attorneys and accountant.

Once the bell rang, Norris could do whatever he wished. Overwhelmed by the occasion? Hardly. He embraced it, not backing off for a second, displaying a combination of speed and power reminiscent of the warrior I used to see in the mirror. I was the one who looked lost, the old, pathetic fighter I promised myself I would never become, hoping to survive the full twelve rounds and be spared the humiliation of ending my career on the canvas of Madison Square Garden.

Norris dropped me in the second, a left hook doing the work, and again in round seven with a right. I landed my share of blows, but there was no power or speed in them and I never put Norris in any real trouble. So inevitable was the outcome that my dad, sitting near the corner, wanted to throw in the towel. He was overruled.

I prefer to think healthy ribs would have made a difference. Who was I kidding? My era was over. It was over after I upset Hagler. Putting away a less-skilled Lalonde and outdueling a thirty-eight-year-old Duran didn't prove a damn thing, and in between was the loss to Tommy Hearns, no matter what the judges said. Now, facing a talented younger opponent, I didn't stand a chance. The surprise was not that I lost. The surprise was that it took this long.

After the verdict was announced, Norris winning easily on every card, I saw no point in waiting a week or two to see how I might feel about the future once the bruises started to heal. I could wait a month or two, and it wouldn't matter. I took the microphone from the ring announcer and made it official: I was retiring as a pro for the fourth, and final, time.

I had been wrong about so many things for so long, and here, with my announcement, I was even wrong about myself. I thought that retirement would devastate me, but to my surprise, I felt overwhelming relief. If I had kept winning and raking in the money, there would have been no incentive for me to quit. I could now move on with the rest of my life.

At least, I thought I could. In late March, nearly two months after the Norris loss, I was reminded the past is not always easy to leave behind. Especially the past I lived.

I was in Los Angeles one afternoon when I received the call from Mike Trainer.

"I need you back here," Mike told me.

"I just got here. I'm with Bern. Can't this wait a few days?"

"No, Ray, it can't wait."

The *Los Angeles Times* was coming out with a story indicating that, according to the court records from my divorce, I admitted to drug and alcohol abuse between 1983 and 1986. It would be pointed out as well that in 1989 I appeared in antidrug public service announcements on TV.

"You need to be ahead of the story," he said. "You need to talk to the press right away."

I never heard such urgency in Mike's voice. He said he would have a private plane take me back to Maryland in a few hours.

After I hung up, the news began to sink in. I had to know this day would come, that I couldn't keep my secret life secret forever. Still, when he told me, I was totally unprepared. Bern volunteered to accompany me to the press conference, but I decided it wouldn't be a good idea. I got myself into this mess, and it was up to me to get out of it as best I could.

The flight back to D.C. seemed to take days instead of hours. I thought I'd go nuts playing out a million different scenarios, wondering: What do the reporters know? And what do I tell them?

I had a few drinks. The irony doesn't escape me—getting wasted while preparing to seek forgiveness for my abuses—but I knew no other way. I was terrified. I was used to fighting for a title, but not for my credibility. A limo driver picked me up at Dulles Airport and took me to my house in Potomac. Mike came over after I settled in. The press conference was set for the next day at the Touchdown Club, the same D.C. establishment where I first met Ali back in 1976.

"I'll write a speech," I told Mike.

"You can't," he said. "You have to speak from the heart. If you try to read from a sheet of paper, people won't believe you."

He was right, as usual. He warned me that the consequences of these revelations would be severe.

"Don't even think about any endorsements after we do this thing," Mike said.

I didn't sleep the whole night. In the morning, during the ride to the club, Mike and I hardly spoke. No magic words came to me, just as none did in the hospital on the night before my eye operation. In no time, we were there.

I took a seat near the podium. I was shaking. I would rather have taken on Mike Tyson than this assignment. I looked at the writers, spotting a lot of familiar faces from much happier times. The day was almost as torturous for some of them as it was for me. They didn't want to bring me down. They were my friends. But they had a story to write.

Gathering my nerves, I stood up and did just what Mike suggested. I told the truth. I said what I did was wrong, and that I was ashamed for letting down my family and fans.

"I can never erase the pain or the scars that I have made through my stupidity," I said. "All I can say is I'm sorry, but that's not enough."

At times I struggled, but I kept my composure. I was surprised at how liberated I felt. I wasn't aware of the energy it took to live a lie all those years. Then, just like that, the session was over, the writers rushing to file, Mike and I left to assess the fallout. Luckily, it was minimal, and he deserved the credit. By strongly urging me to come clean immediately, instead of waiting for the press to probe deeper, we took control of the situation. The public forgave me and so did corporate America. In time, I was doing endorsements again.

B ack in Los Angeles, Bern and I were growing closer. I was spending so much time in California, I bought a condo in Santa Monica. For years, after the pain I caused to Juanita and the children, I told myself I would never marry again. I obviously was not very good at it. Then came Bern, and I couldn't imagine not sharing the rest of my life with her.

For her birthday in April 1992, we were with about a hundred friends at a party on the pier in the D.C. area when I proposed in front of everyone. She said yes. I was never happier. In August 1993, we tied the knot in the gardens of our lovely new house in California. With my fighting days over, I worked on an exercise video and a Nintendo video game, and kept up my responsibilities as a member of the Governor's Council on Physical Fitness and Sports. I also hadn't given up on the idea of acting. I had done my share of it in the ring.

The future was without limitations. No one could hurt me. No one except myself.

I continued to drink, heavily at times. Having a woman who loved me was not enough. It wasn't the first time, either.

I embarrassed myself more often than I care to remember. Once, in Monte Carlo, it was arranged for me to meet Nelson Mandela the following morning at eleven. I could not have been more excited. I knew of no greater man for how he survived all those years in prison and yet emerged without any desire for revenge. All he wanted was peace and equality for the country he loved.

So what did I do to prepare? I got plastered, naturally.

At 11:15 the next morning, I heard someone banging on my door. Before I was fully awake, several members of Mandela's security detail had broken in.

"Mr. Mandela is waiting for you," one of them said.

I had overslept. I had stood up Nelson Mandela!

I jumped in the shower, combed my hair, and somehow arrived in his suite before noon. I probably set a record for apologies. He was incredibly understanding.

"That's okay, son," Mr. Mandela said when he embraced me.

He went on to say how much he admired me. I stopped him before he went any further.

"Sir," I said, "you are the one who is to be admired."

Over the years, Bern tried to get me to stop drinking, and for brief periods I did. But I always went back.

In the fall of 1996, I chose a new outlet—or, rather, a familiar one. I decided to fight again.

What was I thinking? At forty, I was an old man in a young man's sport. For that matter, I was an old man when Norris whipped me in 1991. What made me believe the outcome would be any different more than five years later? If anything, my reflexes would be slower, my footwork less fluid, my body less able to absorb pain. I was lucky to walk out of the Garden in one piece. I might not be as lucky the next time.

In looking back, though, I told myself Norris defeated me because of the injury to my ribs, not because he was a superior fighter. I also was a victim of my own success, the victory over Hagler convincing me I could pull off another shocker anytime I put my mind to it. The public would think I was deluded. The press would predict disaster. Come fight night, I would be the one standing, my arms raised in the air, overcoming the odds once more, the skeptics left to scramble for an explanation.

For several years I had attended a lot of fights and almost always walked away with the same conclusion: I can beat *that* guy.

One of those guys was Hector "Macho" Camacho. I was doing the TV commentary in June 1996 when Camacho won a decision over a forty-five-year-old Duran in Atlantic City. Afterward, Camacho proposed that he and I fight next. I did not give it much thought but J. D. Brown did, and by October we had a deal, the match slated, after an initial delay, for March 1, also in Atlantic City, with my purse being a guaranteed $4 million plus a share of the pay-per-view revenue. People said I came back for the money. Nothing could have been further from the truth. I came back for the challenge. That's what fighters do. It's what we do better than anything else.

As usual, almost everyone around me was opposed to my return, including Bern.

"We have a great life," she told me. "You don't need to do this."

Bern didn't understand. She couldn't. Only fighters know what it feels like to yearn for that place we go to when preparing for battle. There is no place like it.

Yet I found a way to get her on board, just as I did with Juanita when she was opposed to my comebacks. I agreed to work with Billy Blanks, a fitness and martial arts expert, who built up the strength in my upper body and legs by having me lift weights for the first time. Blanks was a strict believer in the Tae Bo workout, as was Bern, which combines tae kwon do and boxing.

I also put in my normal amount of time in the screening room. I was encouraged by what I saw. Despite being six years older, I was quicker and stronger than Camacho, the International Boxing Council middle-weight and welterweight champion. With the body shots I planned to throw, I'd wear him down just as I outlasted my sparring partners every day at camp in Chandler, Arizona, near Phoenix. It made no difference that since my most recent retirement he'd fought twenty-eight times, for a total of 219 rounds. I beat Hagler after being away for three years, and Camacho was no Hagler. In his youth, Camacho was filled with a lot of promise. His youth was a long time ago.

Things could not have been going any better, until, suddenly, they could not have gotten any worse. On January 31, doing an exercise Blanks taught me in which I stepped onto a bench with weights on the back of my shoulder, I felt a sharp twinge in my right calf.

I saw a doctor that very afternoon. The diagnosis was a torn muscle.

"You should be out of action for four to six weeks," he said, "but then you will be fine."

"Doc, you do not seem to understand," I said. "I'm *fighting* in six weeks. Just give me something so it doesn't hurt."

As with the cracked ribs before the Norris fight, there was little doubt that I should have asked for an immediate postponement, but I wasn't going to give in this time, either. The bout had already been put off due to problems with the original promoters, forcing us to make a new arrangement with Titan Sports, the pay-per-view firm operated by wrestling's Vince McMahon. Another postponement, and it's possible I would have come to my senses and used the injury as an excuse to back out for good. I preferred fooling myself. That was one of my best talents.

It became necessary to fool the press and the public as well while I rested the leg. If word of the torn muscle got out, there would be calls for the fight to be delayed, if not canceled. I couldn't let that happen.

The idea we came up with was brilliant, practically out of a Hitchcock film. We closed camp, pretending to work on a secret strategy. A number of fans managed to peek through the cracks in the tent, believing they saw me working out. What they really saw was Roger in a hood. I was on the other side of town visiting the doctor to build up the muscles in my leg. I sneaked in much later to do any interviews. No one ever found out. The leg gradually improved, though it was still far less than 100 percent, keeping me from running or sparring for weeks. The extent of my exercise was riding on a stationary bike. J.D. suggested I have the doctor give me a few shots, but I told him to wait until fight night. I needed the leg to be good for only an hour, maybe less.

Those final days were strange. The entire original cast was gone, including Juice, Ollie, Joe, and Pepe, who was replaced by my new trainer, Adrian Davis. Adrian was certainly capable, though there was no real trust between us. There couldn't be. Trust takes years, not weeks. Even Mike Trainer was not around. He looked over the contract, but that was all he did.

The night was a total disaster—and it started long before the opening bell.

For some unknown reason, my mom and dad and siblings were given seats about five rows from ringside, while Bern sat in the front row. My parents were never that far back for any of my fights. My mom, to no one's surprise, was furious and didn't hesitate to make her feelings known. Neither did my sister Bunny. I didn't see what took place, though from what I was told, Bunny attempted to slap Bern in the face, believing she had been responsible for the seating arrangement. She wasn't. It was J.D. who made the error. It didn't matter. When she couldn't get her way, Momma left and missed the whole fight.

I was having my own problems. The shots the doctor had given me in the calf made it go completely numb. I was going to have to fight on one leg. I also got concerned when Roger held his hands out for me to hit. I missed. I never missed.

Once the fight got under way, I didn't have a chance. Camacho was in total control, backing me into the ropes. I fell to the floor late in the first round, but it was the result of a shove.

In the second, I rallied a bit, landing a right jab to Camacho's nose and a right hook to his head. Perhaps there was hope for me yet. If I was not the fighter I once was, neither was he. In round three, though, that illusion disappeared in a hurry. Camacho nailed me with a left hook to the cheek and a right to the face. From then on, I was helpless, the end coming in the fifth. Camacho sent me to the deck early in the round and proceeded to throw about a dozen punches in a row before the ref, Joe Cortez, stopped it. Thank God he did. Lying flat on my back in the Atlantic City Convention Center would have been the worst possible way to end my boxing carrer. I was humbled enough as it was, requiring assistance to climb the two steps to the dais for the postfight press conference.

At least there would be no more comebacks. If losing to Norris did not do it, losing to Camacho would surely end any fantasies I might have had of recapturing my former glory. I could now attend the International Boxing Hall of Fame induction ceremony, scheduled, appropriately, for June, and be resigned to the fact that it was finally over.

Or could I? Within days, amazingly enough, I was busy plotting another comeback. I convinced myself that the loss to Camacho, like the one to Norris, was due to injuries, and to prove money wasn't the issue, I planned to donate the entire purse to charity. The problem was: Who would I fight? It couldn't be a bum. The public wouldn't pay the big bucks for the closed-circuit telecast, especially after the awful show I gave them against Camacho. Nor could it be a top-ten contender. No matter how motivated I might be, I'd be in no shape to take on anyone that good, not without another fight or two.

In the end, sanity, thank goodness, prevailed and nothing came of my plans. Prior to the Camacho fight, J.D. held discussions with people representing Oscar De La Hoya, the light welterweight champion, which were subsequently dropped. I was lucky I didn't beat Camacho. I can't begin to imagine what Oscar, still in his early twenties, would have done to a has-been like me. Yet as the months went by, the Camacho loss depressed me to no end. *You dumb fuck,* I kept asking myself, *how could you have been beaten so badly?* It was on my mind when I went to sleep and when I woke up. I kept searching for a way to fix it, even if that meant I'd have to get back in the ring.

I should have been happy. Bern and I were building a nice life for ourselves, excited by the arrival of our baby girl, Camille, in the fall of 1997, and then came a son, Daniel, three years later.

My new business ventures were moving along, too. In 2001, I launched a boxing promotional company in association with ESPN. In 2004, I was named the cohost, with Sylvester Stallone, of a new NBC reality series, *The Contender*, in which promising young fighters worked on their craft in hopes of becoming a world champion. The show put me back in the public eye. It also helped me finally get over the Camacho loss.

Then why, in the summer of 2006, was I on the set of *Live with Regis and Kelly* in New York with the most painful hangover I could remember? And why, on Christmas Eve of the year before, was I out cold, lying on my kitchen floor.

The answer, as Juanita and Bern had told me, is that I was still an alcoholic, and it was not the outcome of the Camacho fight I was anxious to fix by drinking. It was the events of a lifetime ago, before I became famous, when two men I trusted took advantage of me, and two parents I loved turned our house into a war zone. For years, I ran—to the gym, to cocaine, to the bottle, to other women, to anything or anyone that would make the pain disappear, which it did, though never for long.

That July, I finally stopped running. I looked at my eyes in the mirror, just as I did in the dressing room before my toughest fights. What I saw I had never seen before, eyes willing to admit I needed help, and before it was too late.

What made me stop? I'm not sure. Perhaps it was the argument I had a few days earlier with my son, Jarrel, now in his early twenties, who was living with us. He was playing loud music in his room and not following our rules. I asked him several times to stop. He didn't. Enough was enough. I told him he'd have to move out.

"You're trying to be a father but you've never been a father to me," he said. "All you are is a fucking machine."

Jarrel then threw me against the wall. I did what I always did when someone tried to push me around. I clenched my fists and got ready to pop him—until I stopped myself, thank God, remembering this was my own son. I walked out. Maybe he was right. Maybe I was a fucking machine.

I couldn't sleep the whole night. The next morning, I made a bunch of calls, and by the end of the week I was sitting in a conference room with about twenty strangers, attending my first Alcoholics Anonymous meeting.

I stayed in the back row, my hat and shades on, head down, trying not to be noticed. It didn't work. Suddenly it was my turn to introduce myself.

"I'm Ray Leonard," I said.

"Your first name is enough," I was told.

I started over.

"I'm Ray," I said.

Everyone laughed.

What I didn't say, however, and wouldn't say for months, was that I was an alcoholic. Being in the same room with these people was one thing. Saying the word was another. Yet I went back almost every day, and began to sense a change inside me. The urge to bury pain with a drink was still there, but I overcame it. Whenever I woke up depressed, a meeting instantly put me in a better mood. I knew I was not alone.

Eventually it became my turn to lead a meeting, and share my struggles with the others. Even then, when I finally did say the *A* word, I said it under my breath. The important thing is that I said it. I saw myself as who I am and will always be, an alcoholic.

*   *   *

B eing sober for the last four years has helped me see a great deal. I see the pain I caused to those I cared about most, and who cared most about me. I blamed the alcohol or the cocaine or the character I created, Sugar Ray, as if I had nothing to do with him. I never blamed myself. Till now.

For years I felt pity for Roger and my closest friend, Derrik Holmes, for the drugs they consumed, which ruined much of their lives. I thought they were weak, but what made me any better? I was blessed in countless ways they never were, and still I fell apart. I beat Duran and Hearns and Hagler, but for the longest time I couldn't beat alcohol and cocaine. I wasn't strong. Not where it counted.

Now here I am, with a second chance to be the husband and father I never was to Juanita and my two older sons. I won't waste it.

I'll never be able to make up for the past, which I'm reminded of every time I gaze into the eyes of Ray Jr. or Jarrel when they watch the love I give to Camille and Daniel. I know what they're thinking: *Where was the love when* we *needed it?* I wish I had an explanation that would make them feel better. I don't. All I can do is be the best father I can to all my kids.

I spend a lot of time these days traveling around the world giving motivational speeches. People come because they remember me as Sugar Ray Leonard, but Sugar Ray is not who I am when I speak. I am Ray Leonard, father of four, survivor of drug and alcohol abuse, who found out what truly matters. I explain that while each of us faces enormous challenges every day, it's not the sins we commit that will define us. It's how we respond to them. If they are lucky, as I have been, they, too, will receive a second chance. I want to make sure they don't blow it, either.

People assume I was happy during my fighting days, and I often was—hanging out with the boys in training camp, studying films of my opponent, walking down the aisle toward the ring. There was no place I would rather have been. I think a lot about those times. When I watch any of my fights on television, I can recall precisely what I was thinking and feeling. I can be Sugar Ray.

Yet those times can't compare to the contentment in my soul at this stage of my life. I beat the toughest opponent of all, myself.

For that, no one awarded me a championship belt. No one put me on the cover of *Sports Illustrated.* And no one filled my head with lies about how superior I am. I am not superior. I never was. I was just blessed with skills our society values.

Don't get me wrong. I have nothing against Sugar Ray. I know how fortunate I was to have him around. Because of him, I saw the world and was introduced to people I never would have met. I escaped the unfortunate fate that befell many of my friends.

Each time I go back for a visit, I'm reminded of how difficult their lives have been, and remain. Despite the progress the neighborhoods have made since I was a kid, there are still sections of town where nothing has changed, where there is no hope for a better tomorrow.

When I was fifteen, I was asked by a local reporter who I wanted to be when I grew up. I did not hesitate.

"I want to be special," I said.

But when I think of Sugar Ray, I am most grateful for a reason that has nothing to do with money and fame.

He was there when I needed a place for my pain and anger. Without him, I can't begin to imagine how my life would have turned out. Because of Sugar Ray, I learned how to accept Ray.

When I look in the mirror, my eyes are warm, caring, at peace.

ACKNOWLEDGMENTS

I had wanted to tell my real story for many years, but something always got in the way. Mostly, it was me. Before I could place my life in any kind of perspective, I needed to understand it myself, to better determine why I made the decisions I did, in and out of the ring, and to figure out what those choices said about who I was, and who I wanted to be. In the spring of 2008, liberated from the dangerous spell that alcohol and drugs had cast over me, my ideas and feelings became more focused, more authentic. It was time, at last, to embark on this most exciting journey.

I knew it would not be easy, that it would open up wounds I had preferred to bury, forever if possible. But I also knew I would never get on with the future if I didn't. The past was ugly. The past was filled with one lie after another. The past made me harbor deep shame and regret for all the people I hurt. Yet the past was mine, and it was my responsibility to claim it more fully as my own, whatever the consequences.

Once the memories flooded in, and they were hard to stop, I became humbled by the amount of family members and friends who've meant so much to me over the years. The list must begin, of course, with my mother and father, who allowed me the freedom to pursue my dream of capturing the Olympic gold medal. Even when the task appeared overwhelming, they did not back off in their belief in me for an instant. I never told them just how much I relied on their faith. Somehow I think they always knew. The same goes for my brothers and sisters. They were always in my corner.

Speaking of my corner, I was blessed with three dedicated men who conditioned me to win—Pepe Correa, Dave Jacobs, and Janks Morton. They put in hour after hour at the gym to help me became a champion. I'm very grateful, as well, for my relationship with Angelo Dundee, whose invaluable words in the corner during the first Hearns fight—"you're blowing it, son"—gave me a defining moment in boxing history. It was a fight I could have easily lost.

When I reflect on my fighting days, I owe a special gratitude to the proud men I fought, who were trying to earn a living just as I was, and to the trainers and managers who prepared them for battle. We were all in it together, even if we were trying to beat one another's brains in. I have run into quite a few of them since I retired, and after we share memories of our youth, we always walk off as friends and that means the world to me. Some of the men I fought have not been as lucky, the sport taking its toll on them as it always does. I pray their remaining days be as comfortable as possible.

As for comfort, I will be forever indebted to my good friend and attorney, Mike Trainer, a man who, at times, wore a lot of hats. Because of Mike, I didn't wind up like so many in my profession. He always put my interests first, and that's rare in boxing. His wife, Jill, was a saint, sparing him when I needed him, which was quite often. Assisting Mike was the amazing Caren Kinder, who was priceless during my career and is now a member of my family along with her husband, Larry.

The boys—Juice, Joe Broddie, Ollie Dunlap, James Anderson, Bobby Stuart, Darrell Foster, etc.—were always there for me as well. I was not the easiest person to be around, especially in the weeks before a fight, but they understood. People who also became such an integral part of my life and career include: Johnny Gill, Donnie Simpson, Eddie Murphy, Lyndie and Kenny G, Michael King, Jeff Wald, Bob Lange, Stephanie Rosenberg, Craig Jones, Ross Greenburg, Jimmy (Ringo) Ryan, Charlie Brotman, Kenny Chevalier, Howard Cosell, Don Gold, Don Glab, Bobby Magruder, Emanuel Steward, Tommy Hearns, and the orginal sponsors of Sugar Ray Leonard, Inc.

A special thanks to Martha Robi, my incredible mother-in-law. She never judged me when I dealt with my demons. She only consoled me. I've very grateful as well to Annette Beale, who is my new Caren Kinder.

Patience was also a virtue with my first wife, Juanita. She gave me more chances than I deserved. I owe a lot to my children, Ray Jr., Jarrel, Camille, and Daniel, who have each showed me how to love and receive love in ways that have enriched my life beyond anything I accomplished as a fighter. I'm so proud of them.

Nobody, though, has been more loving and kind than my wife, Bernadette. She rescued me when I was completely lost. To have her in my life every day, a beacon of strength and warmth, is a blessing I can't put into words.

Writing a book is no different from preparing for a title fight: It requires a high-quality team and I was fortunate to have the very best: president Clare Ferraro, editorial director Wendy Wolf, production editor Noirin Lucas, and publicists Shannon Twomey and Carolyn Coleburn. I can't say enough, as well, about Maggie Riggs, who kept each train on time despite the inevitable pitfalls. Leading the way was Viking's senior editor Joshua Kendall, whose passion for the project was a source of constant inspiration from day one. His vision can be found throughout these pages.

My assistant, Katie Diest, was indispensable, helping out with the research and reaching the people who added key details to the narrative. I don't know what I would have done without her.

Special thanks to my former agent, Lon Rosen, who gave me the final push that I needed, and to Jay Mandel of William Morris–Endeavor, who guided us to the finish line.

Finally, I want to express my appreciation to co-writer Michael Arkush, and his wife, Pauletta Walsh, who enthusiastically supported the project from the beginning. Michael met with me on a regular basis from the spring of 2009 through the fall of 2010. We also made trips to Maryland, New York, and Las Vegas. From our initial meeting, he pushed me to reveal my emotions when I did not want to go there, *especially* when I did not want to go there. Michael is a true friend.

Ray Leonard
January 2011

INDEX